SHADOW ROADS

— VOLUME ONE —

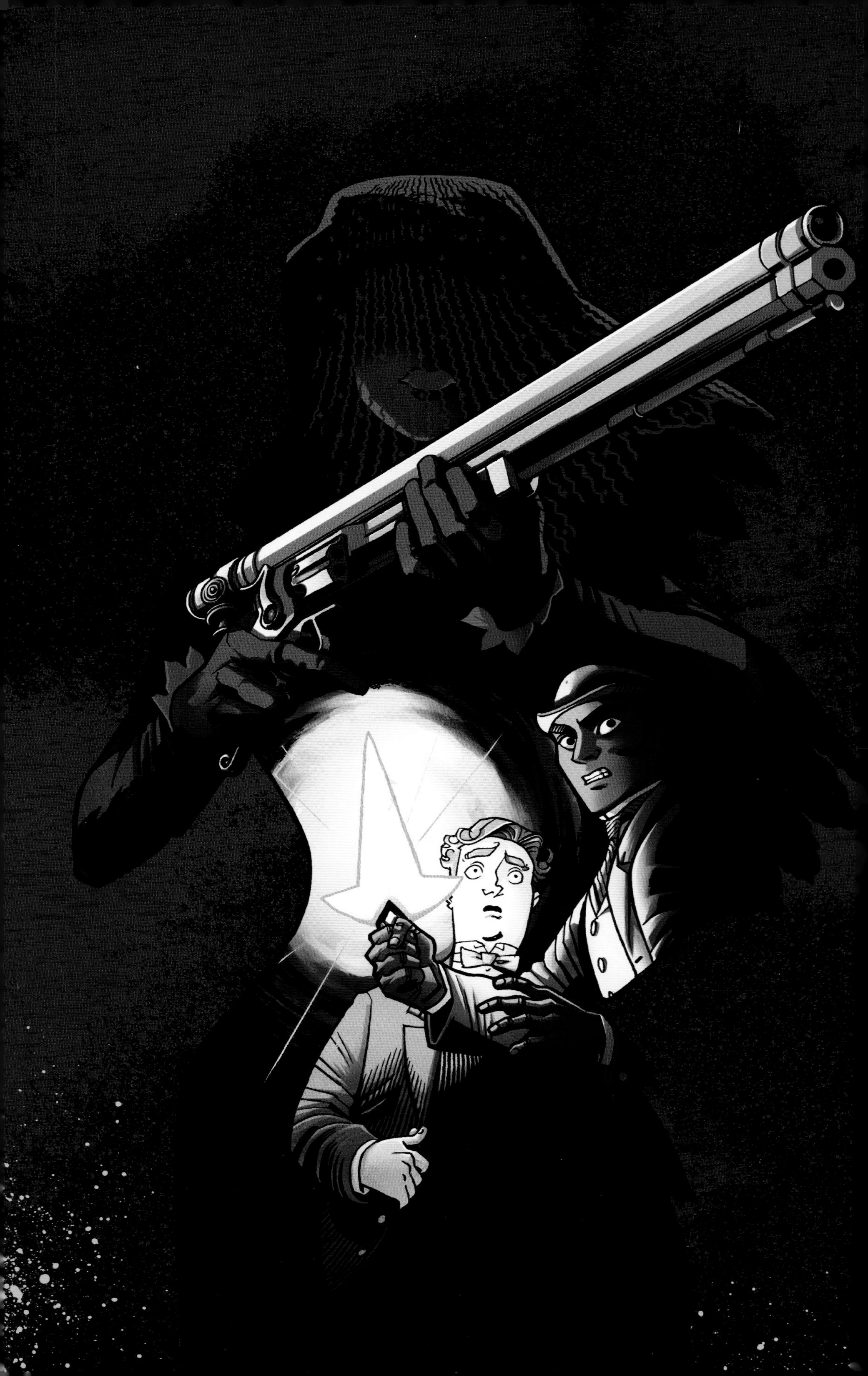

SHADOW ROADS

— VOLUME ONE —

WRITTEN BY
CULLEN BUNN
&
BRIAN HURTT

ILLUSTRATED BY
A.C. ZAMUDIO

COLORED BY
CARLOS N. ZAMUDIO

LETTERED BY
CRANK!

DESIGNED BY
KEITH WOOD

EDITED BY
CHARLIE CHU
WITH
SARAH GAYDOS

ONI PRESS

AN ONI PRESS PUBLICATION

—Published by Oni Press, Inc.—

Joe Nozemack *founder & chief financial officer* · James Lucas Jones *publisher*

Sarah Gaydos *editor in chief* · Charlie Chu *v.p. of creative & business development*

Brad Rooks *director of operations* · Melissa Meszaros *director of publicity*

Margot Wood *director of sales* · Sandy Tanaka *marketing design manager*

Amber O'Neill *special projects manager* · Troy Look *director of design & production*

Kate Z. Stone *senior graphic designer* · Sonja Synak *graphic designer*

Angie Knowles *digital prepress lead* · Robin Herrera *senior editor*

Ari Yarwood *senior editor* · Desiree Wilson *associate editor*

Kate Light *editorial assistant* · Michelle Nguyen *executive assistant*

Jung Lee *logistics coordinator*

SHADOW ROADS VOLUME 1, June 2019. Published by Oni Press, Inc.
1319 SE Martin Luther King Jr. Blvd., Suite 240, Portland, OR 97214.
Shadow Roads is ™ & © 2019 Cullen Bunn & Brian Hurtt. All Rights Reserved.
Oni Press logo and icon are ™ & © 2019 Oni Press, Inc. All Rights Reserved.
Oni Press logo and icon artwork created by Keith A. Wood. The events,
institutions, and characters presented in this book are fictional. Any
resemblance to actual persons, living or dead, is purely coincidental.
No portion of this publication may be reproduced, by any means,
without the express written permission of the copyright holders.

This volume collects *Shadow Roads* issues #1-5.

Oni Press, Inc.
1319 SE Martin Luther King Jr. Blvd.
Suite 240
Portland, OR 97214
USA

onipress.com
facebook.com/onipress
twitter.com/onipress
onipress.tumblr.com
instagram.com/onipress

cullenbunn.com · @cullenbunn
brihurtt.com · @brihurtt
aczamudio.blogspot.com · @aczamudio
ink-imp.blogspot.com · @inkimpnick
crankcast.net · @ccrank

First edition: June 2019

ISBN: 978-1-62010-634-1
eISBN: 978-1-62010-635-8

Library of Congress Control Number: 2018963238

10 9 8 7 6 5 4 3 2 1

Printed in China

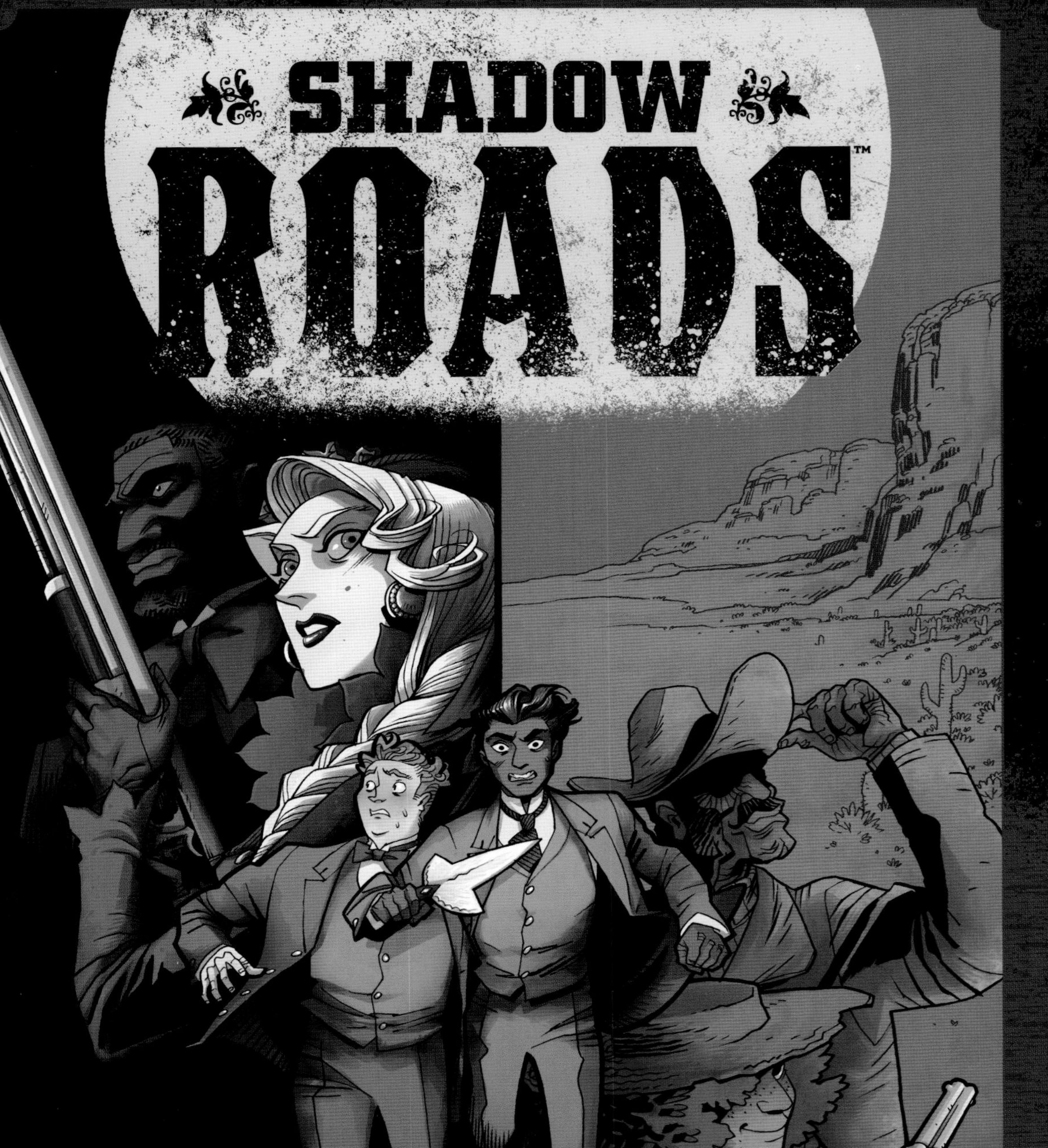
SHADOW
ROADS™

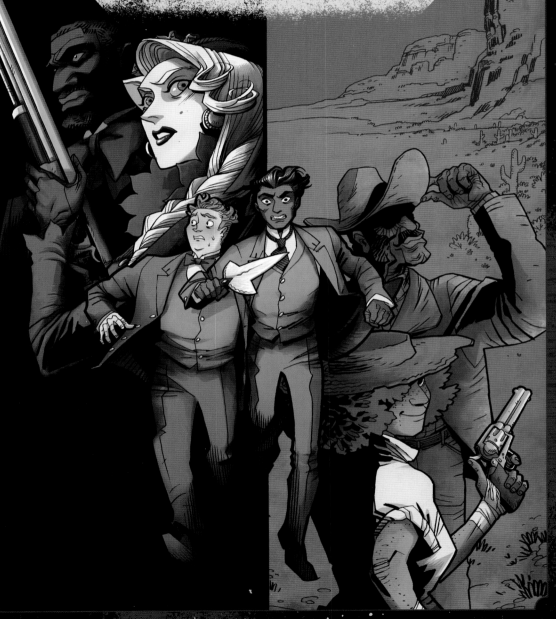

CHAPTER 1

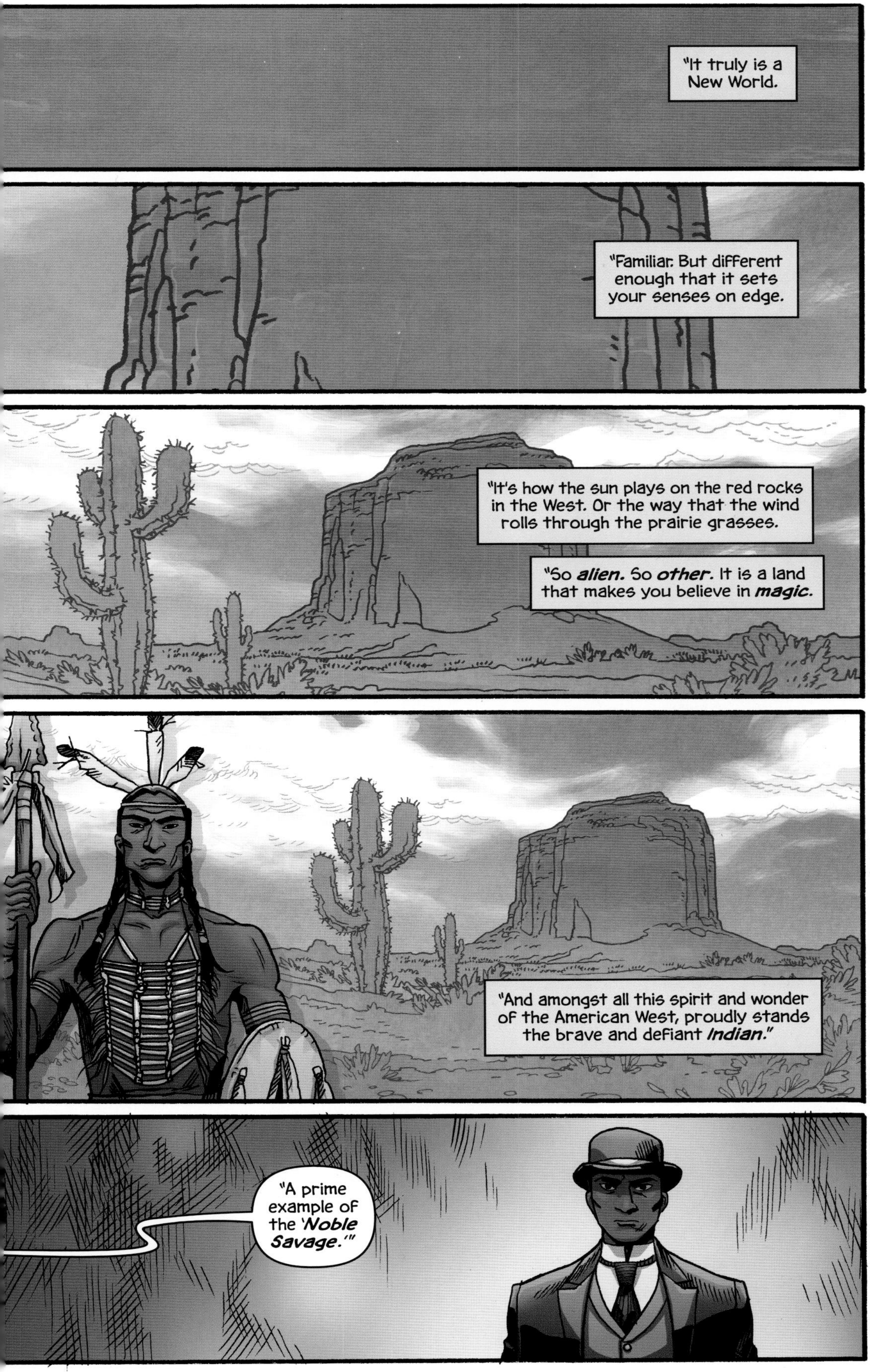
"It truly is a New World.
"Familiar. But different enough that it sets your senses on edge.
"It's how the sun plays on the red rocks in the West. Or the way that the wind rolls through the prairie grasses.
"So *alien.* So *other*. It is a land that makes you believe in *magic.*
"And amongst all this spirit and wonder of the American West, proudly stands the brave and defiant *Indian.*"
"A prime example of the '*Noble Savage.*'"

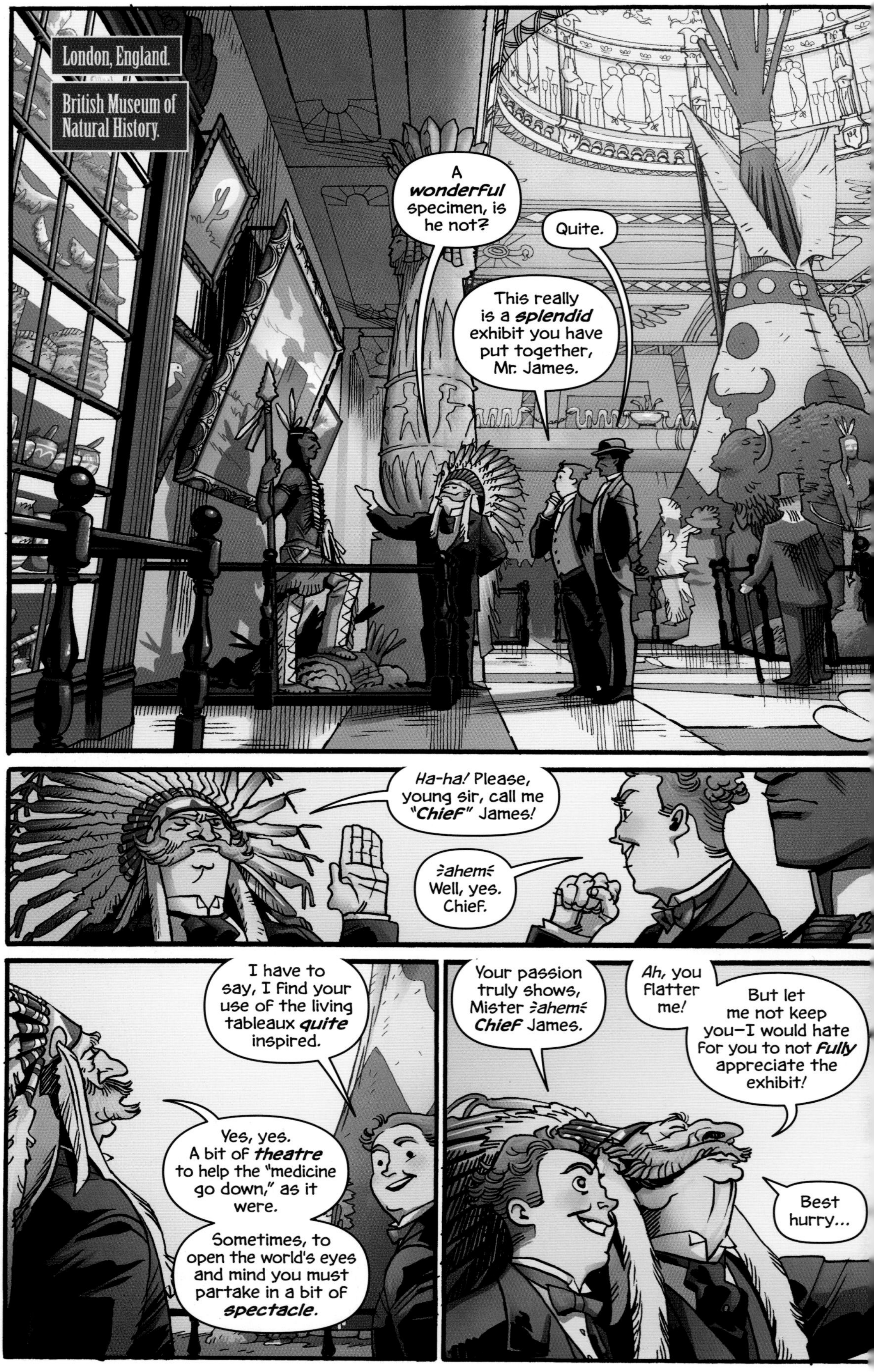
London, England.
British Museum of Natural History.
A *wonderful* specimen, is he not?
Quite.
This really is a *splendid* exhibit you have put together, Mr. James.
Ha-ha! Please, young sir, call me *"Chief"* James!
ahem Well, yes. Chief.
I have to say, I find your use of the living tableaux *quite* inspired.
Yes, yes. A bit of *theatre* to help the "medicine go down," as it were.
Sometimes, to open the world's eyes and mind you must partake in a bit of *spectacle*.
Your passion truly shows, Mister *ahem* *Chief* James.
Ah, you flatter me!
But let me not keep you—I would hate for you to not *fully* appreciate the exhibit!
Best hurry...

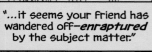

"...it seems your friend has wandered off—*enraptured* by the subject matter."

Henry!

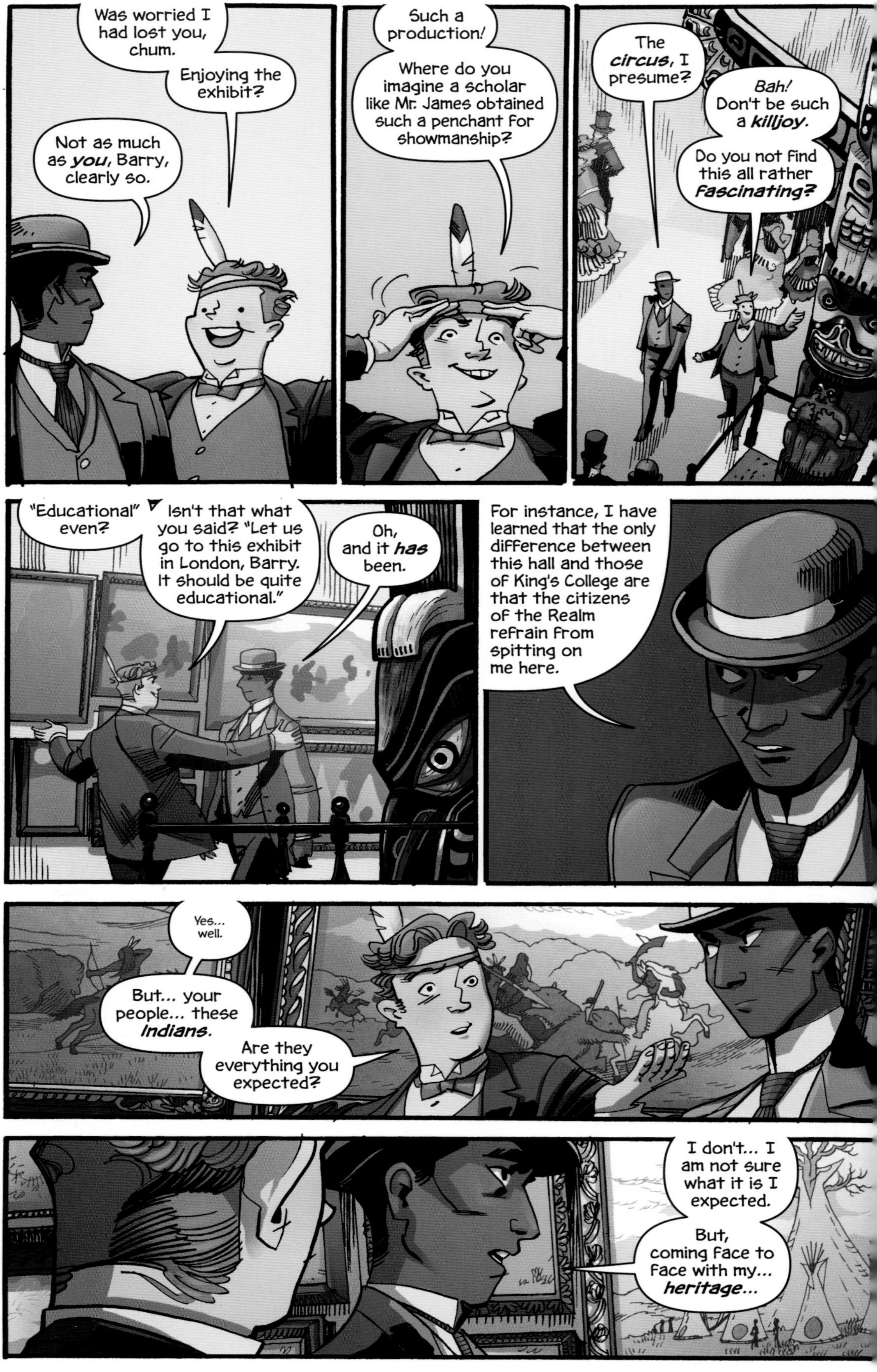

Was worried I had lost you, chum.
Enjoying the exhibit?
Not as much as *you*, Barry, clearly so.
Such a production!
Where do you imagine a scholar like Mr. James obtained such a penchant for showmanship?
The *circus*, I presume?
Bah! Don't be such a *killjoy*.
Do you not find this all rather *fascinating?*
"Educational" even?
Isn't that what you said? "Let us go to this exhibit in London, Barry. It should be quite educational."
Oh, and it *has* been.
For instance, I have learned that the only difference between this hall and those of King's College are that the citizens of the Realm refrain from spitting on me here.
Yes... well.
But... your people... these *Indians*.
Are they everything you expected?
I don't... I am not sure what it is I expected.
But, coming face to face with my... *heritage*...

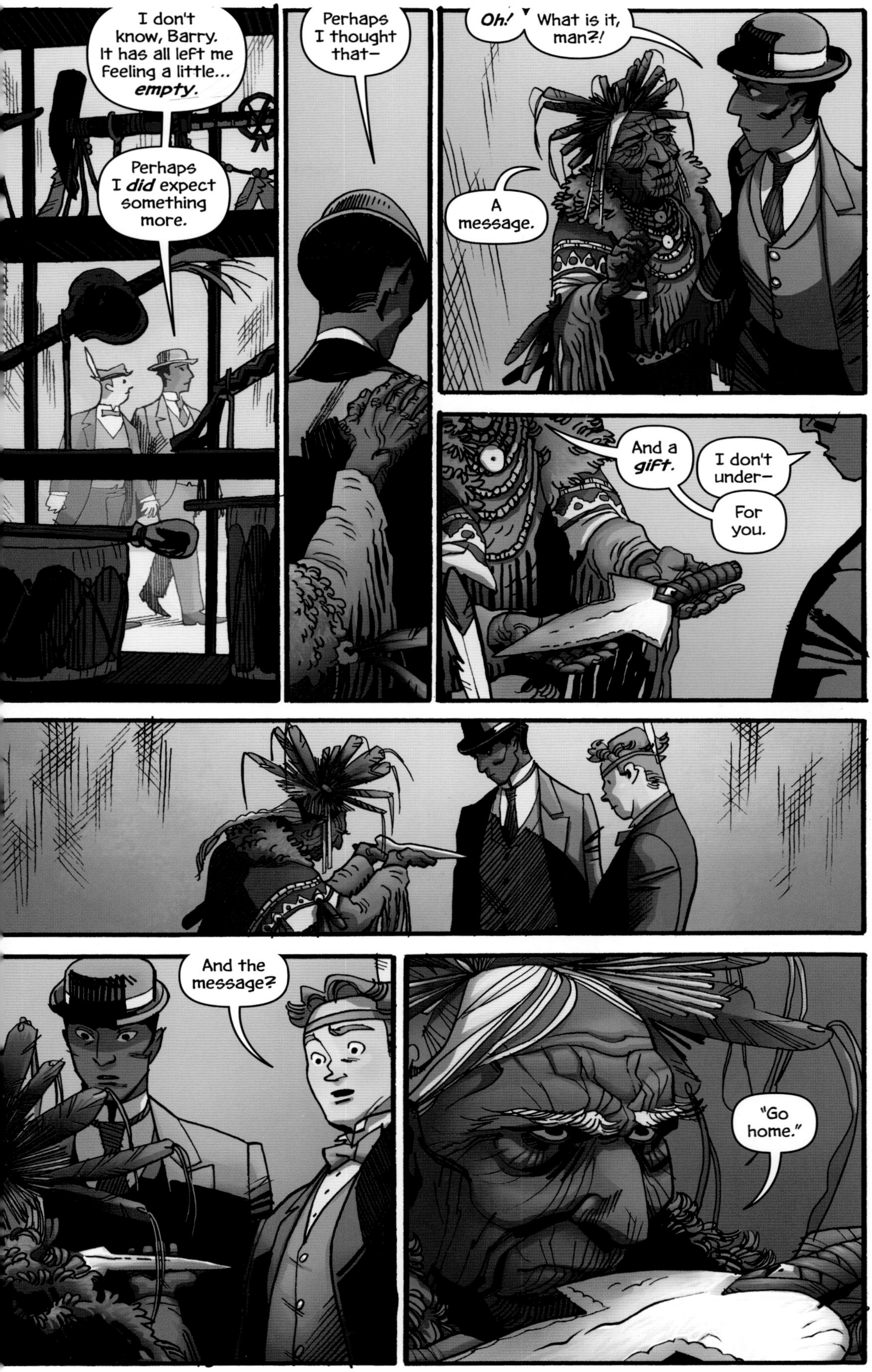
I don't know, Barry. It has all left me feeling a little... *empty*.
Perhaps I *did* expect something more.
Perhaps I thought that–
Oh!
What is it, man?!
A message.
And a *gift*.
I don't under–
For you.
And the message?
"Go home."

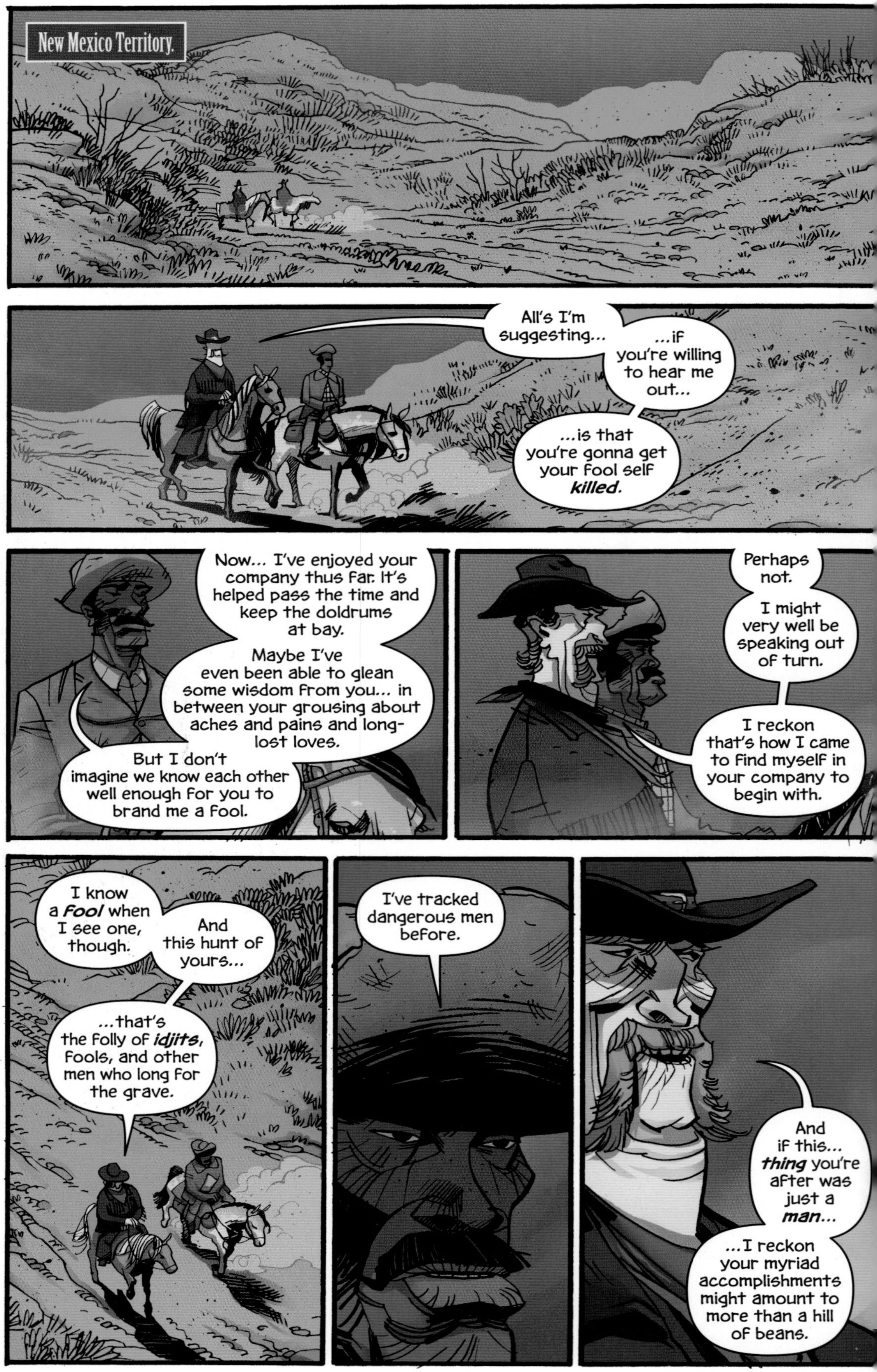
New Mexico Territory.
All's I'm suggesting...
...if you're willing to hear me out...
...is that you're gonna get your fool self *killed*.
Now... I've enjoyed your company thus far. It's helped pass the time and keep the doldrums at bay.
Maybe I've even been able to glean some wisdom from you... in between your grousing about aches and pains and long-lost loves.
But I don't imagine we know each other well enough for you to brand me a fool.
Perhaps not.
I might very well be speaking out of turn.
I reckon that's how I came to find myself in your company to begin with.
I know a *fool* when I see one, though.
And this hunt of yours...
...that's the folly of *idjits*, fools, and other men who long for the grave.
I've tracked dangerous men before.
And if this... *thing* you're after was just a *man*...
...I reckon your myriad accomplishments might amount to more than a hill of beans.

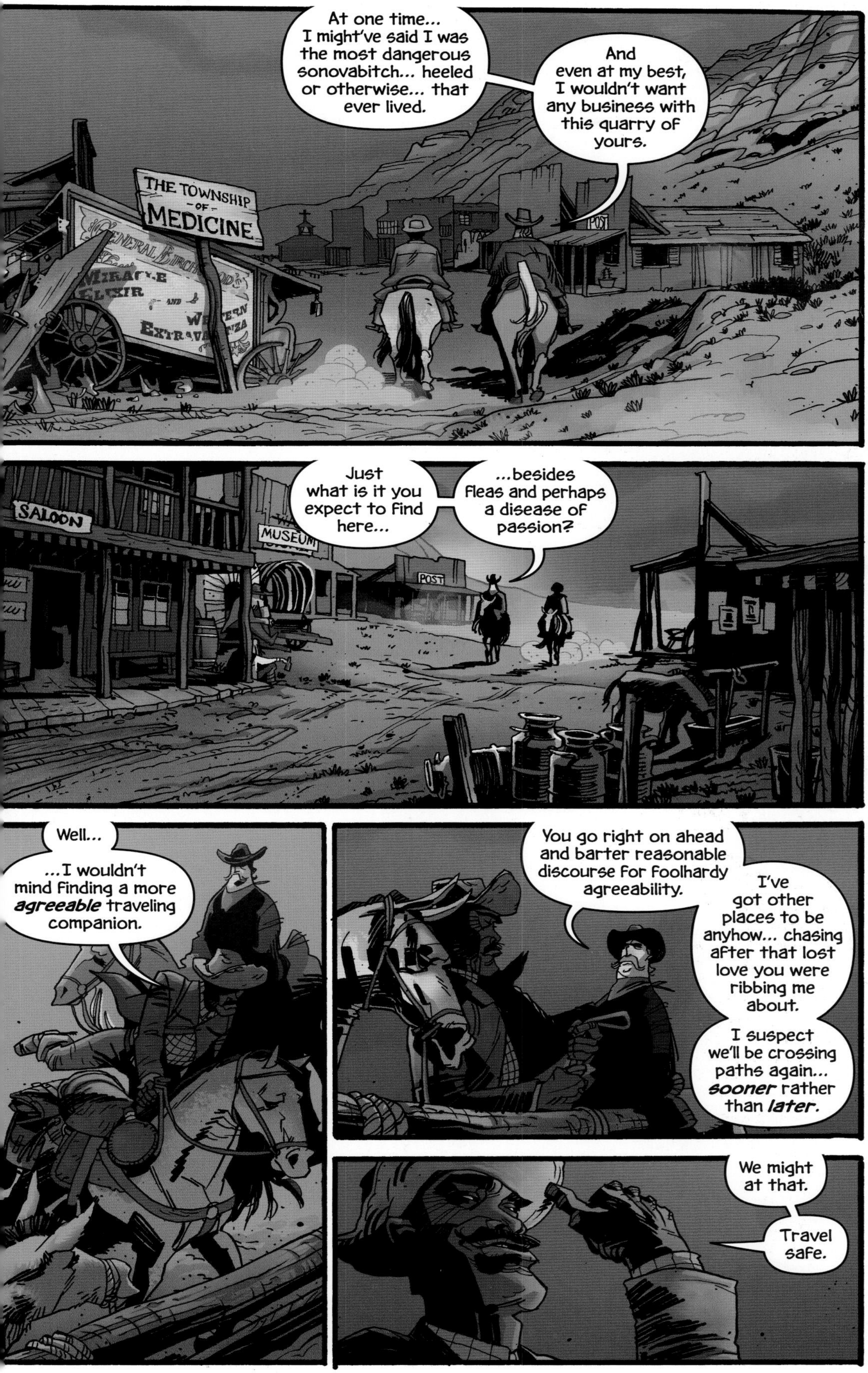
At one time... I might've said I was the most dangerous sonovabitch... heeled or otherwise... that ever lived.
And even at my best, I wouldn't want any business with this quarry of yours.
THE TOWNSHIP -OF- MEDICINE
POST
SALOON
MUSEUM
Just what is it you expect to find here...
...besides fleas and perhaps a disease of passion?
POST
Well...
...I wouldn't mind finding a more *agreeable* traveling companion.
You go right on ahead and barter reasonable discourse for foolhardy agreeability.
I've got other places to be anyhow... chasing after that lost love you were ribbing me about.
I suspect we'll be crossing paths again... *sooner* rather than *later.*
We might at that.
Travel safe.

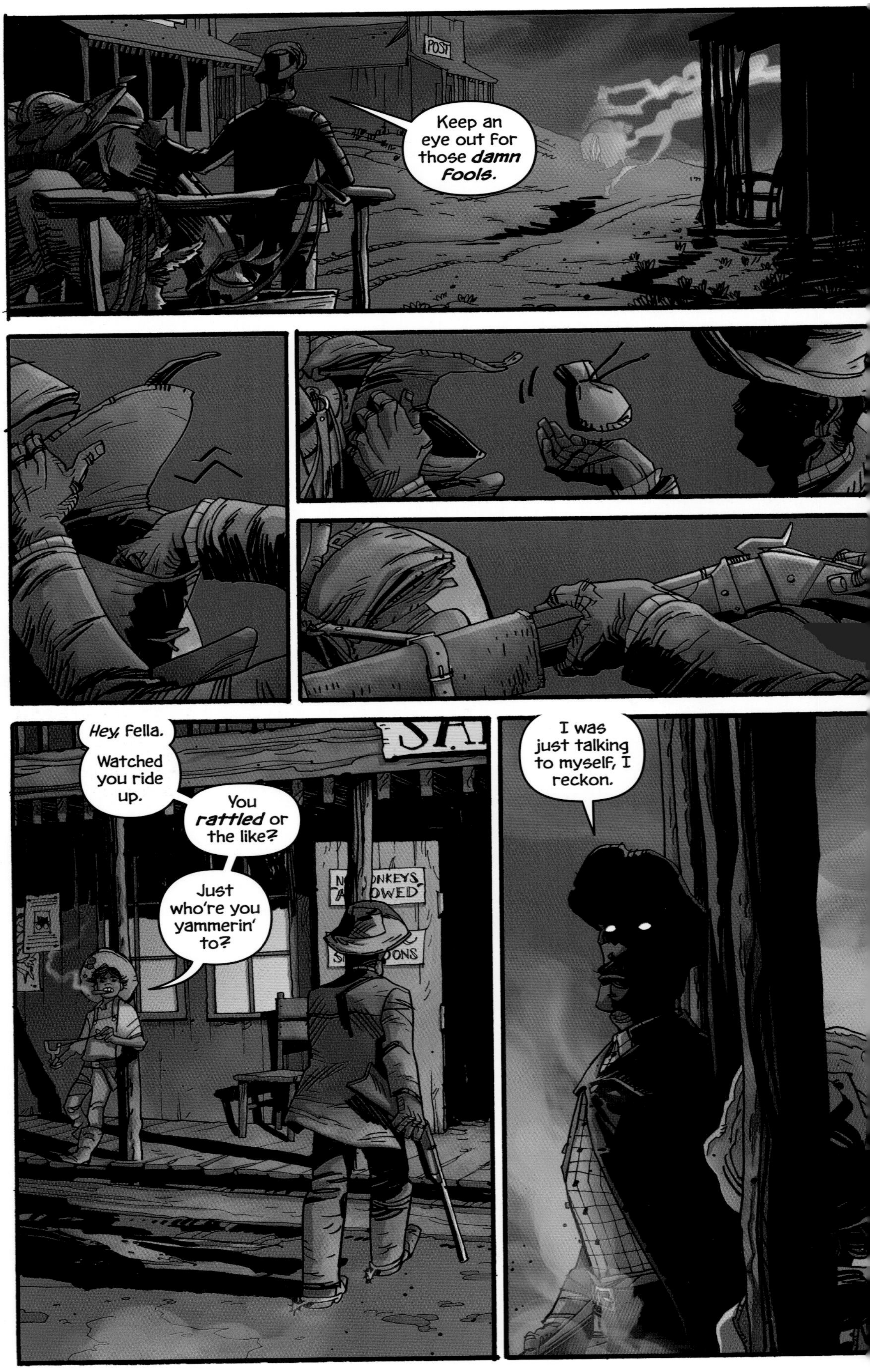
POST
Keep an eye out for those *damn fools.*
Hey, fella.
Watched you ride up.
You *rattled* or the like?
Just who're you yammerin' to?
I was just talking to myself, I reckon.

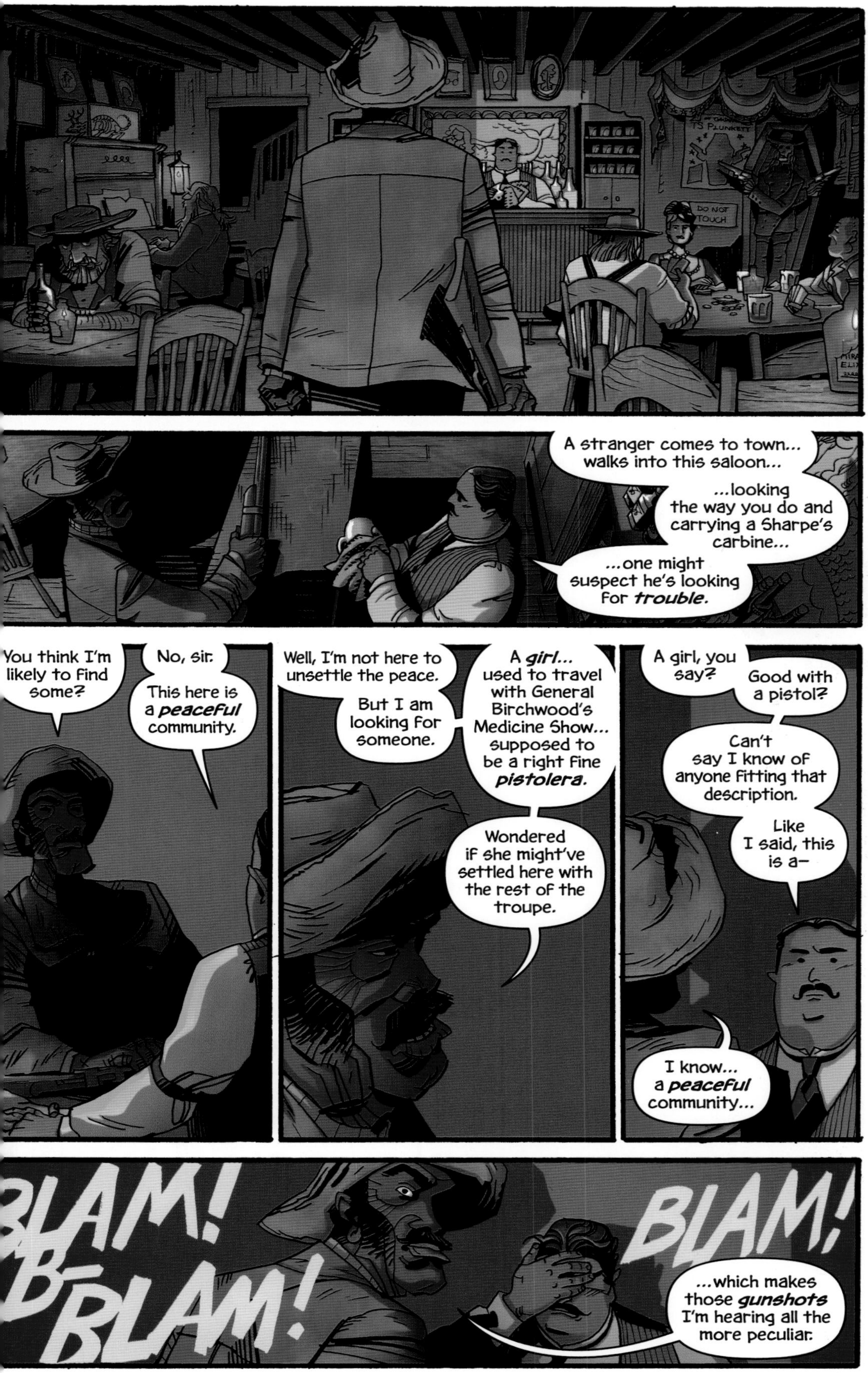
TS PLUNKETT
DO NOT TOUCH
A stranger comes to town... walks into this saloon...
...looking the way you do and carrying a Sharpe's carbine...
...one might suspect he's looking for *trouble.*
You think I'm likely to find some?
No, sir.
This here is a *peaceful* community.
Well, I'm not here to unsettle the peace.
But I am looking for someone.
A *girl...* used to travel with General Birchwood's Medicine Show... supposed to be a right fine *pistolera.*
Wondered if she might've settled here with the rest of the troupe.
A girl, you say?
Good with a pistol?
Can't say I know of anyone fitting that description.
Like I said, this is a–
I know... a *peaceful* community...
BLAM!
B-BLAM!
BLAM!
...which makes those *gunshots* I'm hearing all the more peculiar.

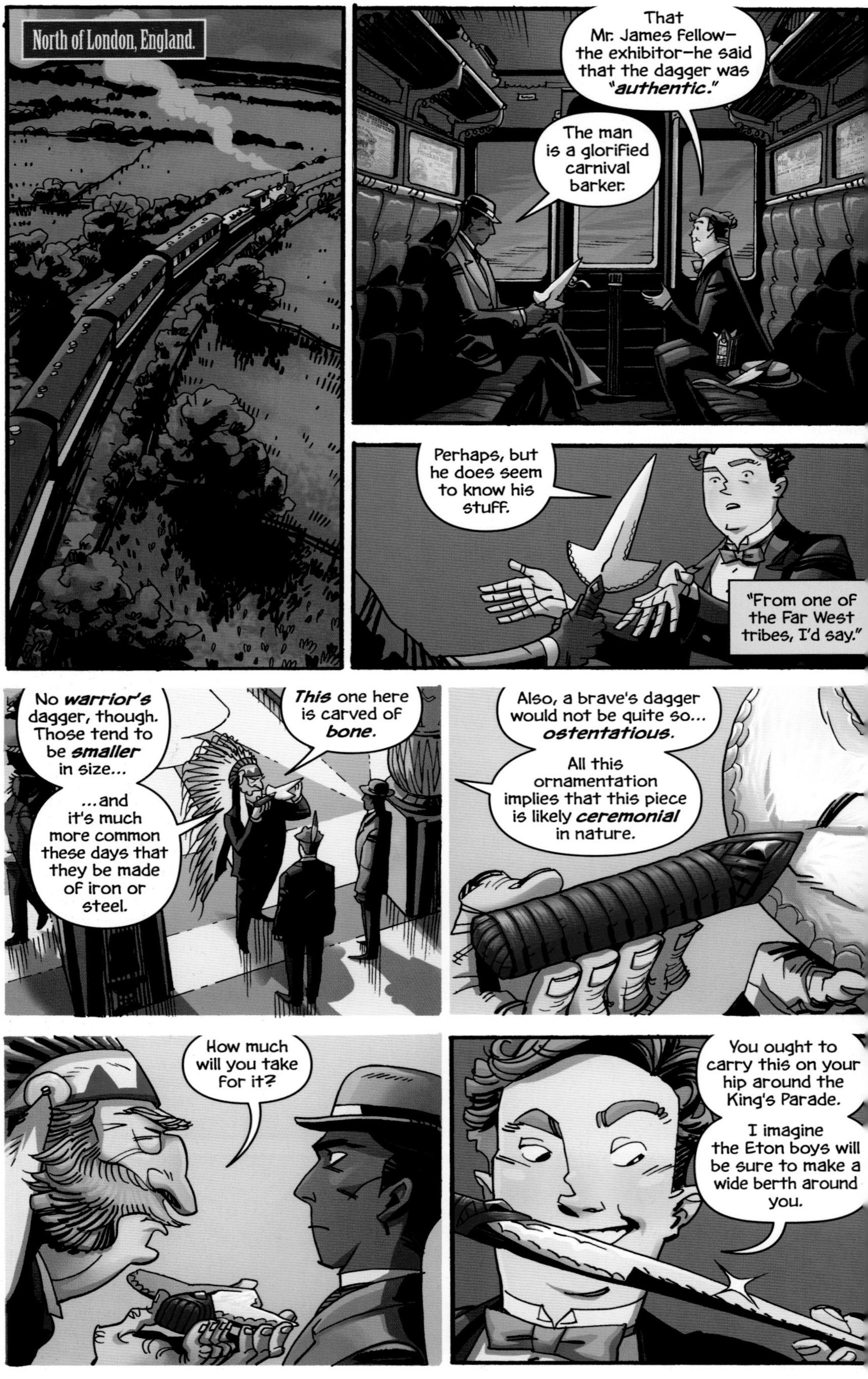
North of London, England.
That Mr. James Fellow—the exhibitor—he said that the dagger was "authentic."
The man is a glorified carnival barker.
Perhaps, but he does seem to know his stuff.
"From one of the Far West tribes, I'd say."
No warrior's dagger, though. Those tend to be smaller in size...
...and it's much more common these days that they be made of iron or steel.
This one here is carved of bone.
Also, a brave's dagger would not be quite so... ostentatious.
All this ornamentation implies that this piece is likely ceremonial in nature.
How much will you take for it?
You ought to carry this on your hip around the King's Parade.
I imagine the Eton boys will be sure to make a wide berth around you.

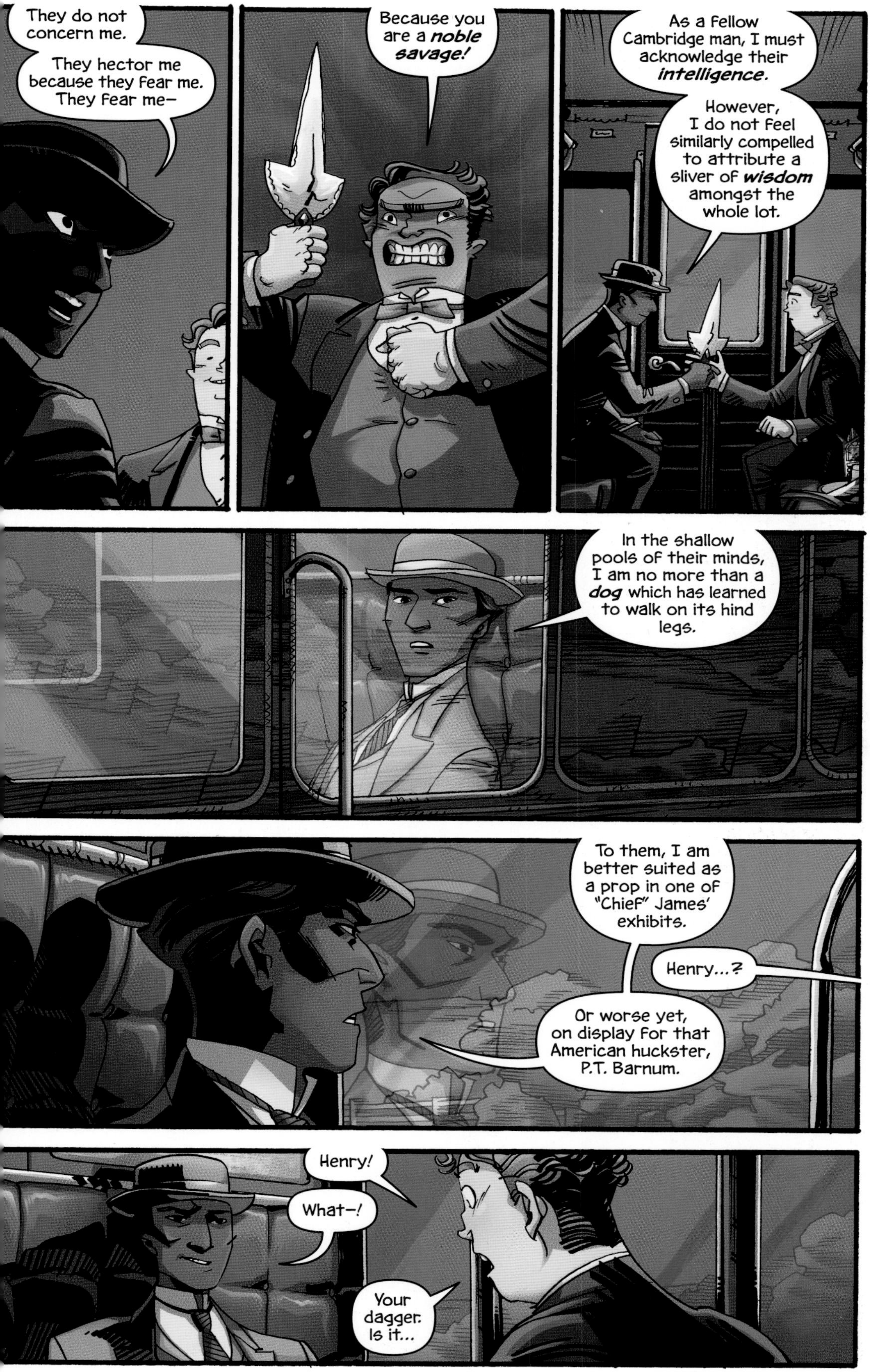
They do not concern me.
They hector me because they fear me. They fear me—
Because you are a *noble savage!*
As a fellow Cambridge man, I must acknowledge their *intelligence.*
However, I do not feel similarly compelled to attribute a sliver of *wisdom* amongst the whole lot.
In the shallow pools of their minds, I am no more than a *dog* which has learned to walk on its hind legs.
To them, I am better suited as a prop in one of "Chief" James' exhibits.
Henry...?
Or worse yet, on display for that American huckster, P.T. Barnum.
Henry!
What—!
Your dagger. Is it...

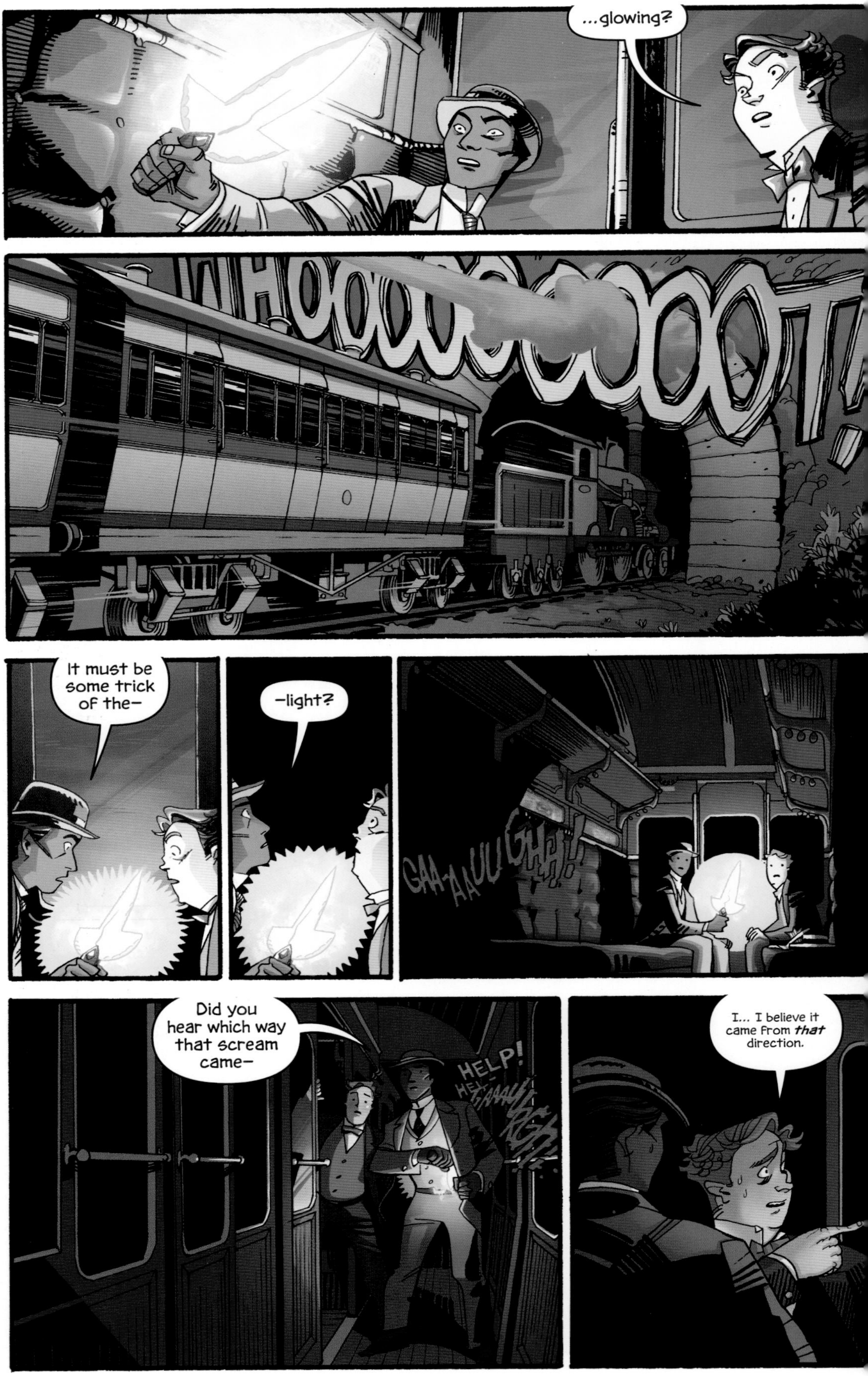
...glowing?
WHOOOOOOOOOT!!
It must be some trick of the–
–light?
GAA-AAUUGHH!!
Did you hear which way that scream came–
HELP!
HEL-AAAUGH!
I... I believe it came from *that* direction.

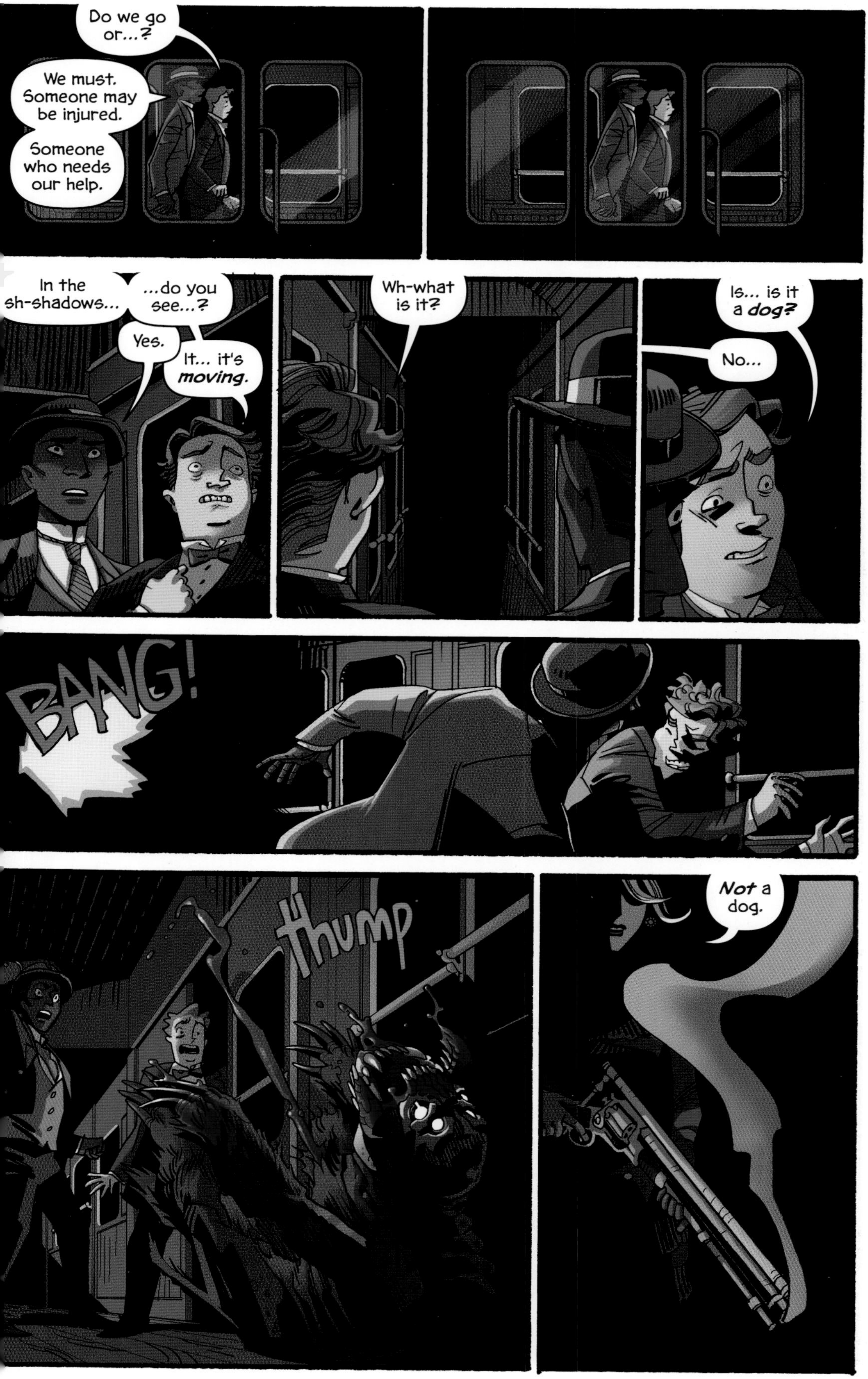
Do we go or...?
We must. Someone may be injured.
Someone who needs our help.
In the sh-shadows...
...do you see...?
Yes.
It... it's *moving*.
Wh-what is it?
Is... is it a *dog?*
No...
BANG!
thump
Not a dog.

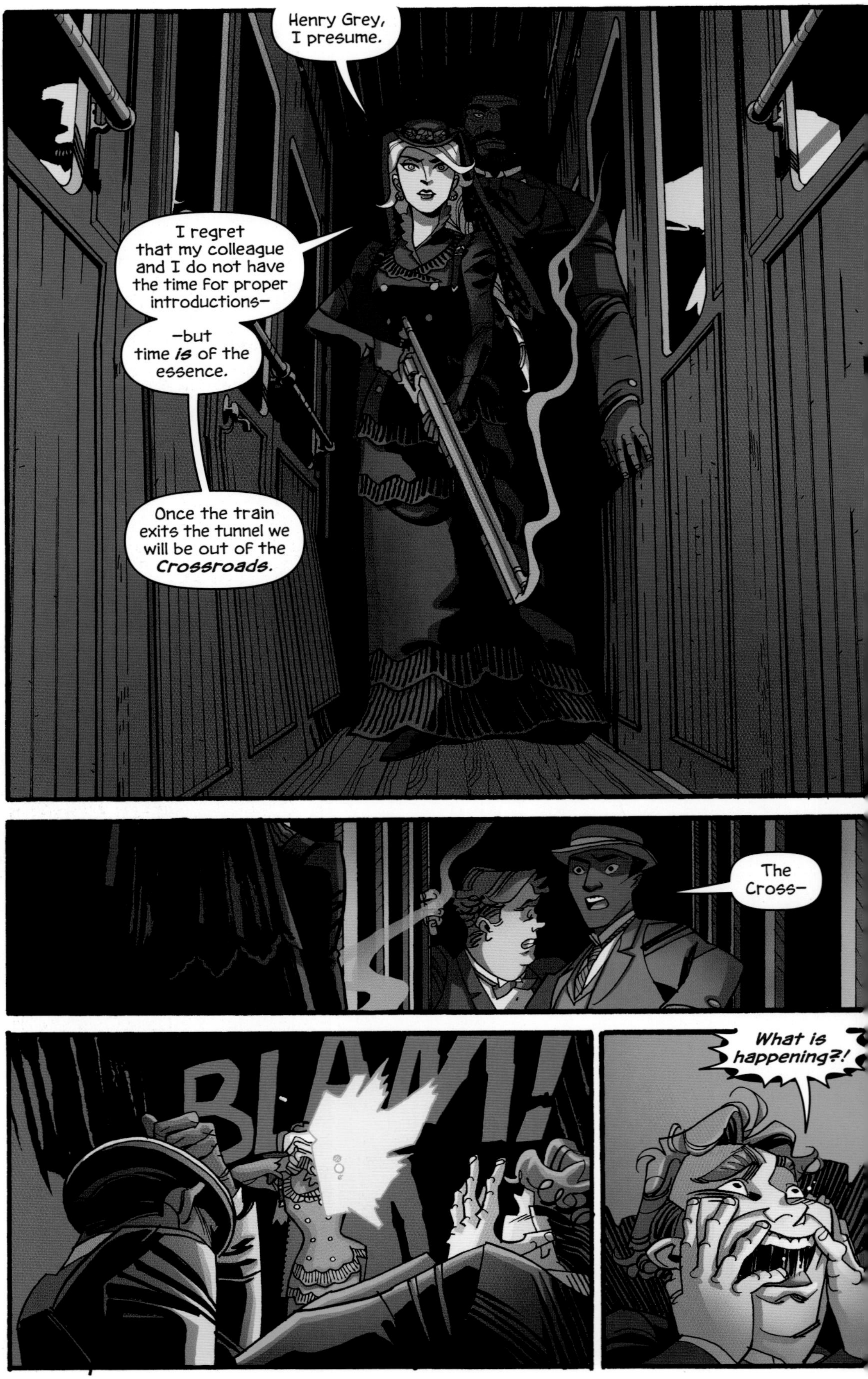
Henry Grey, I presume.
I regret that my colleague and I do not have the time for proper introductions–
–but time *is* of the essence.
Once the train exits the tunnel we will be out of the ***Crossroads.***
The Cross–
BLAM!
What is happening?!

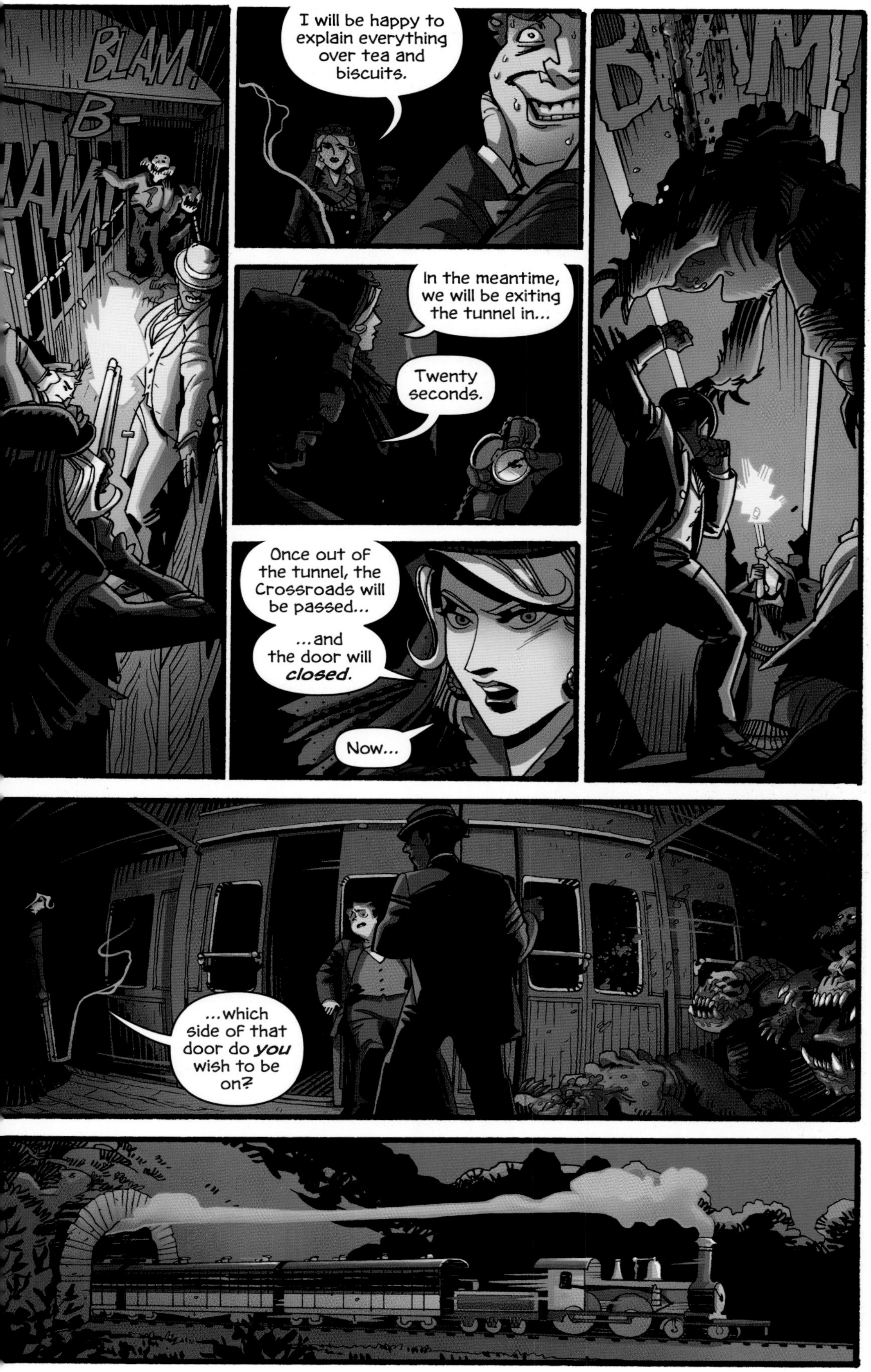
BLAM!
B-BLAM!
I will be happy to explain everything over tea and biscuits.
BLAM!
In the meantime, we will be exiting the tunnel in...
Twenty seconds.
Once out of the tunnel, the Crossroads will be passed...
...and the door will *closed*.
Now...
...which side of that door do *you* wish to be on?

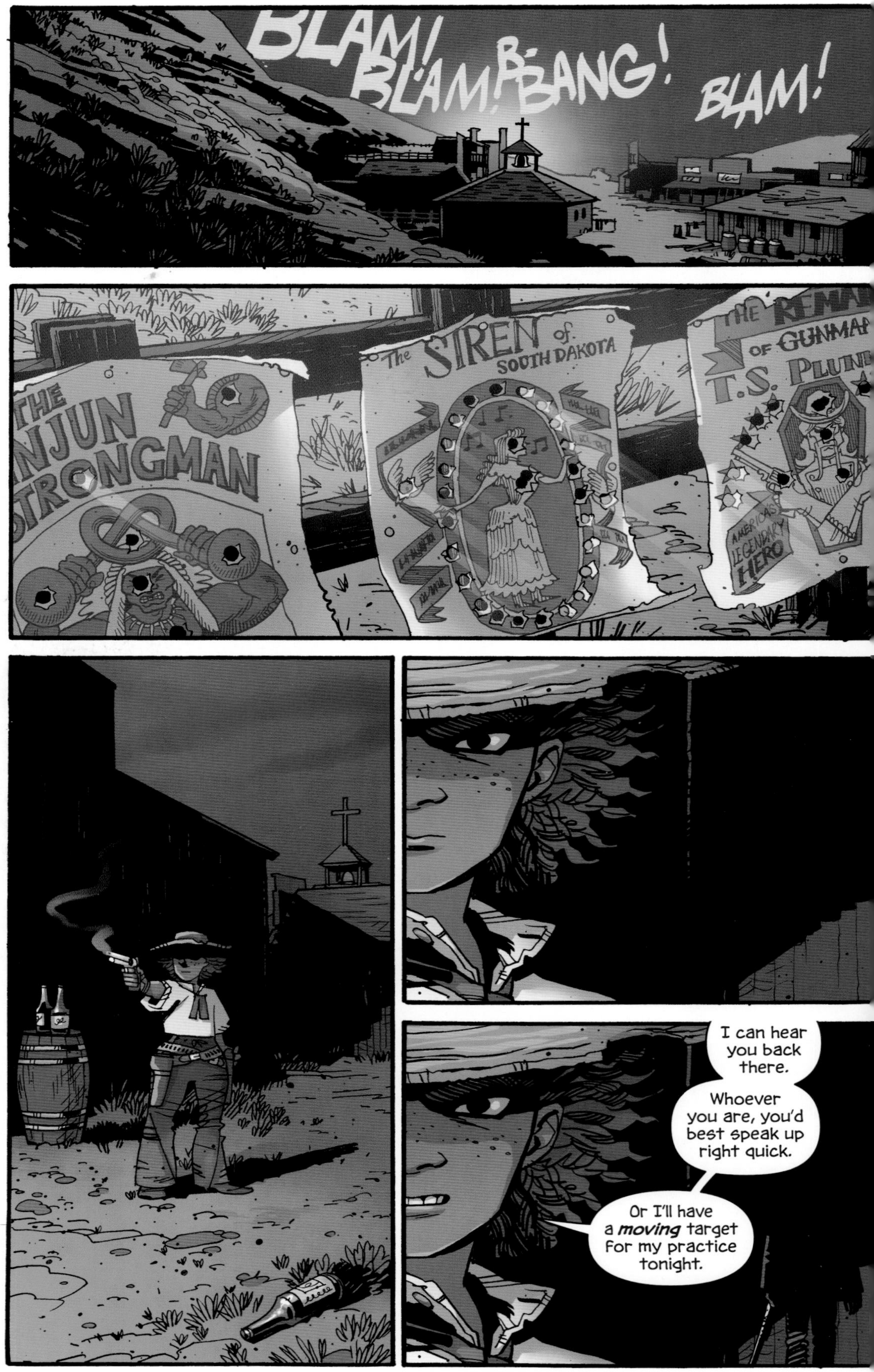
BLAM! BLAM! B-BANG! BLAM!
THE
NJUN
STRONGMAN
The SIREN of SOUTH DAKOTA
THE
OF GUNMA
T.S. PLUN
AMERICA'S LEGENDARY HERO
I can hear you back there.
Whoever you are, you'd best speak up right quick.
Or I'll have a ***moving*** target for my practice tonight.

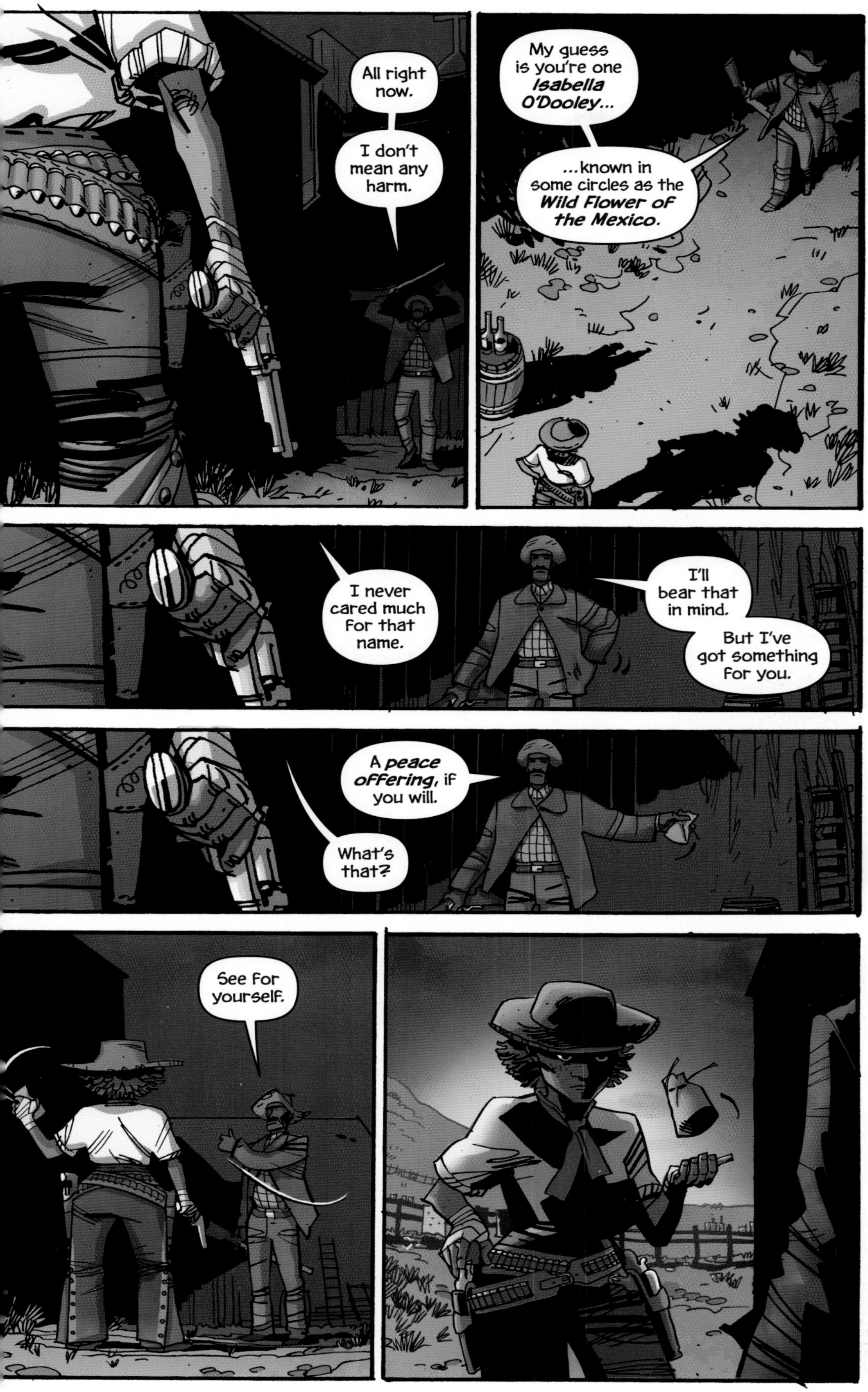
All right now.
I don't mean any harm.
My guess is you're one *Isabella O'Dooley...*
...known in some circles as the *Wild Flower of the Mexico.*
I never cared much for that name.
I'll bear that in mind.
But I've got something for you.
A *peace offering,* if you will.
What's that?
See for yourself.

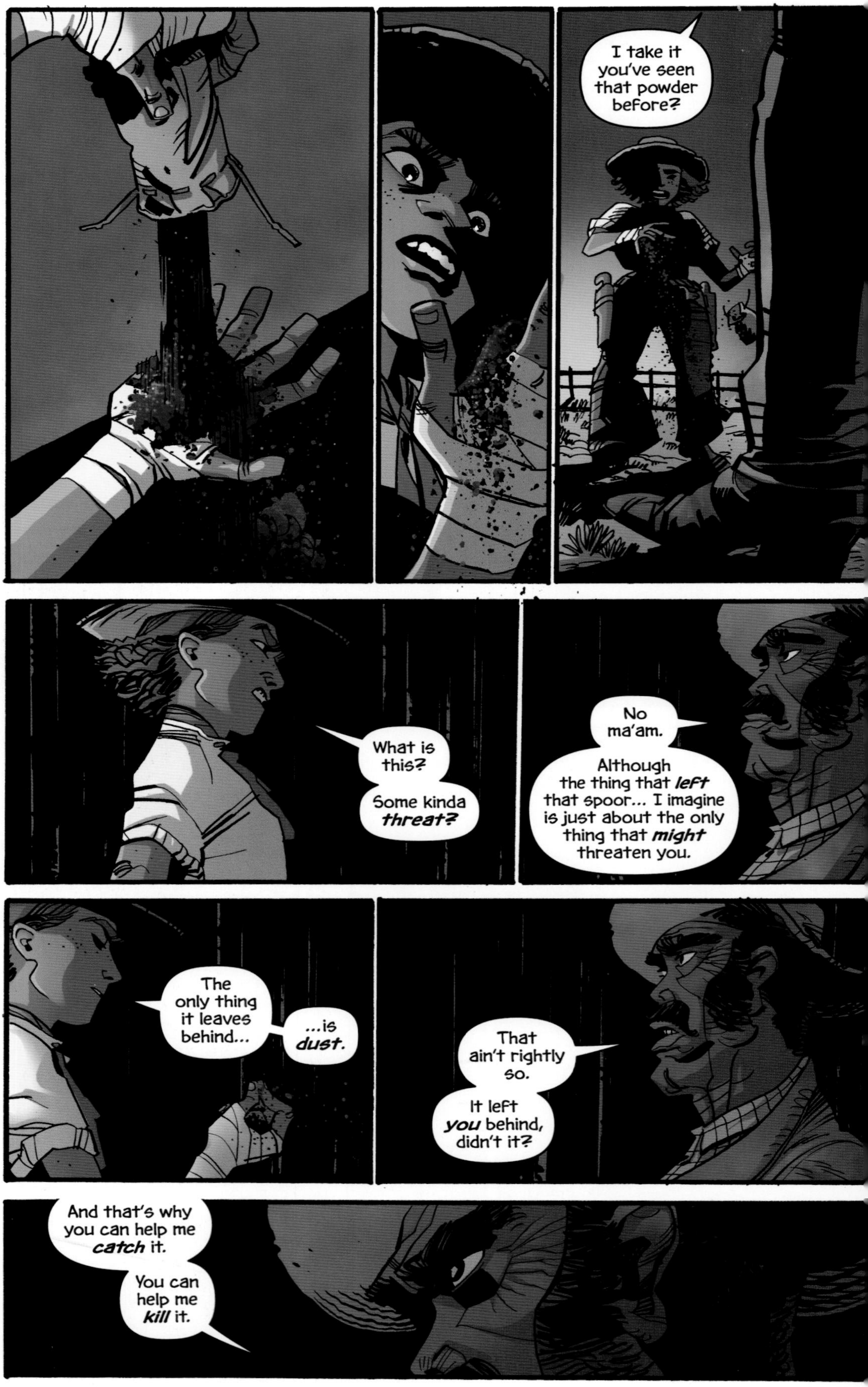
I take it you've seen that powder before?
What is this?
Some kinda *threat?*
No ma'am.
Although the thing that *left* that spoor... I imagine is just about the only thing that *might* threaten you.
The only thing it leaves behind...
...is *dust.*
That ain't rightly so.
It left *you* behind, didn't it?
And that's why you can help me *catch* it.
You can help me *kill* it.

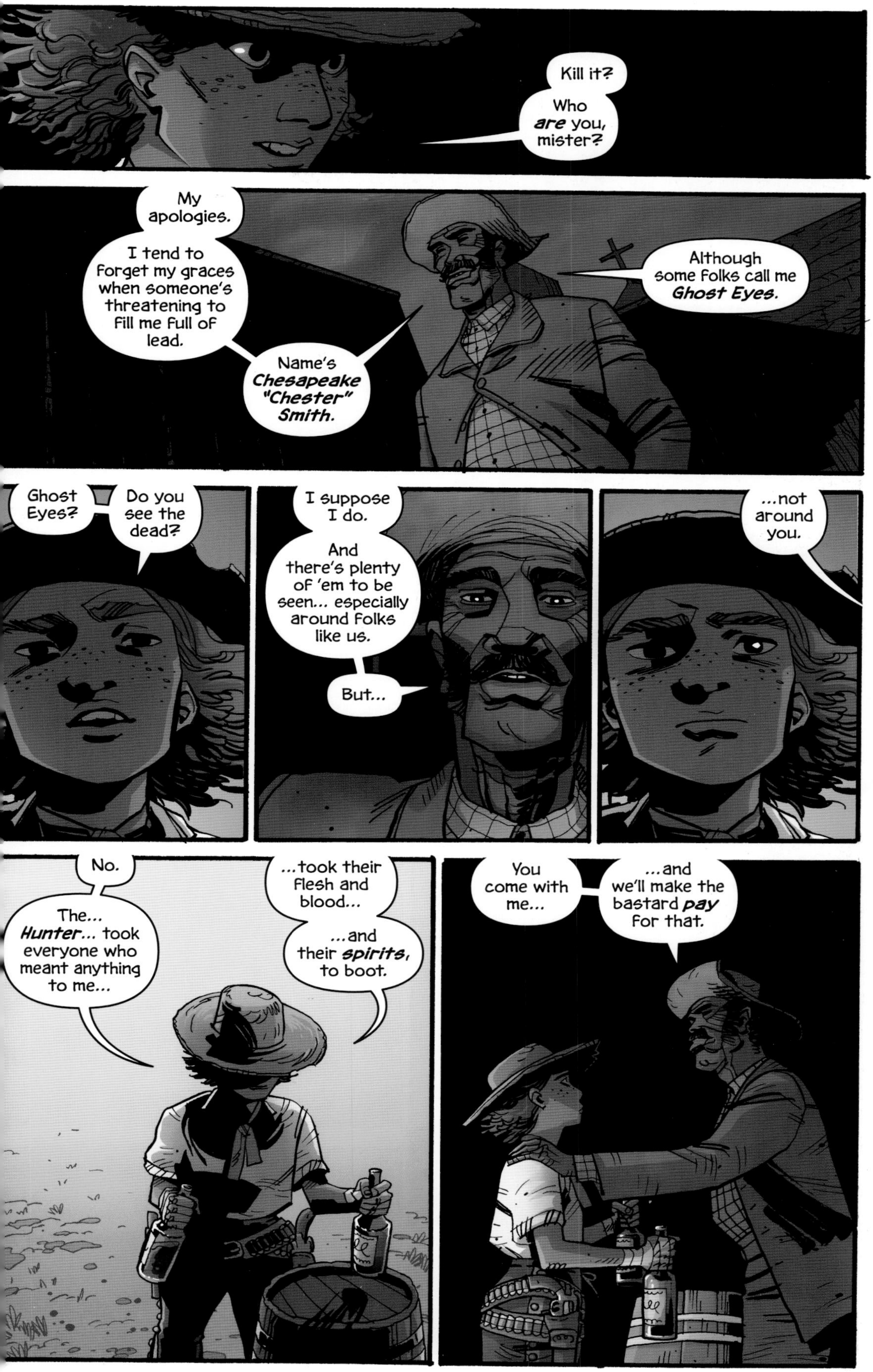
Kill it?
Who *are* you, mister?
My apologies.
I tend to forget my graces when someone's threatening to fill me full of lead.
Name's *Chesapeake "Chester" Smith.*
Although some folks call me *Ghost Eyes.*
Ghost Eyes?
Do you see the dead?
I suppose I do.
And there's plenty of 'em to be seen... especially around folks like us.
But...
...not around you.
No.
The... *Hunter*... took everyone who meant anything to me...
...took their flesh and blood...
...and their *spirits,* to boot.
You come with me...
...and we'll make the bastard *pay* for that.

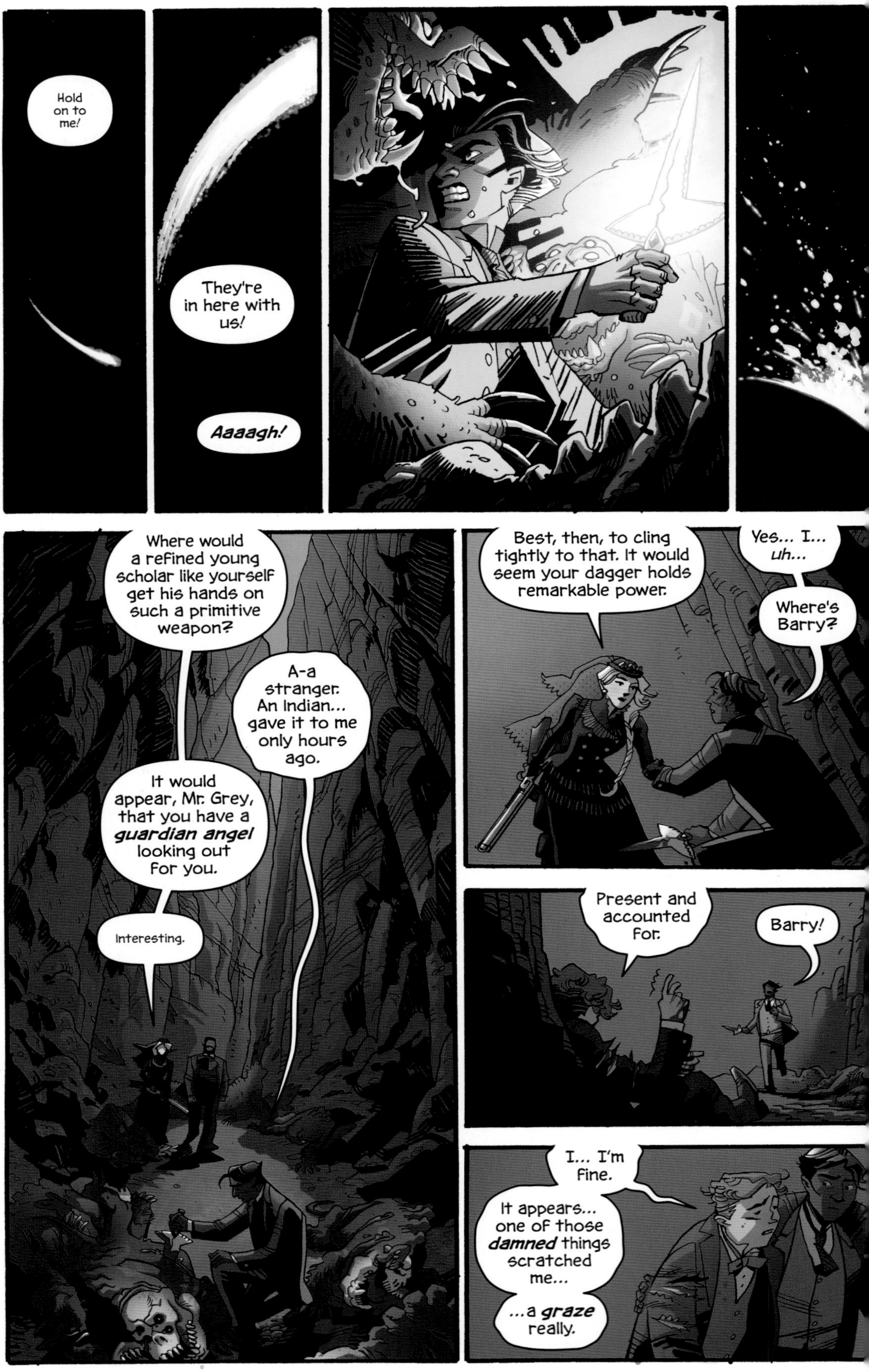

Hold on to me!
They're in here with us!
Aaaagh!
Where would a refined young scholar like yourself get his hands on such a primitive weapon?
A-a stranger. An Indian... gave it to me only hours ago.
It would appear, Mr. Grey, that you have a guardian angel looking out for you.
Interesting.
Best, then, to cling tightly to that. It would seem your dagger holds remarkable power.
Yes... I... uh...
Where's Barry?
Present and accounted for.
Barry!
I... I'm fine.
It appears... one of those damned things scratched me...
...a graze really.

I don't understand... did we...

...did we **Fall** off the train?

I do not believe so, friend. Not as such, at least.

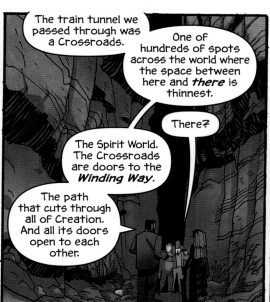

The train tunnel we passed through was a Crossroads.

One of hundreds of spots across the world where the space between here and **there** is thinnest.

There?

The Spirit World. The Crossroads are doors to the **Winding Way**.

The path that cuts through all of Creation. And all its doors open to each other.

What sort of mumbo-jumbo—

Fine.

So we stepped off a moving train, **somewhere** in Essex, and now...

...well... now we are **where** exactly, Ms....?

Redmayne. Ms. **Abigail Redmayne**.

And this is—

Kalfu.

Cal... foo?

Ms. Redmayne.

Mr. Kalfu.

Might I ask where exactly it is that you have brought us?

Why... I've brought you where you are **needed**, Mr. Grey.

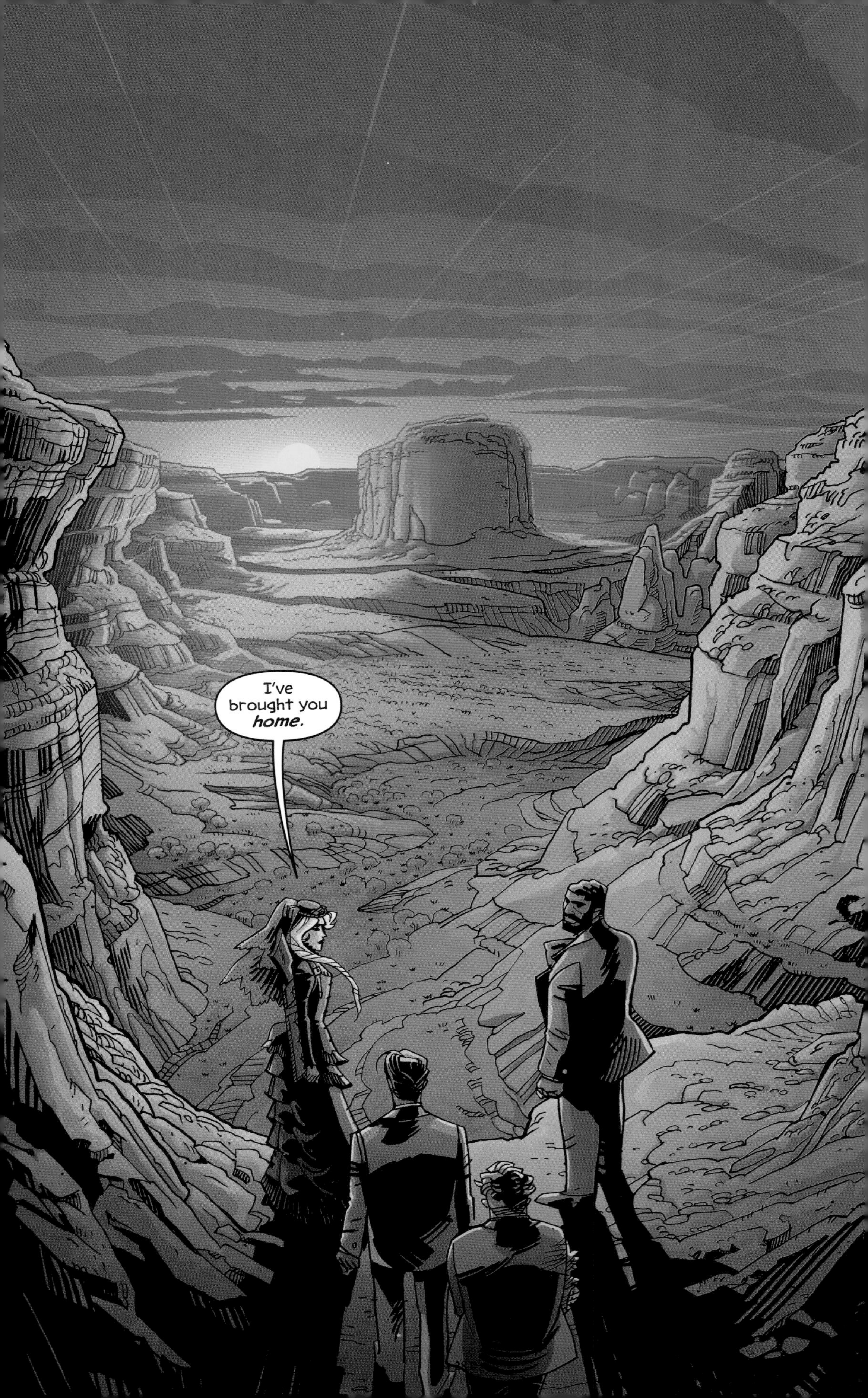
I've brought you *home*.

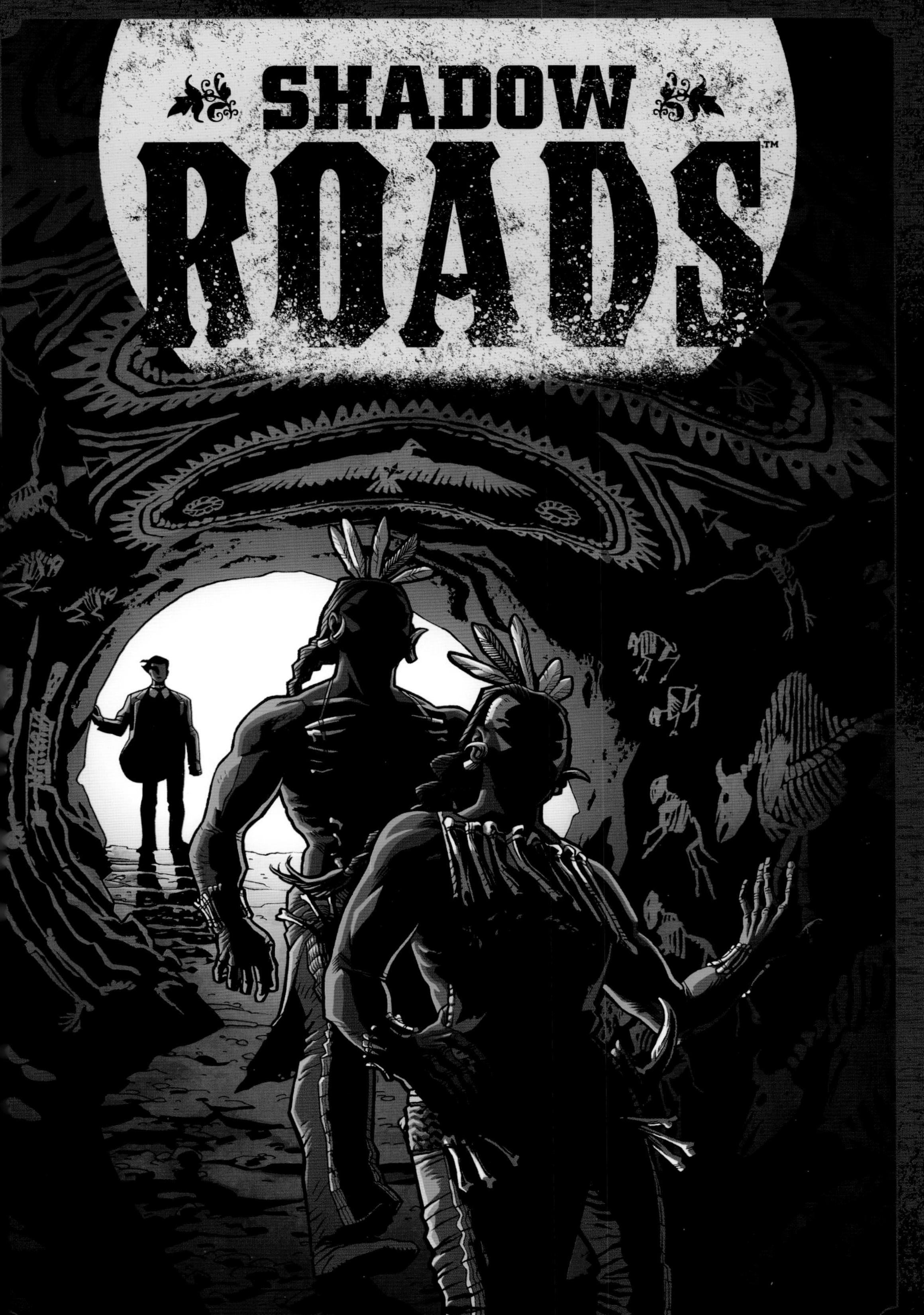
SHADOW
ROADS™

CHAPTER 2

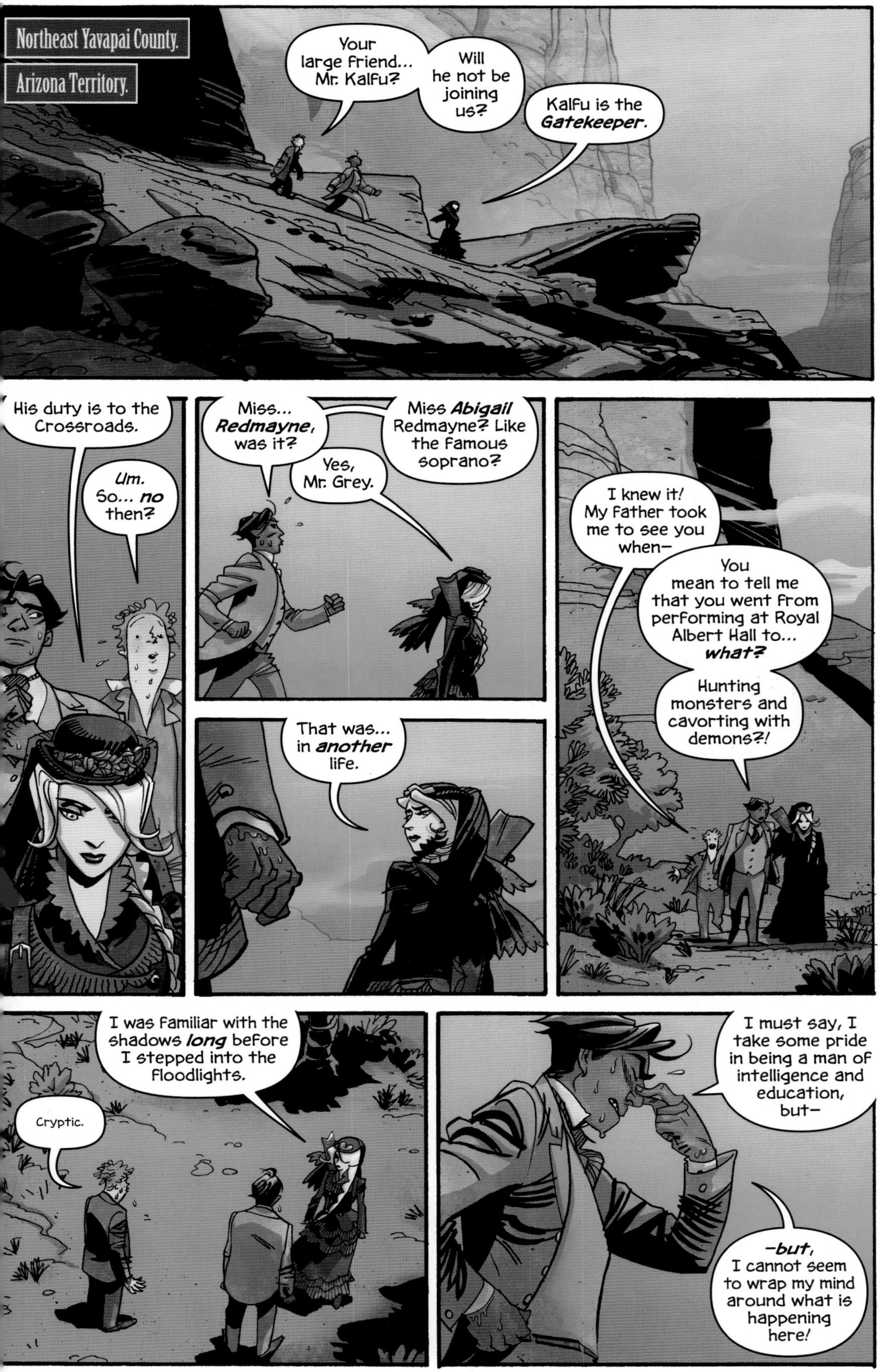
Northeast Yavapai County.
Arizona Territory.
Your large friend... Mr. Kalfu?
Will he not be joining us?
Kalfu is the *Gatekeeper*.
His duty is to the Crossroads.
Um. So... *no* then?
Miss... *Redmayne*, was it?
Yes, Mr. Grey.
Miss *Abigail* Redmayne? Like the famous soprano?
That was... in *another* life.
I knew it! My father took me to see you when—
You mean to tell me that you went from performing at Royal Albert Hall to... *what?*
Hunting monsters and cavorting with demons?!
I was familiar with the shadows *long* before I stepped into the floodlights.
Cryptic.
I must say, I take some pride in being a man of intelligence and education, but—
—but, I cannot seem to wrap my mind around what is happening here!

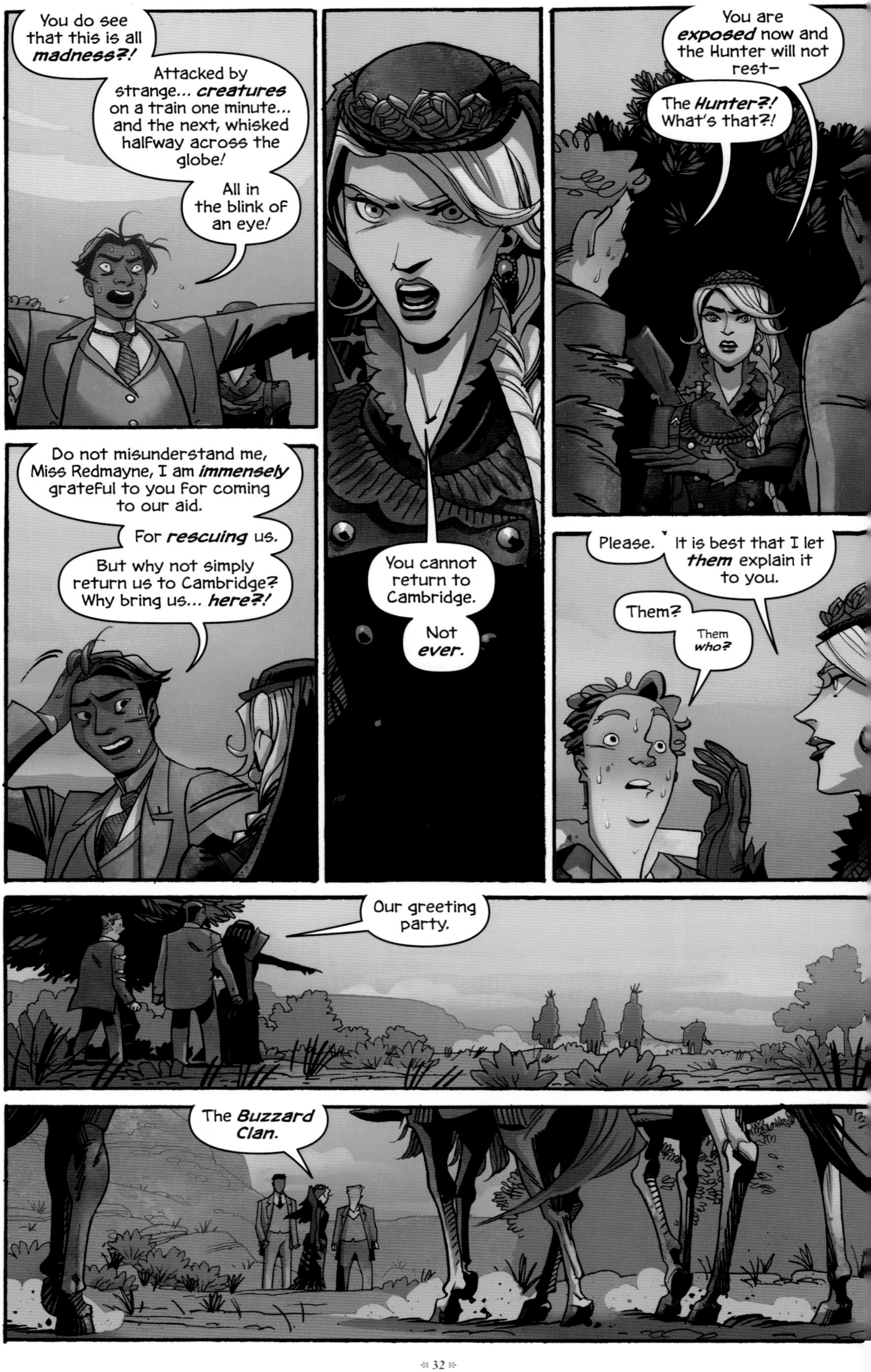
You do see that this is all *madness?!*
Attacked by strange... *creatures* on a train one minute... and the next, whisked halfway across the globe!
All in the blink of an eye!
You are *exposed* now and the Hunter will not rest—
The *Hunter?!* What's that?!
Do not misunderstand me, Miss Redmayne, I am *immensely* grateful to you for coming to our aid.
For *rescuing* us.
But why not simply return us to Cambridge? Why bring us... *here?!*
You cannot return to Cambridge.
Not *ever*.
Please.
It is best that I let *them* explain it to you.
Them?
Them *who?*
Our greeting party.
The *Buzzard Clan.*

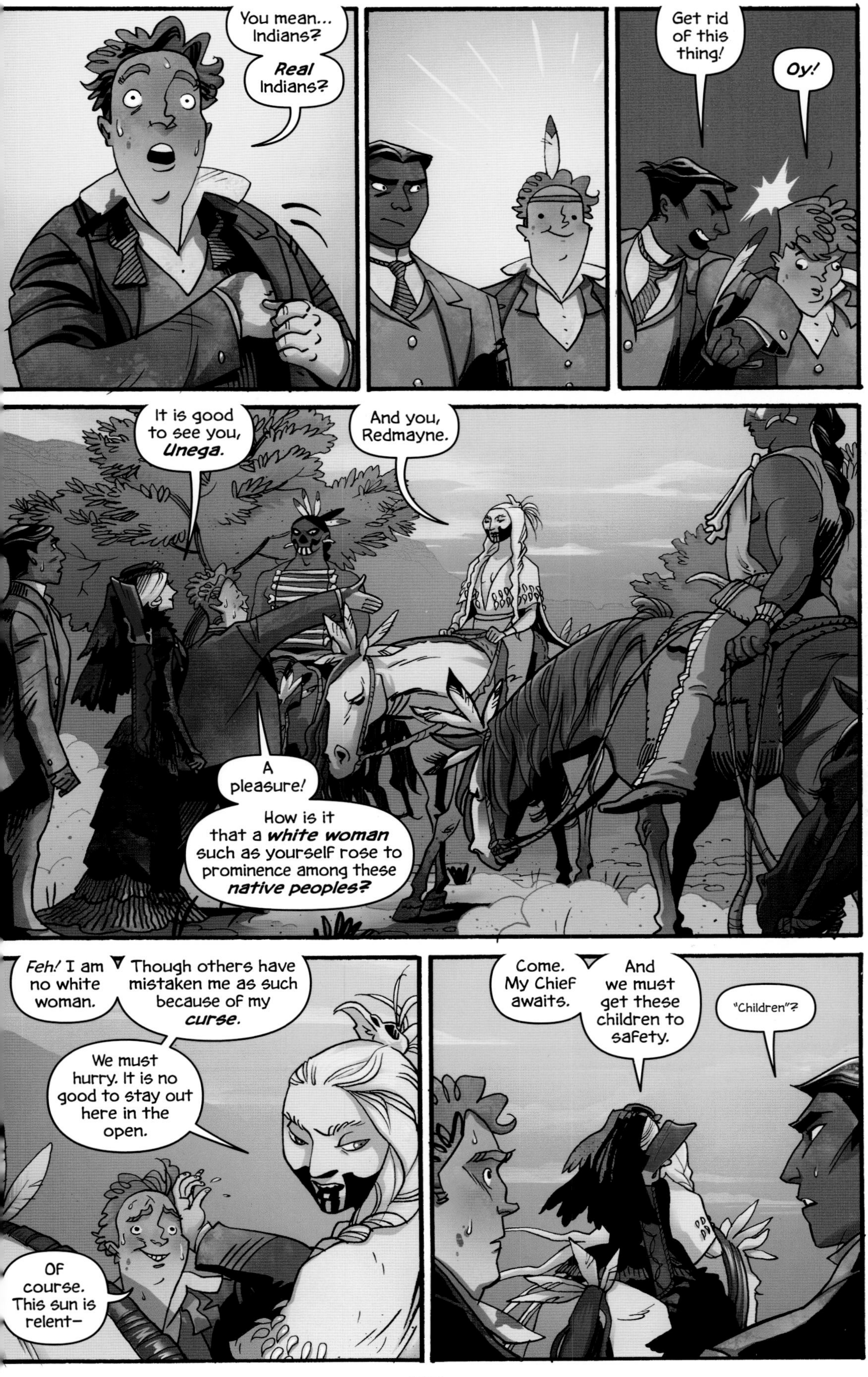

You mean... Indians?
Real Indians?
Get rid of this thing!
Oy!
It is good to see you, Unega.
And you, Redmayne.
A pleasure!
How is it that a white woman such as yourself rose to prominence among these native peoples?
Feh! I am no white woman.
Though others have mistaken me as such because of my curse.
We must hurry. It is no good to stay out here in the open.
Of course. This sun is relent—
Come. My Chief awaits.
And we must get these children to safety.
"Children"?

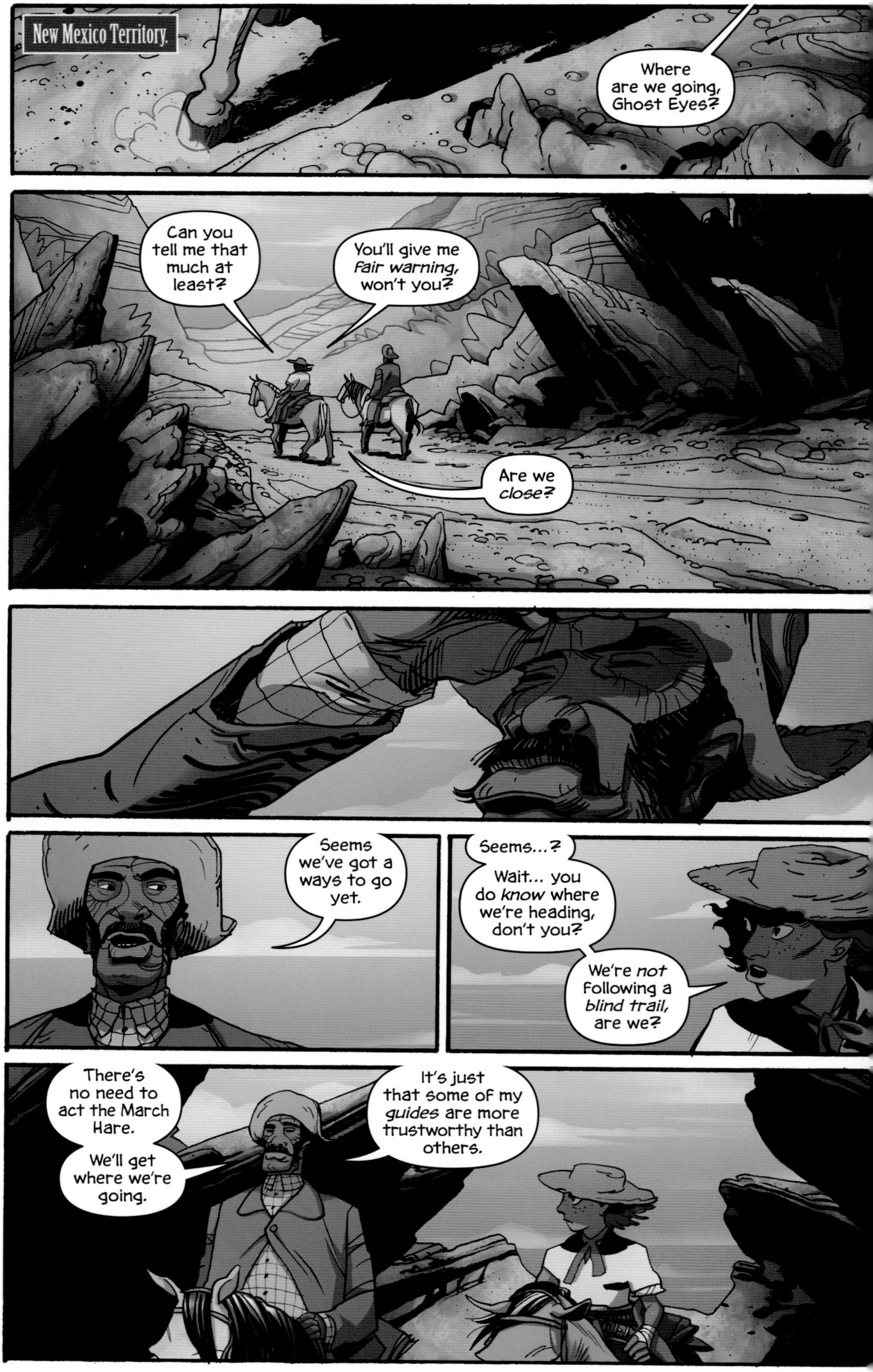
New Mexico Territory.
Where are we going, Ghost Eyes?
Can you tell me that much at least?
You'll give me *fair warning,* won't you?
Are we *close?*
Seems we've got a ways to go yet.
Seems...?
Wait... you do *know* where we're heading, don't you?
We're *not* following a *blind trail,* are we?
There's no need to act the March Hare.
We'll get where we're going.
It's just that some of my *guides* are more trustworthy than others.

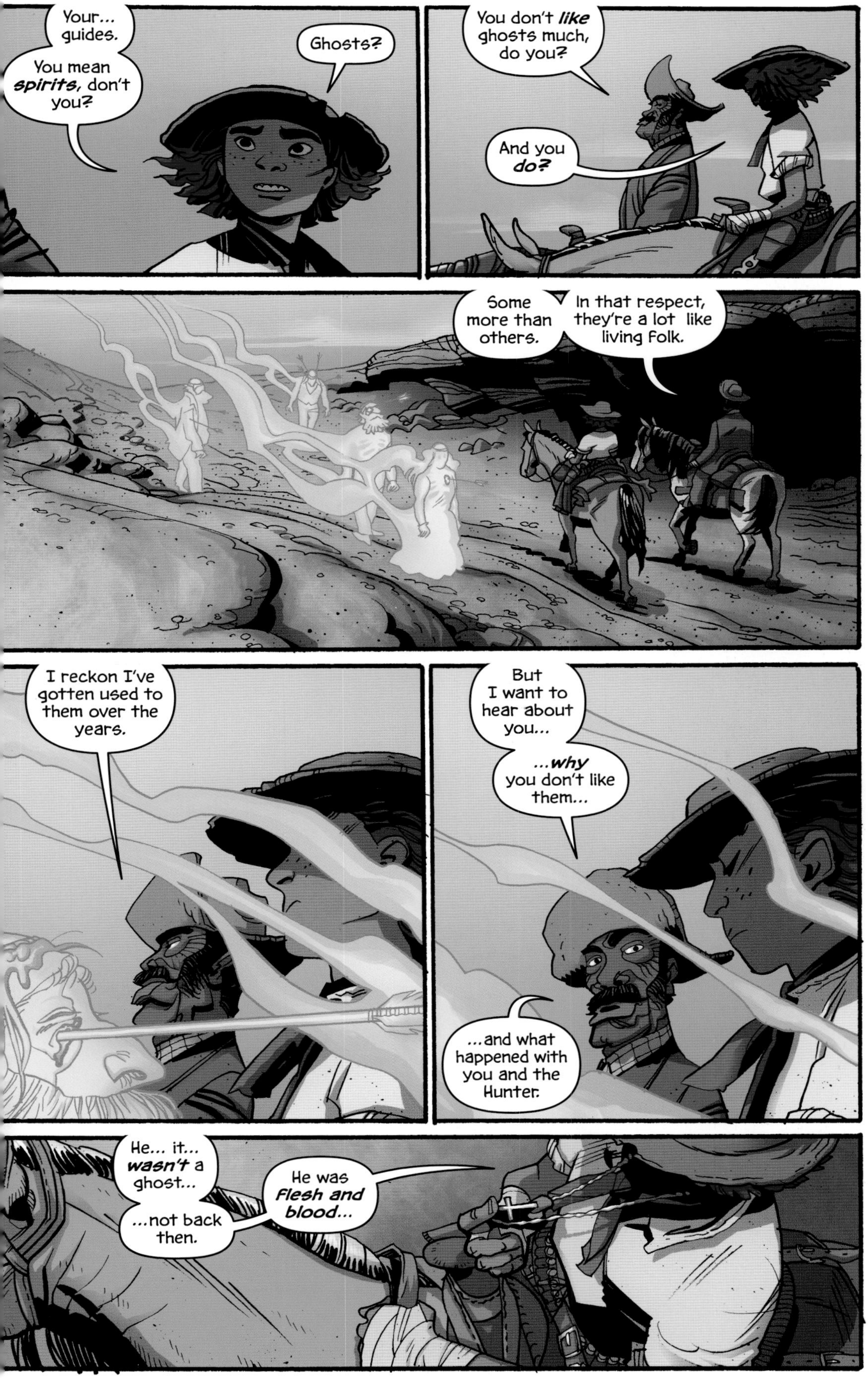
Your... guides.
You mean *spirits*, don't you?
Ghosts?
You don't *like* ghosts much, do you?
And you *do?*
Some more than others.
In that respect, they're a lot like living folk.
I reckon I've gotten used to them over the years.
But I want to hear about you...
...*why* you don't like them...
...and what happened with you and the Hunter.
He... it... *wasn't* a ghost...
...not back then.
He was *flesh and blood...*

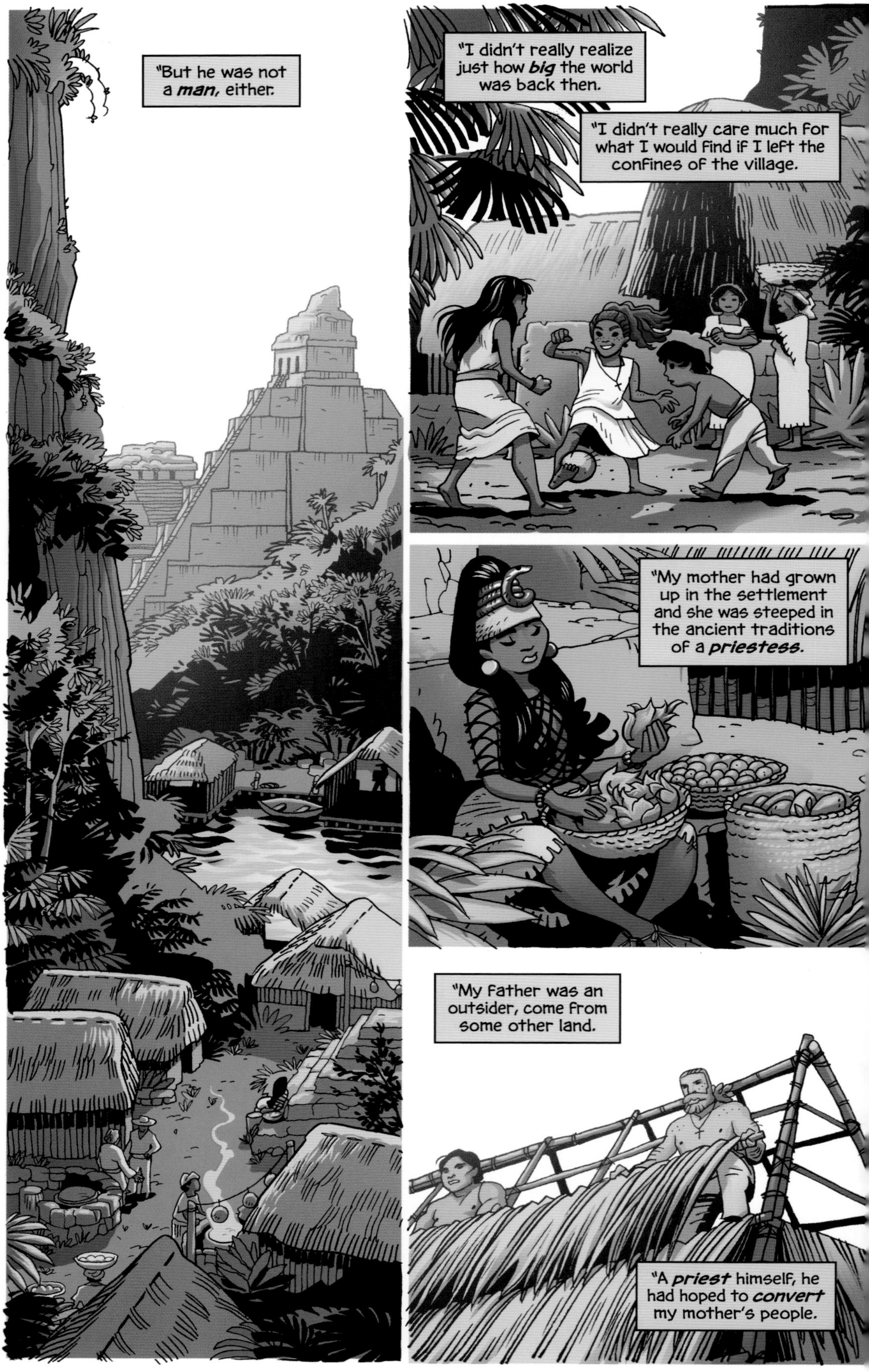
"But he was not a *man,* either.
"I didn't really realize just how *big* the world was back then.
"I didn't really care much for what I would find if I left the confines of the village.
"My mother had grown up in the settlement and she was steeped in the ancient traditions of a *priestess.*
"My father was an outsider, come from some other land.
"A *priest* himself, he had hoped to *convert* my mother's people.

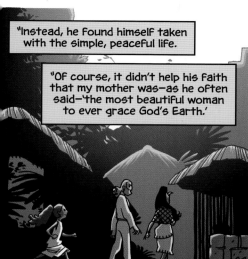

"Instead, he found himself taken with the simple, peaceful life.

"Of course, it didn't help his faith that my mother was—as he often said—'the most beautiful woman to ever grace God's Earth.'

"I was *happy*.

"Like I said, I didn't rightly know how much bigger the world was.

"Bigger.

"And so *much darker*.

"The screams woke me up on the night it happened...

"...the night the *Hunter* came for us."

Just... just stay here.

I'll see what's going on... and I'll let you know if it's *safe.*

"Those were the last words my father spoke to me.

"But the *screams*... we heard those for a *long time* to come."

Mother... *don't!*

Don't go out there!

It's all right, child.

I just need to—

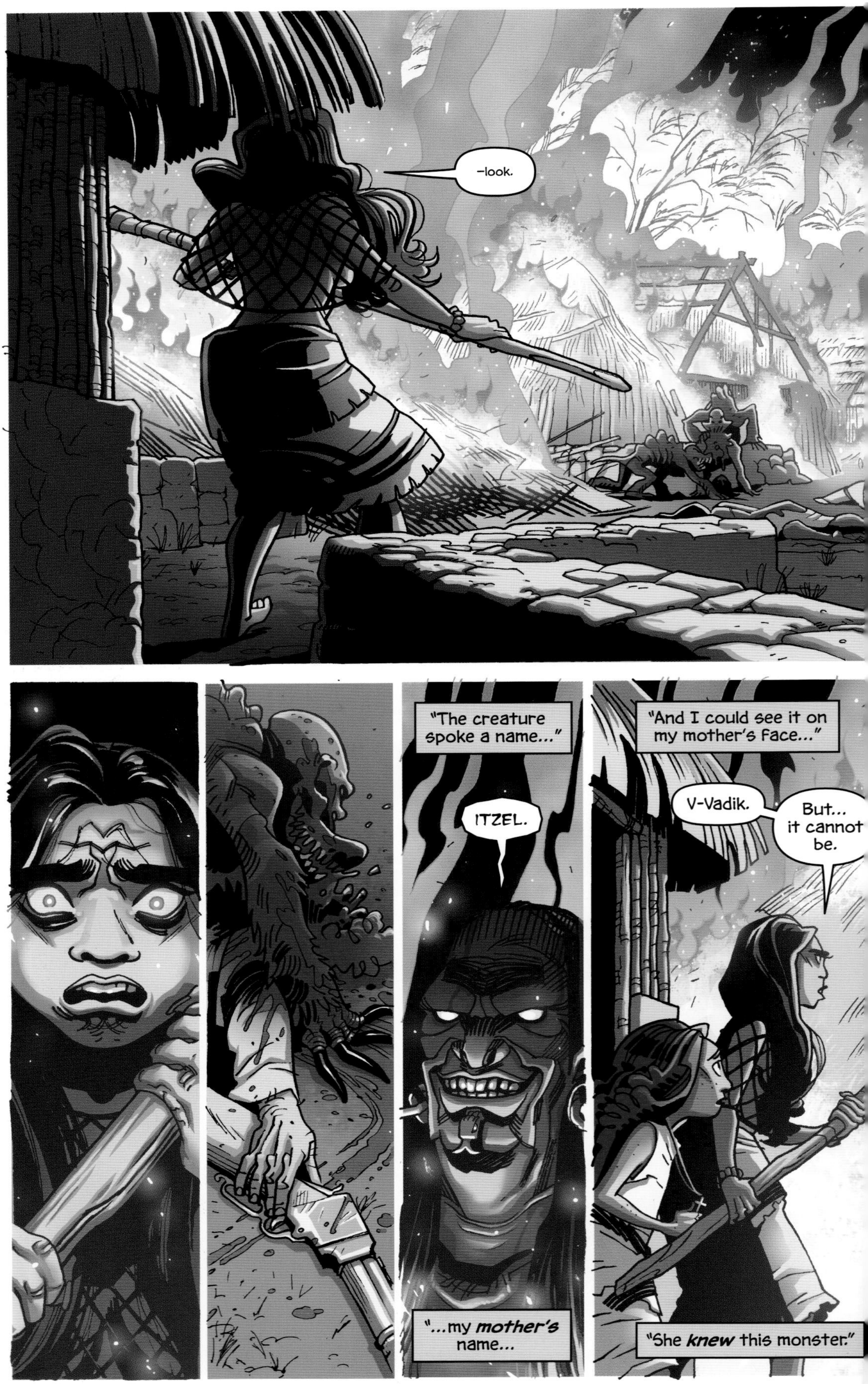
–look.
"The creature spoke a name..."
ITZEL.
"...my mother's name...
"And I could see it on my mother's face..."
V-Vadik.
But... it cannot be.
"She knew this monster."

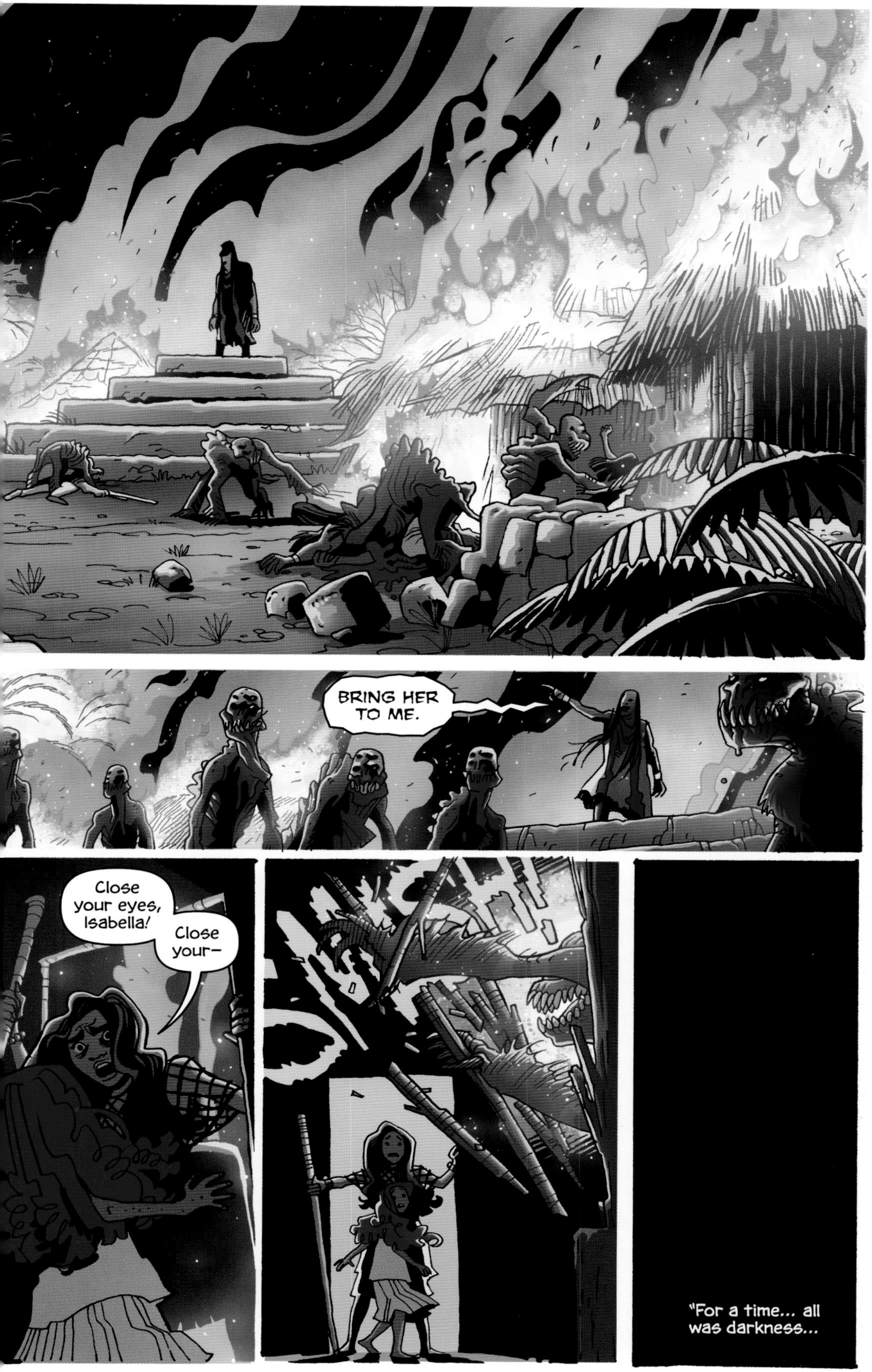
BRING HER TO ME.
Close your eyes, Isabella!
Close your–
"For a time... all was darkness...

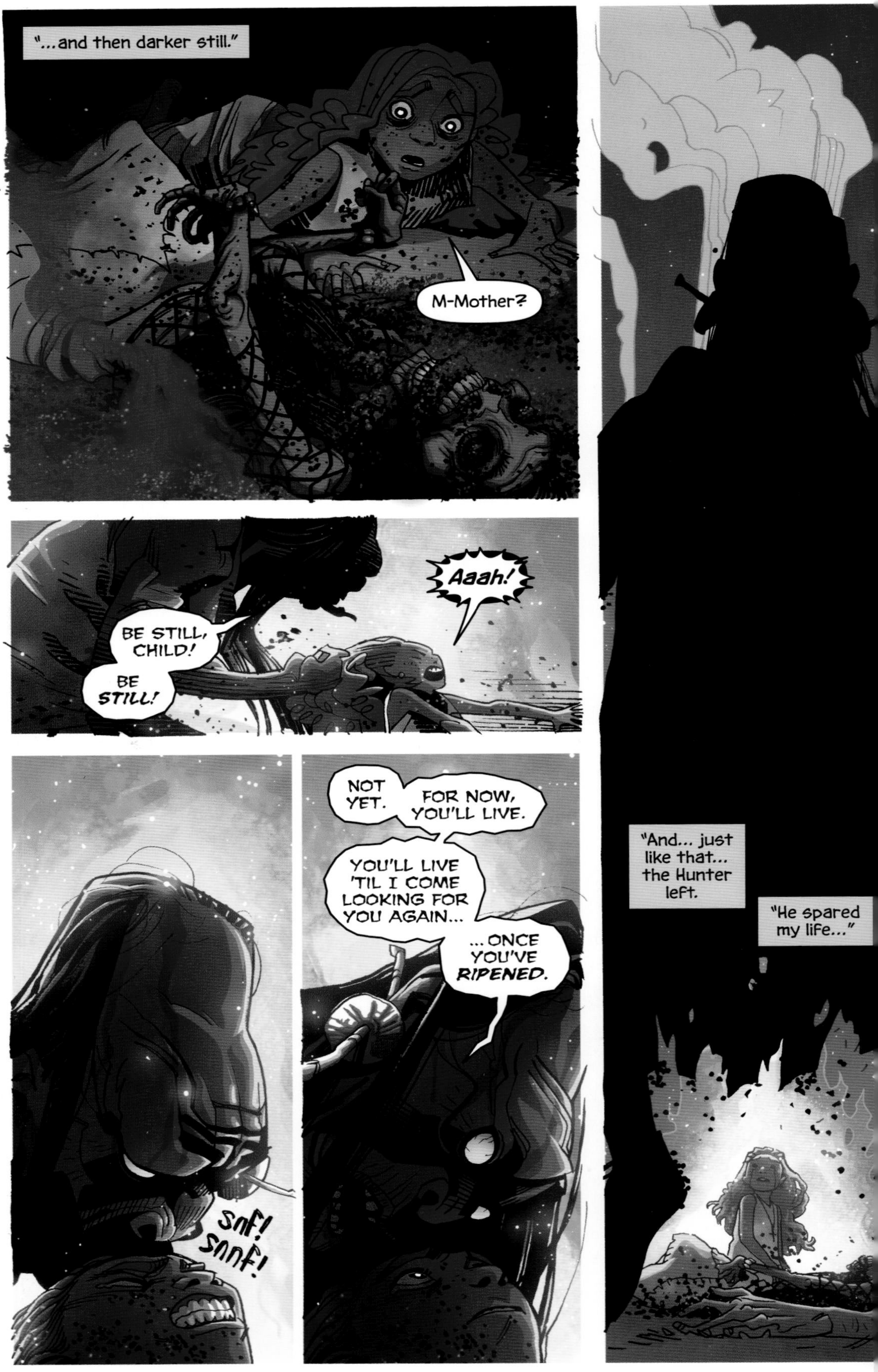
"...and then darker still."
M-Mother?
Aaah!
BE STILL, CHILD!
BE STILL!
snf! snnf!
NOT YET.
FOR NOW, YOU'LL LIVE.
YOU'LL LIVE 'TIL I COME LOOKING FOR YOU AGAIN...
...ONCE YOU'VE RIPENED.
"And... just like that... the Hunter left.
"He spared my life..."

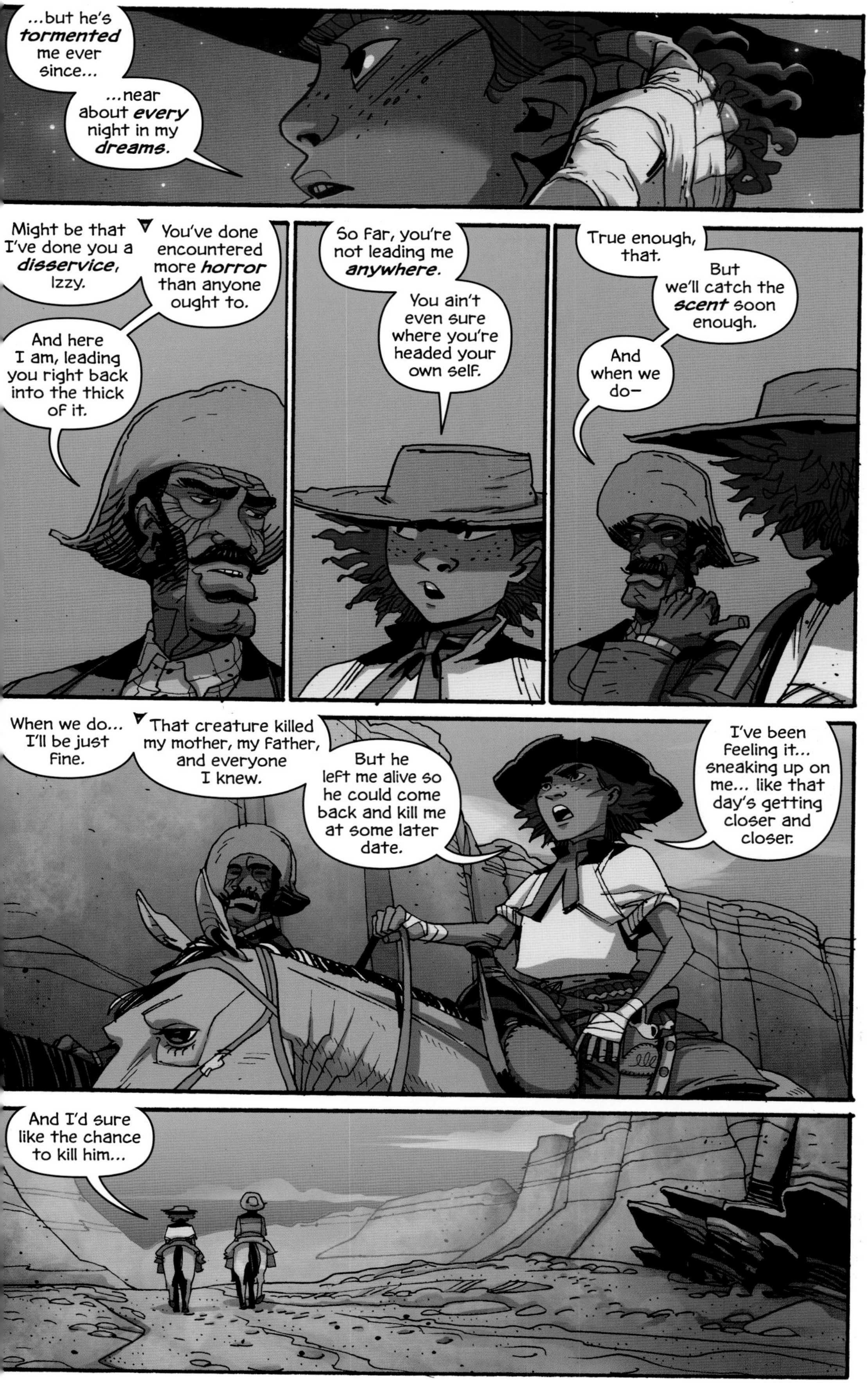
...but he's *tormented* me ever since...
...near about *every* night in my *dreams*.
Might be that I've done you a *disservice*, Izzy.
You've done encountered more *horror* than anyone ought to.
And here I am, leading you right back into the thick of it.
So far, you're not leading me *anywhere*.
You ain't even sure where you're headed your own self.
True enough, that.
But we'll catch the *scent* soon enough.
And when we do—
When we do... I'll be just fine.
That creature killed my mother, my father, and everyone I knew.
But he left me alive so he could come back and kill me at some later date.
I've been feeling it... sneaking up on me... like that day's getting closer and closer.
And I'd sure like the chance to kill him...

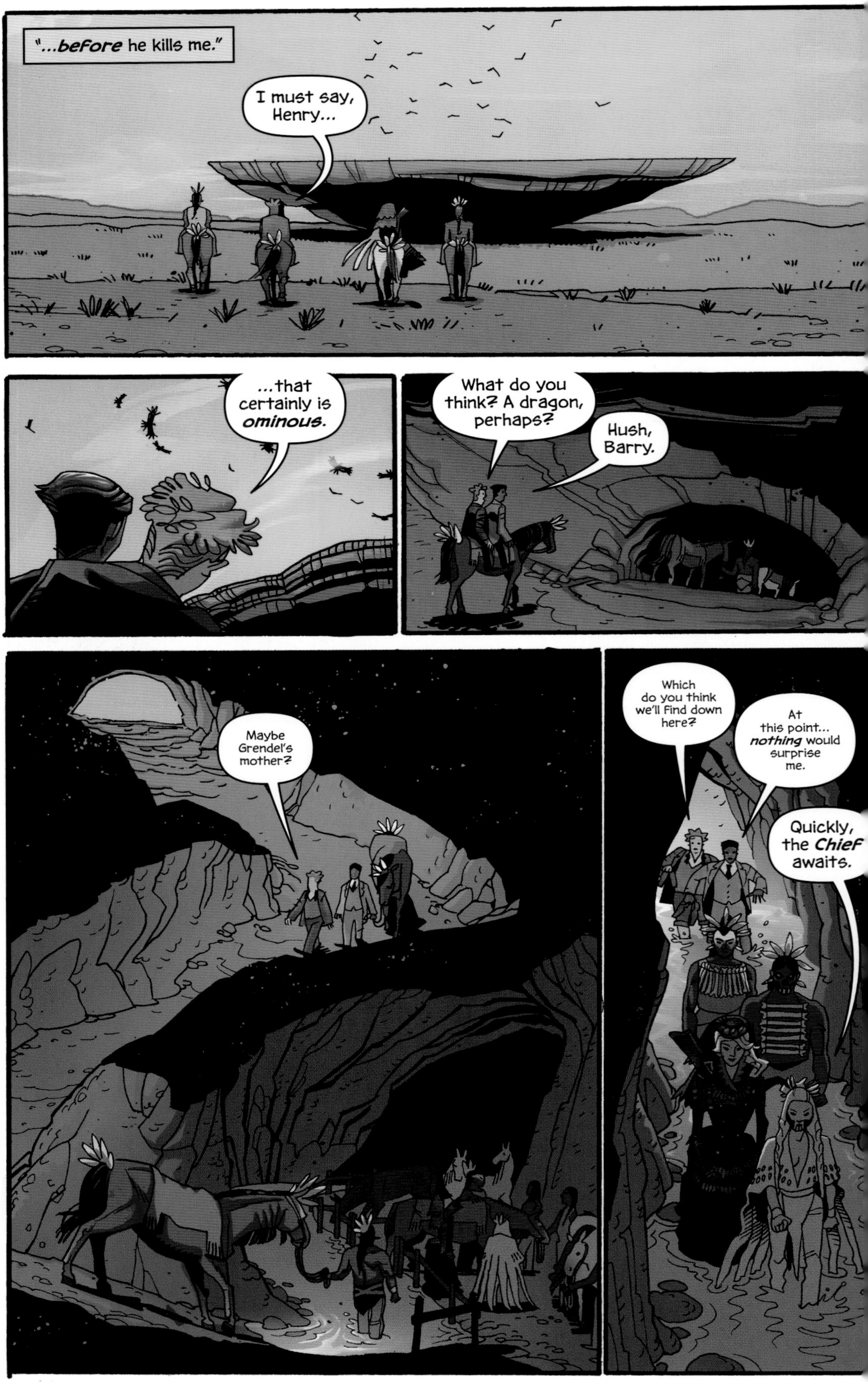
"...before he kills me."
I must say, Henry...
...that certainly is ominous.
What do you think? A dragon, perhaps?
Hush, Barry.
Maybe Grendel's mother?
Which do you think we'll find down here?
At this point... nothing would surprise me.
Quickly, the Chief awaits.

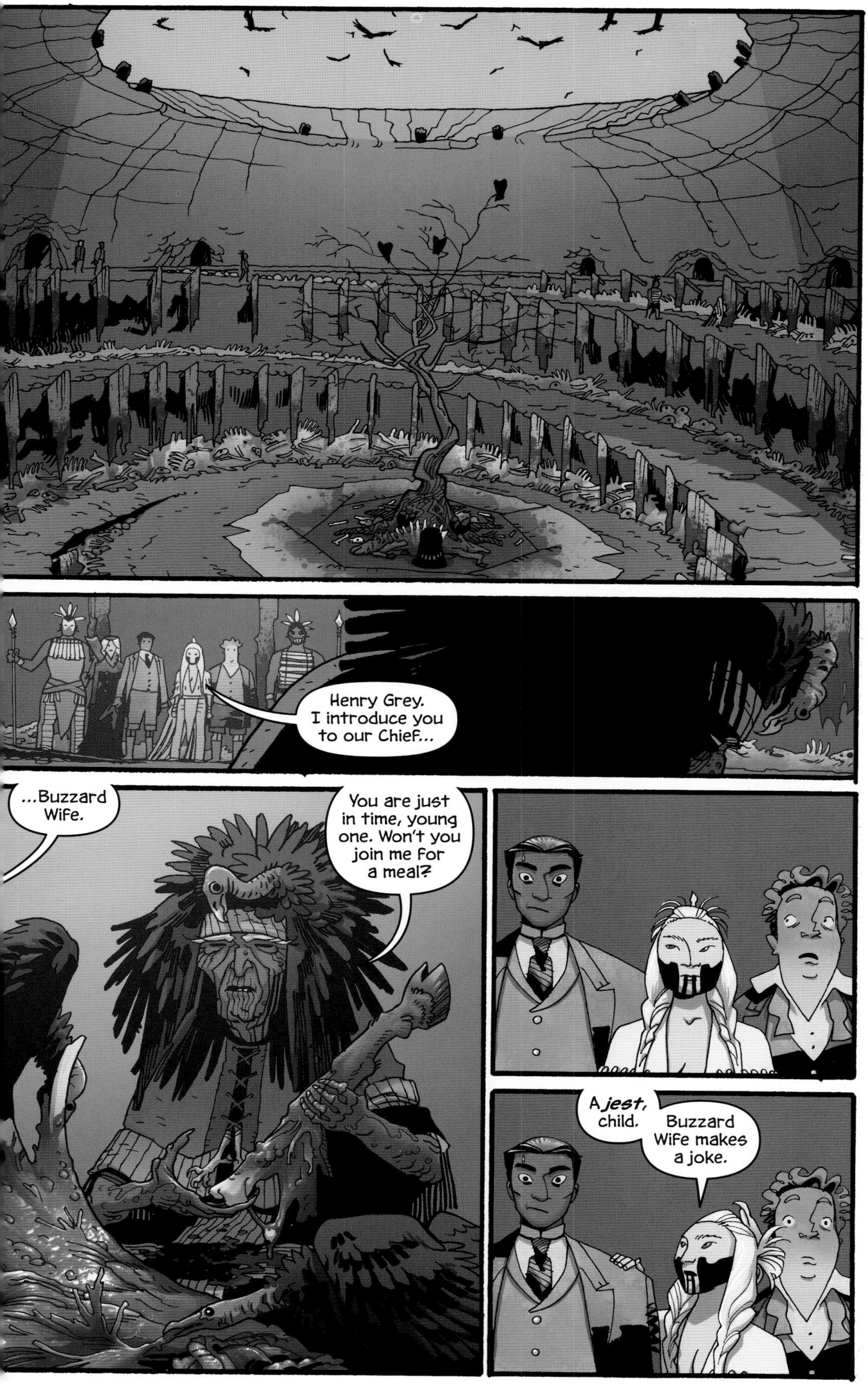
Henry Grey. I introduce you to our Chief...
...Buzzard Wife.
You are just in time, young one. Won't you join me for a meal?
A *jest,* child.
Buzzard Wife makes a joke.

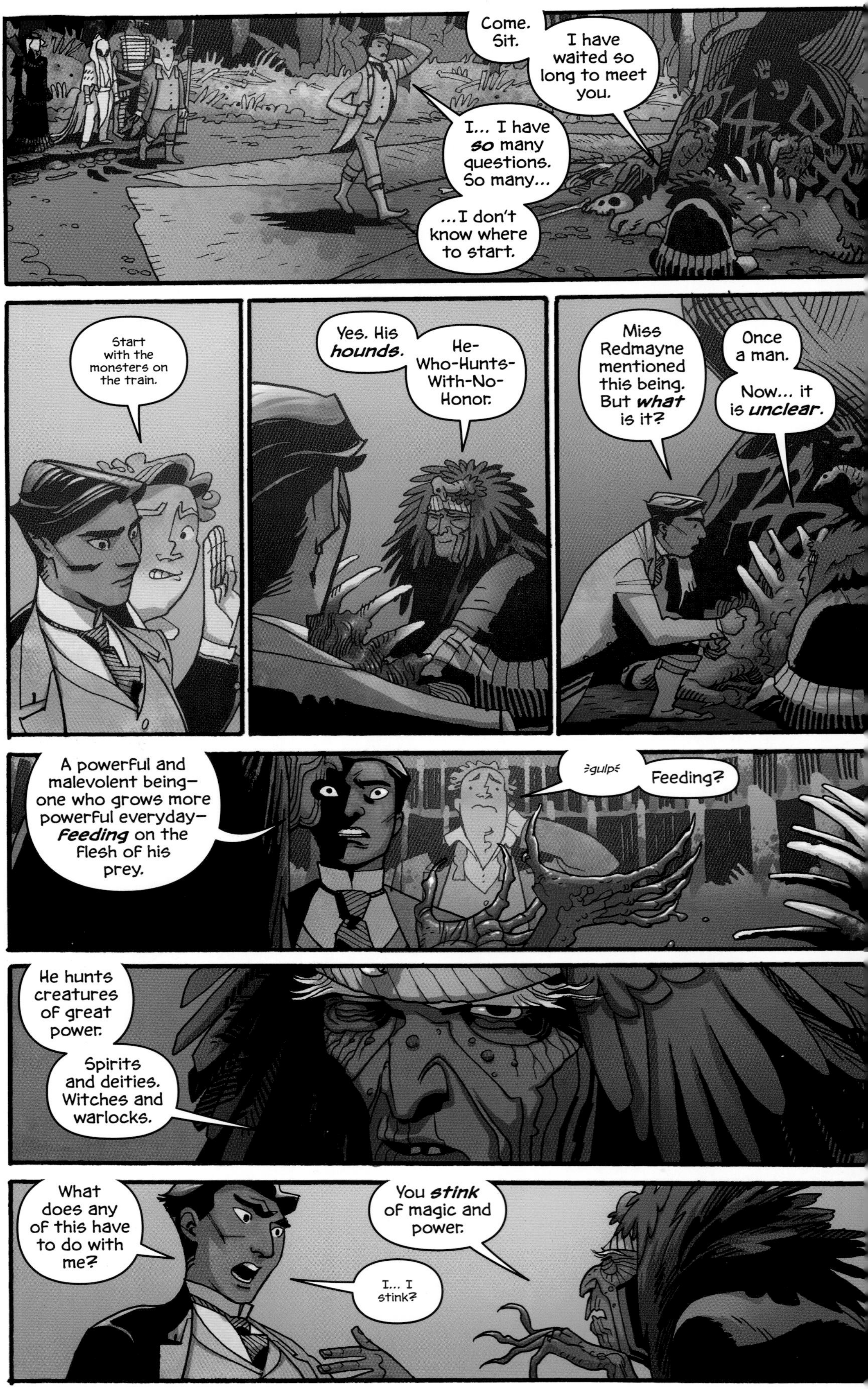
Come. Sit.
I have waited so long to meet you.
I... I have so many questions. So many...
...I don't know where to start.
Start with the monsters on the train.
Yes. His hounds.
He-Who-Hunts-With-No-Honor.
Miss Redmayne mentioned this being. But what is it?
Once a man.
Now... it is unclear.
A powerful and malevolent being—one who grows more powerful everyday—feeding on the flesh of his prey.
gulp
Feeding?
He hunts creatures of great power.
Spirits and deities. Witches and warlocks.
What does any of this have to do with me?
You stink of magic and power.
I... I stink?

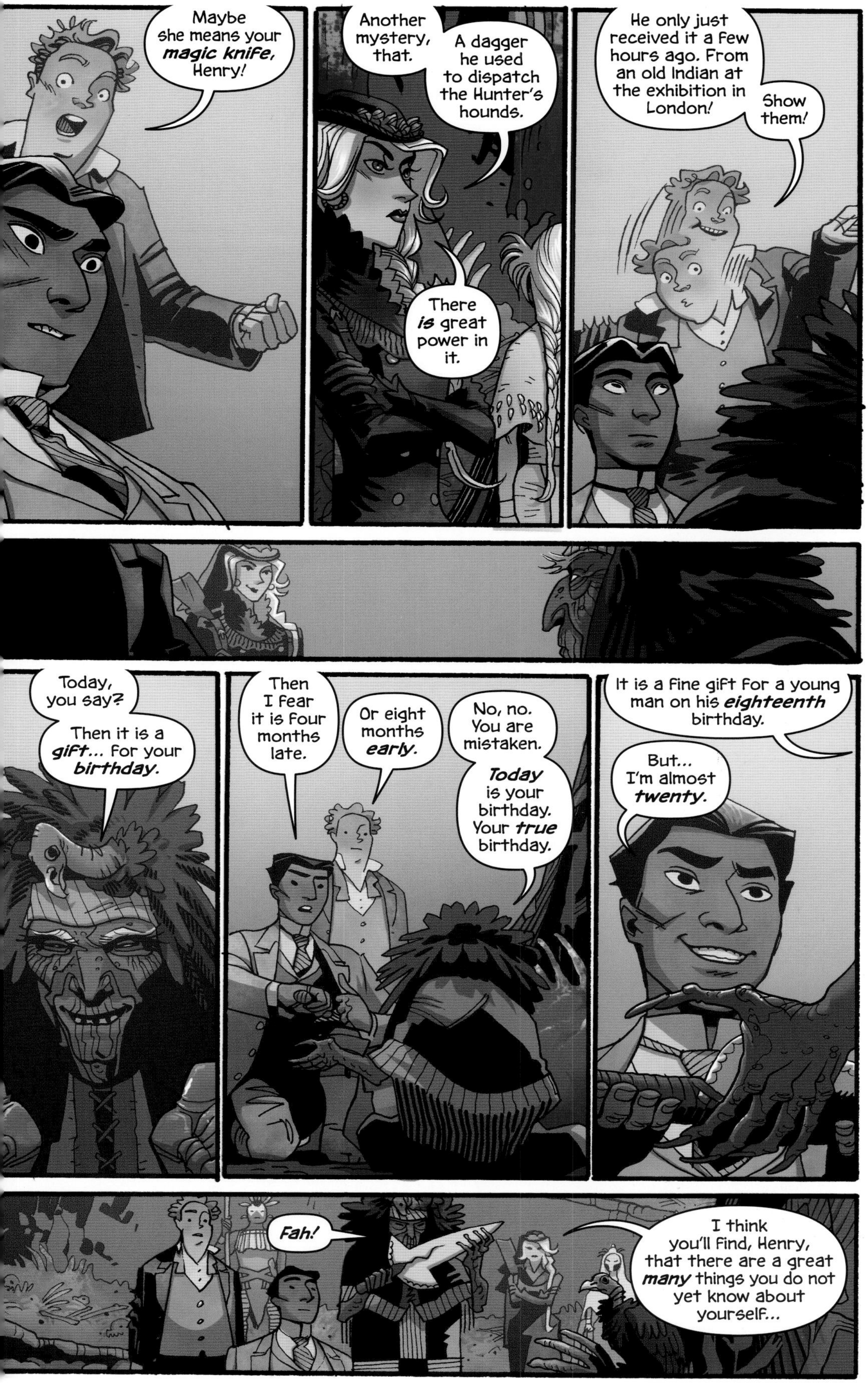
Maybe she means your *magic knife,* Henry!
Another mystery, that.
A dagger he used to dispatch the Hunter's hounds.
There *is* great power in it.
He only just received it a few hours ago. From an old Indian at the exhibition in London!
Show them!
Today, you say?
Then it is a *gift*... for your *birthday*.
Then I fear it is four months late.
Or eight months *early*.
No, no. You are mistaken.
Today is your birthday. Your *true* birthday.
It is a fine gift for a young man on his *eighteenth* birthday.
But... I'm almost *twenty*.
Fah!
I think you'll find, Henry, that there are a great *many* things you do not yet know about yourself...

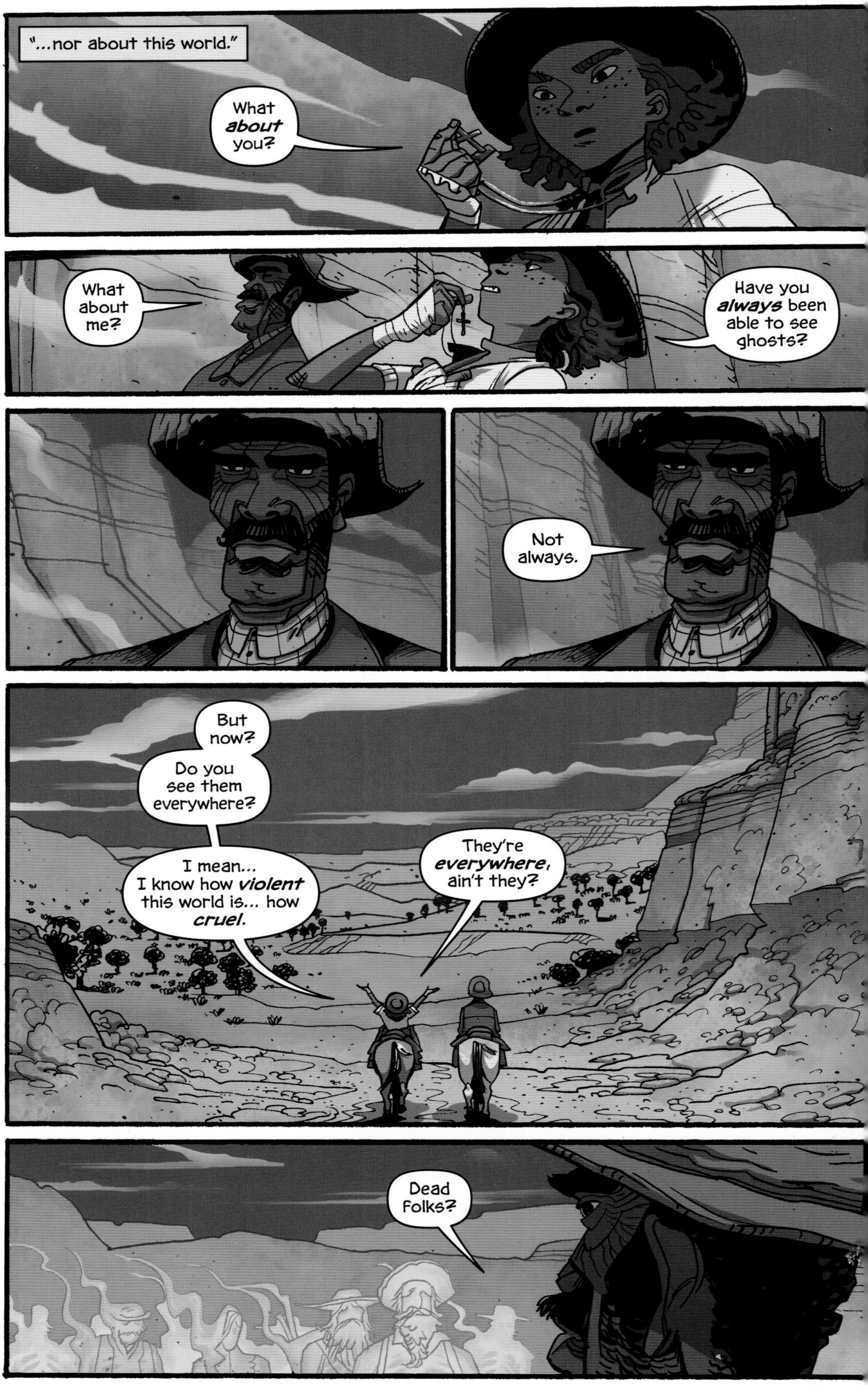
"...nor about this world."
What *about* you?
What about me?
Have you *always* been able to see ghosts?
Not always.
But now?
Do you see them everywhere?
I mean... I know how *violent* this world is... how *cruel*.
They're *everywhere*, ain't they?
Dead folks?

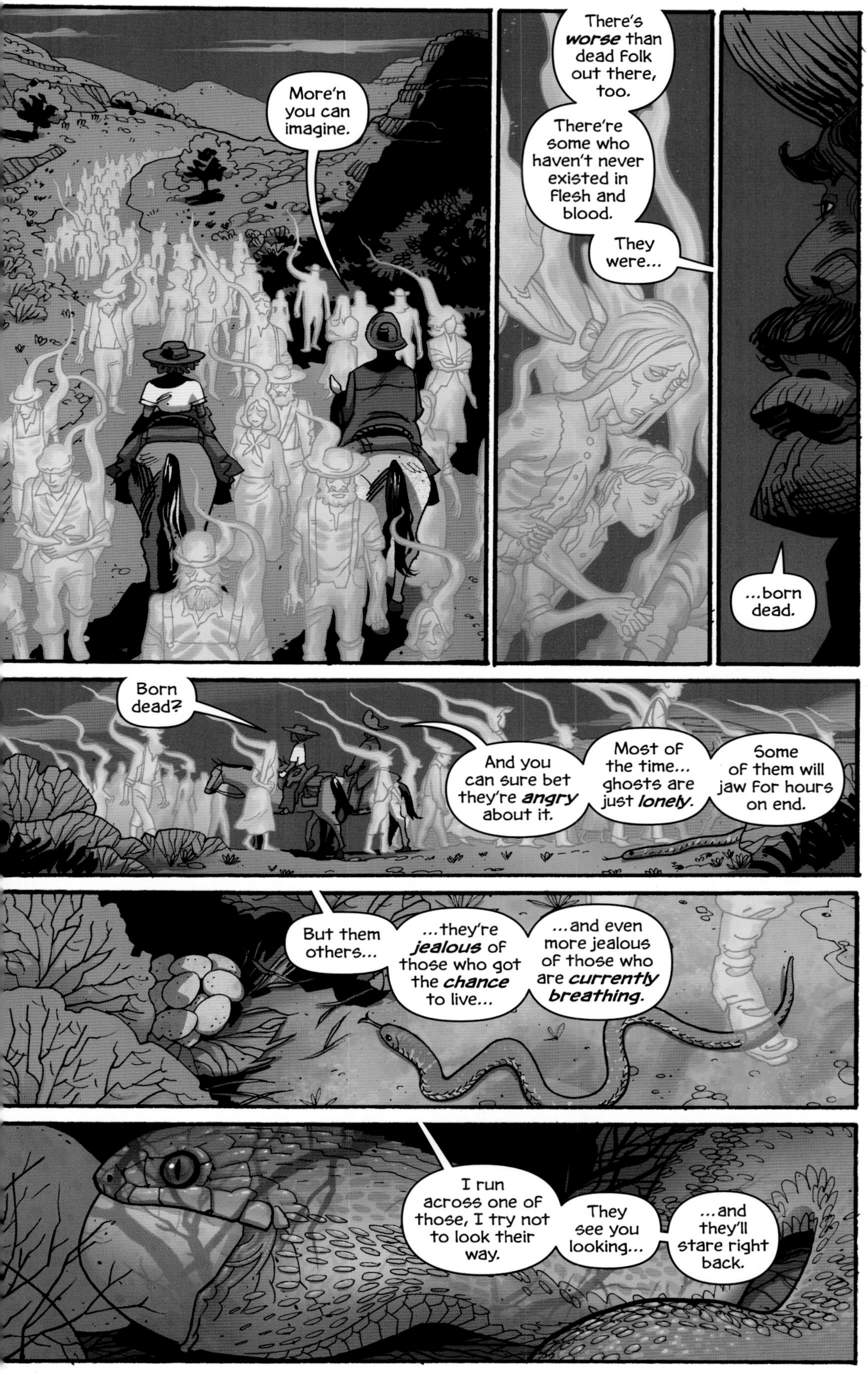
More'n you can imagine.
There's *worse* than dead folk out there, too.
There're some who haven't never existed in flesh and blood.
They were...
...born dead.
Born dead?
And you can sure bet they're *angry* about it.
Most of the time... ghosts are just *lonely*.
Some of them will jaw for hours on end.
But them others...
...they're *jealous* of those who got the *chance* to live...
...and even more jealous of those who are *currently breathing*.
I run across one of those, I try not to look their way.
They see you looking...
...and they'll stare right back.

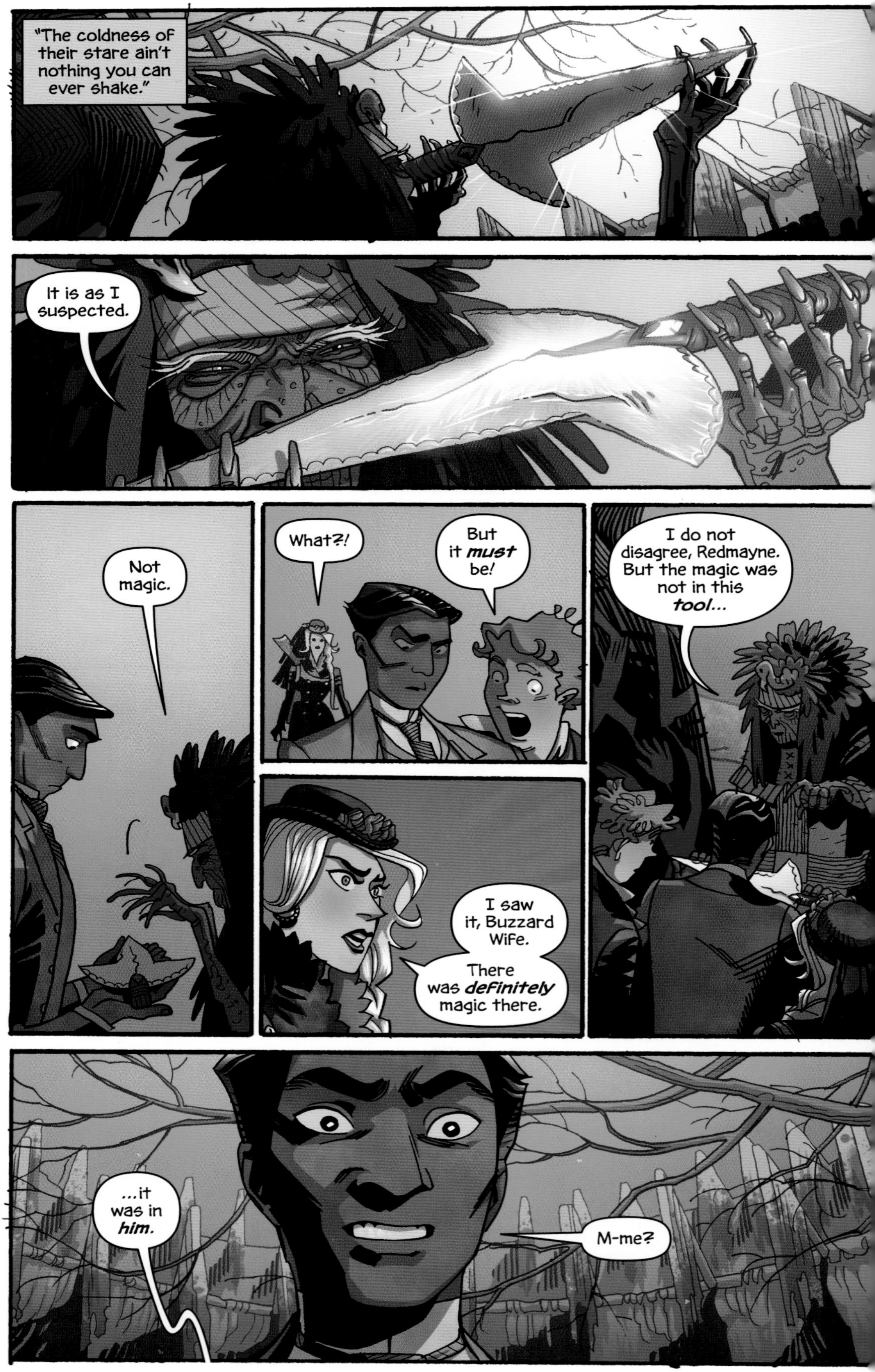
"The coldness of their stare ain't nothing you can ever shake."
It is as I suspected.
Not magic.
What?!
But it *must* be!
I saw it, Buzzard Wife.
There was *definitely* magic there.
I do not disagree, Redmayne. But the magic was not in this *tool*...
...it was in *him*.
M-me?

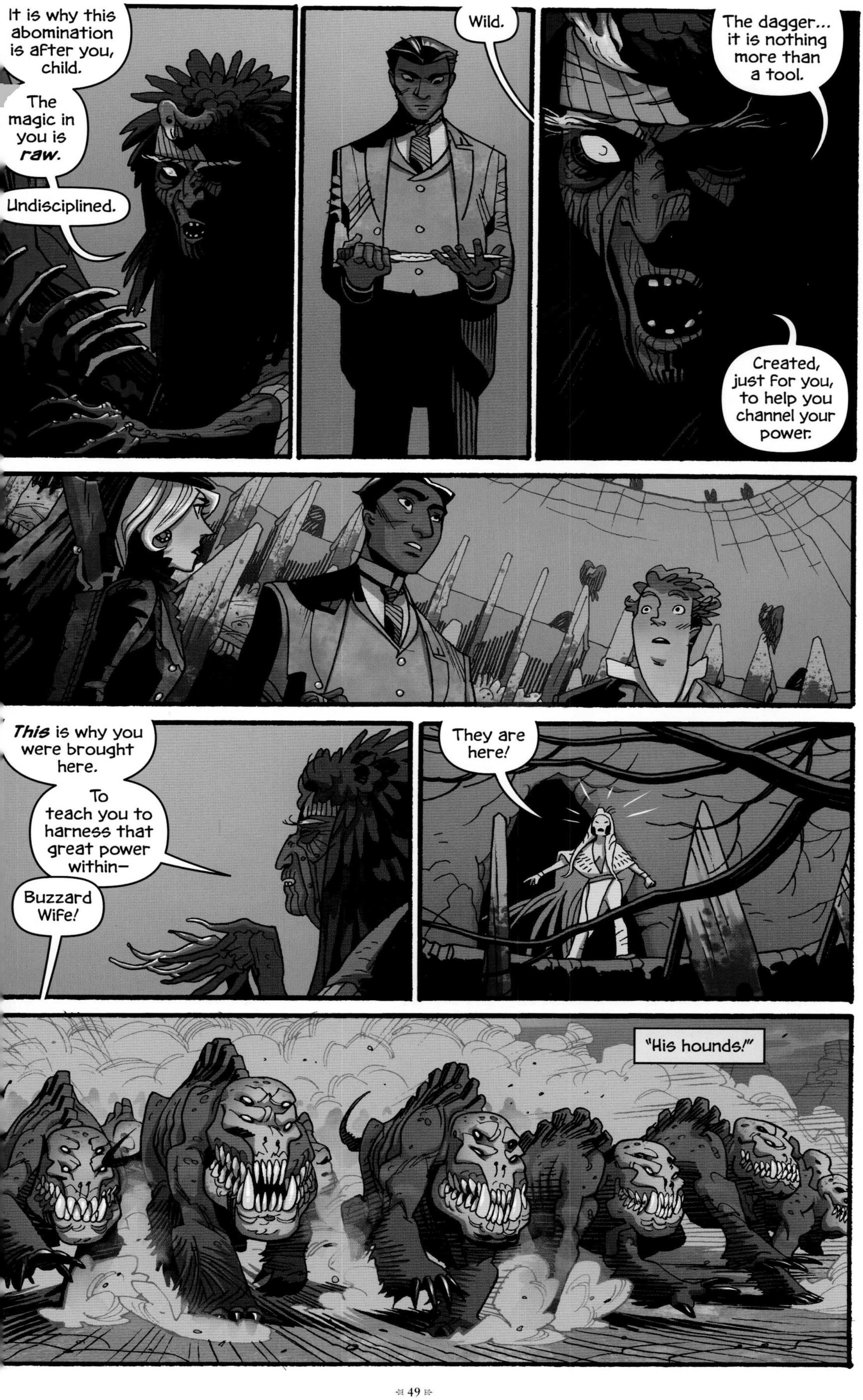
It is why this abomination is after you, child.
The magic in you is *raw*.
Undisciplined.
Wild.
The dagger... it is nothing more than a tool.
Created, just for you, to help you channel your power.
This is why you were brought here.
To teach you to harness that great power within—
Buzzard Wife!
They are here!
"His hounds!"

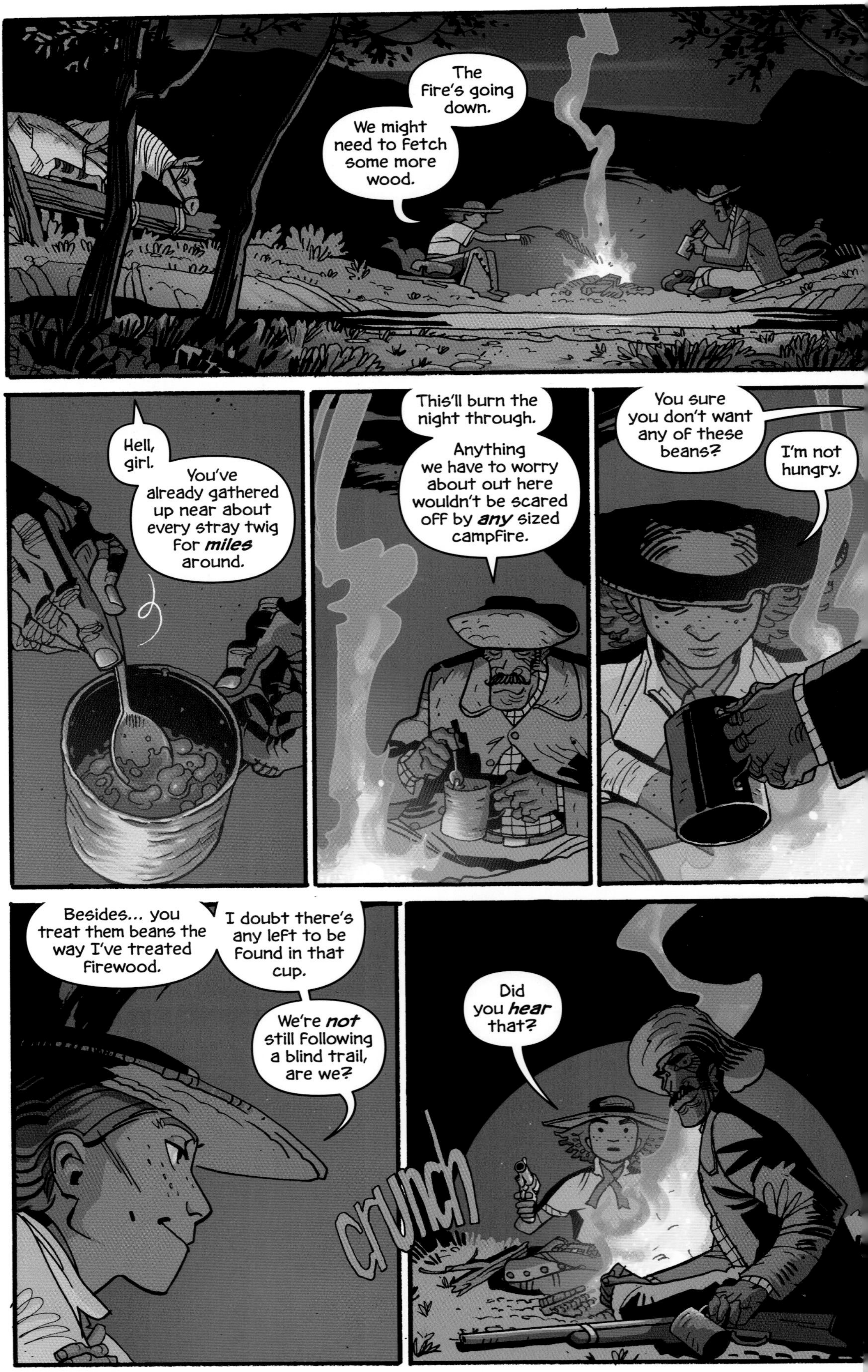
The fire's going down.
We might need to fetch some more wood.
Hell, girl.
You've already gathered up near about every stray twig for *miles* around.
This'll burn the night through.
Anything we have to worry about out here wouldn't be scared off by *any* sized campfire.
You sure you don't want any of these beans?
I'm not hungry.
Besides... you treat them beans the way I've treated firewood.
I doubt there's any left to be found in that cup.
We're *not* still following a blind trail, are we?
Did you *hear* that?
crunch

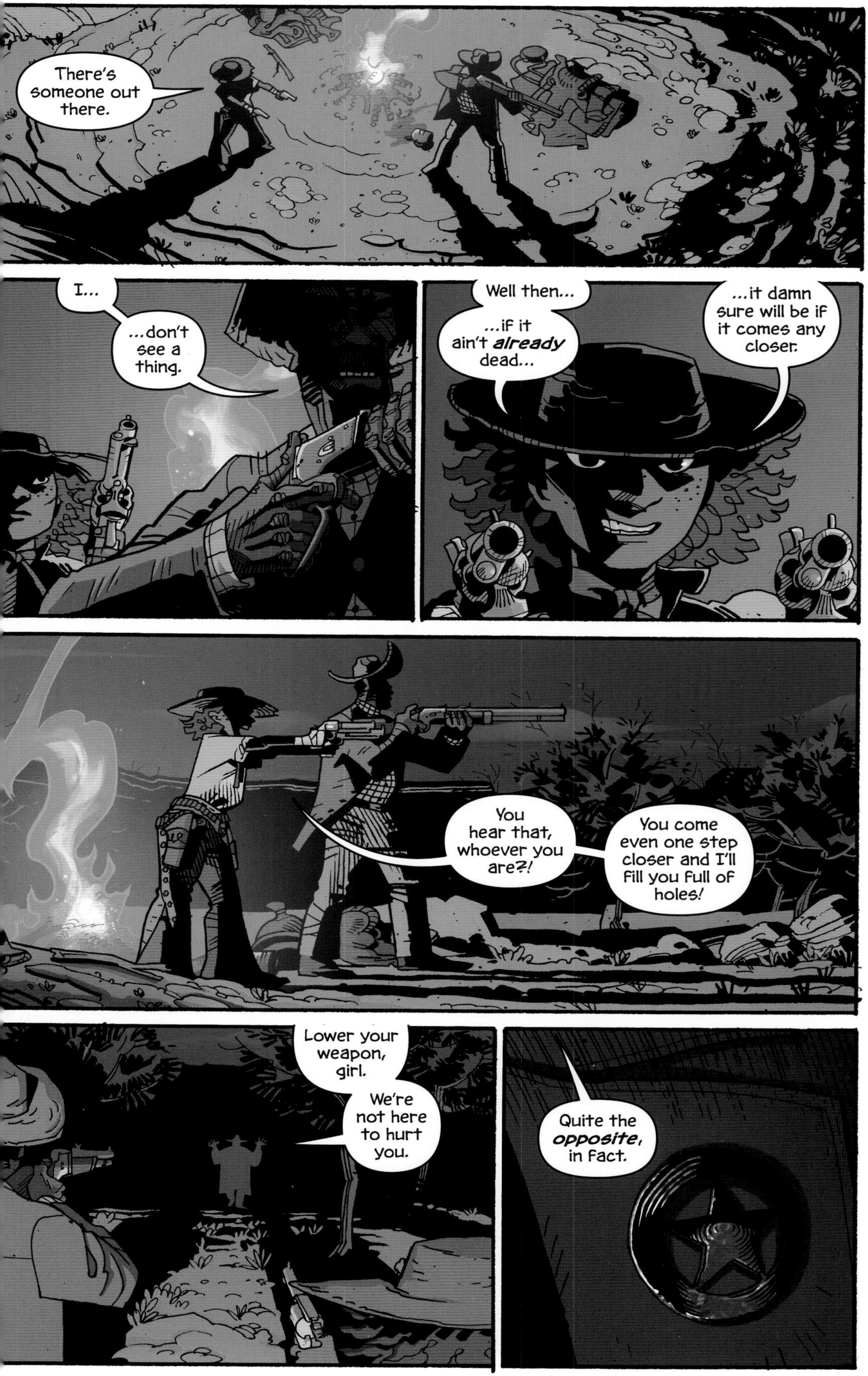
There's someone out there.
I...
...don't see a thing.
Well then...
...if it ain't *already* dead...
...it damn sure will be if it comes any closer.
You hear that, whoever you are?!
You come even one step closer and I'll fill you full of holes!
Lower your weapon, girl.
We're not here to hurt you.
Quite the *opposite*, in fact.

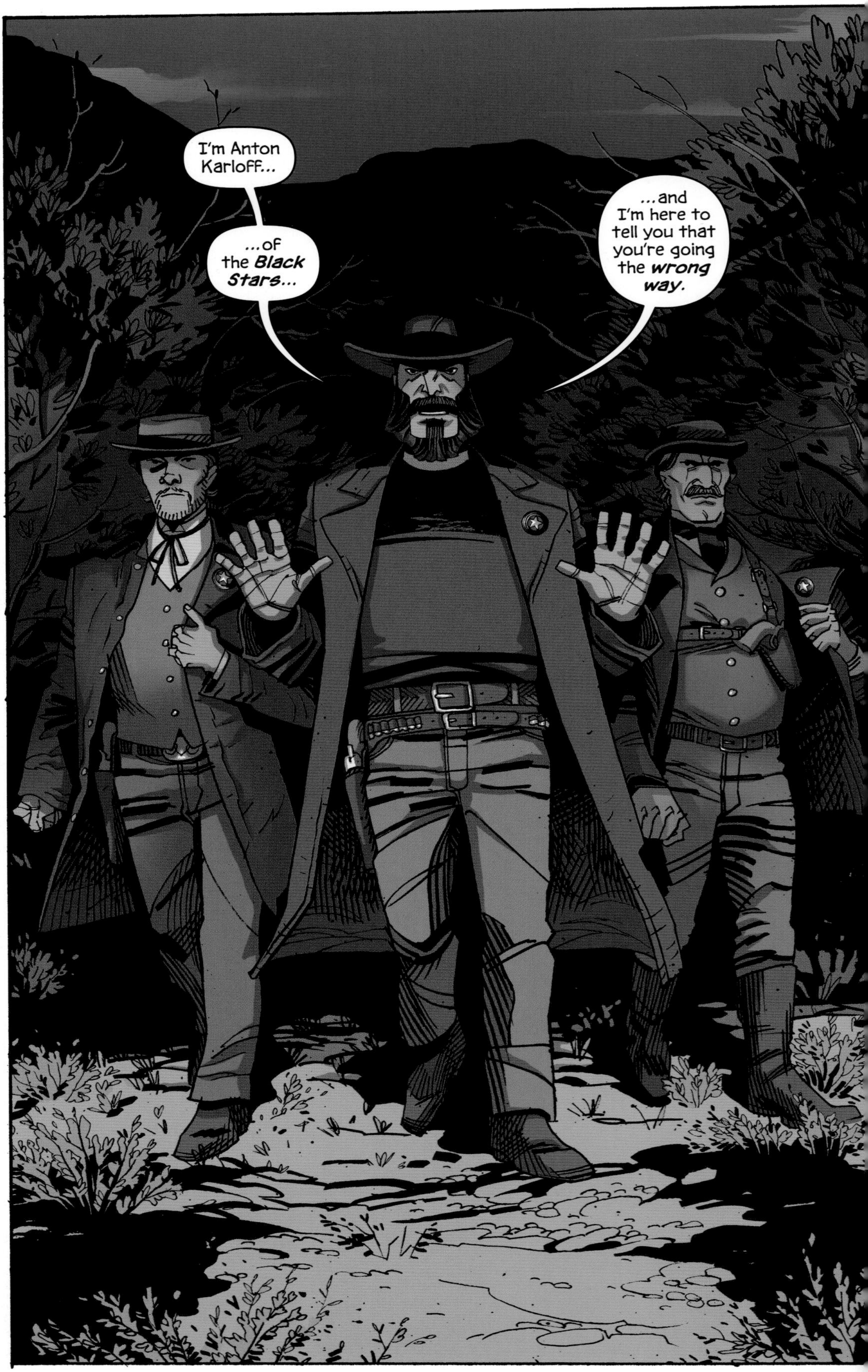
I'm Anton Karloff...
...of the *Black Stars*...
...and I'm here to tell you that you're going the *wrong way*.

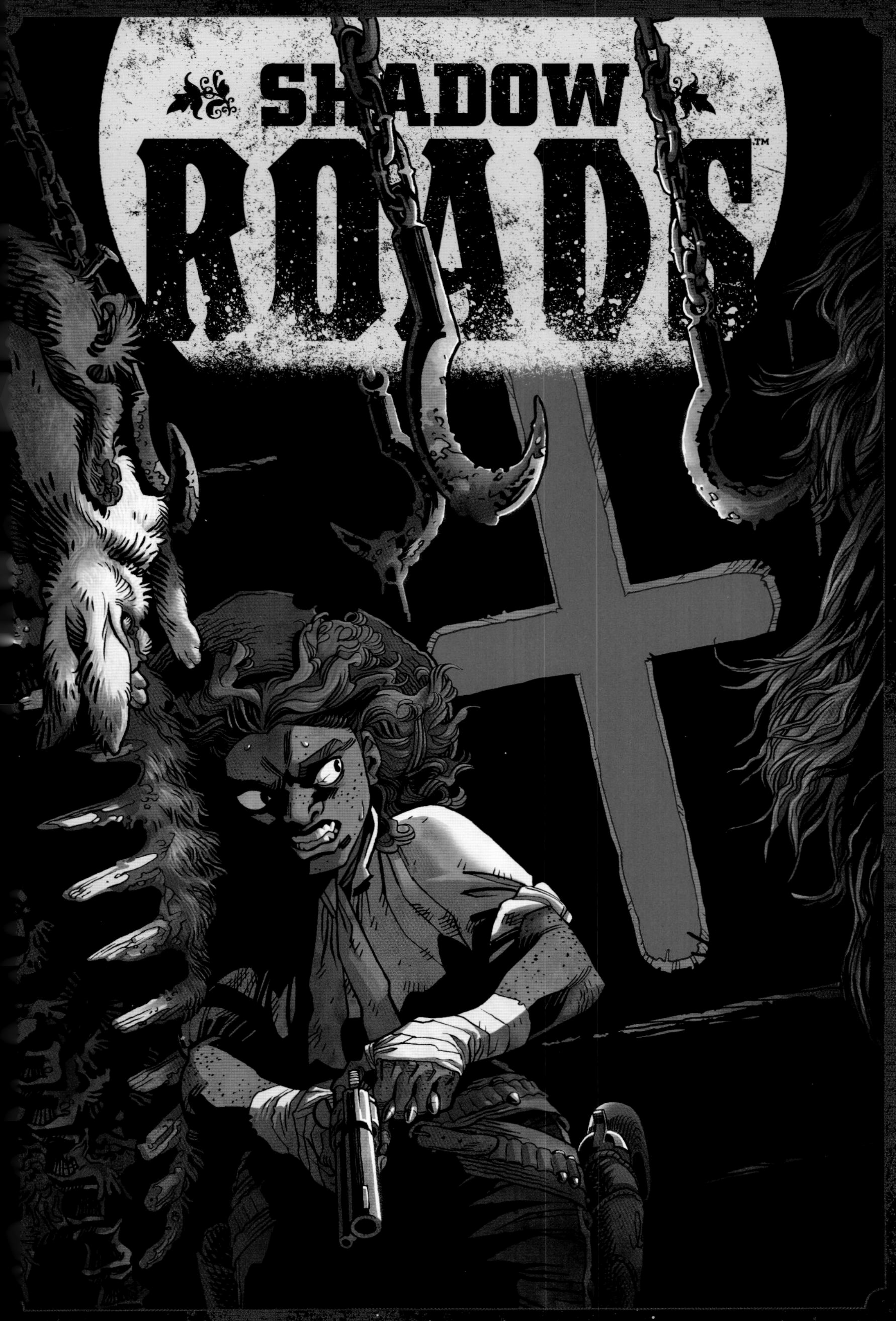
SHADOW
ROADS™

CHAPTER 3

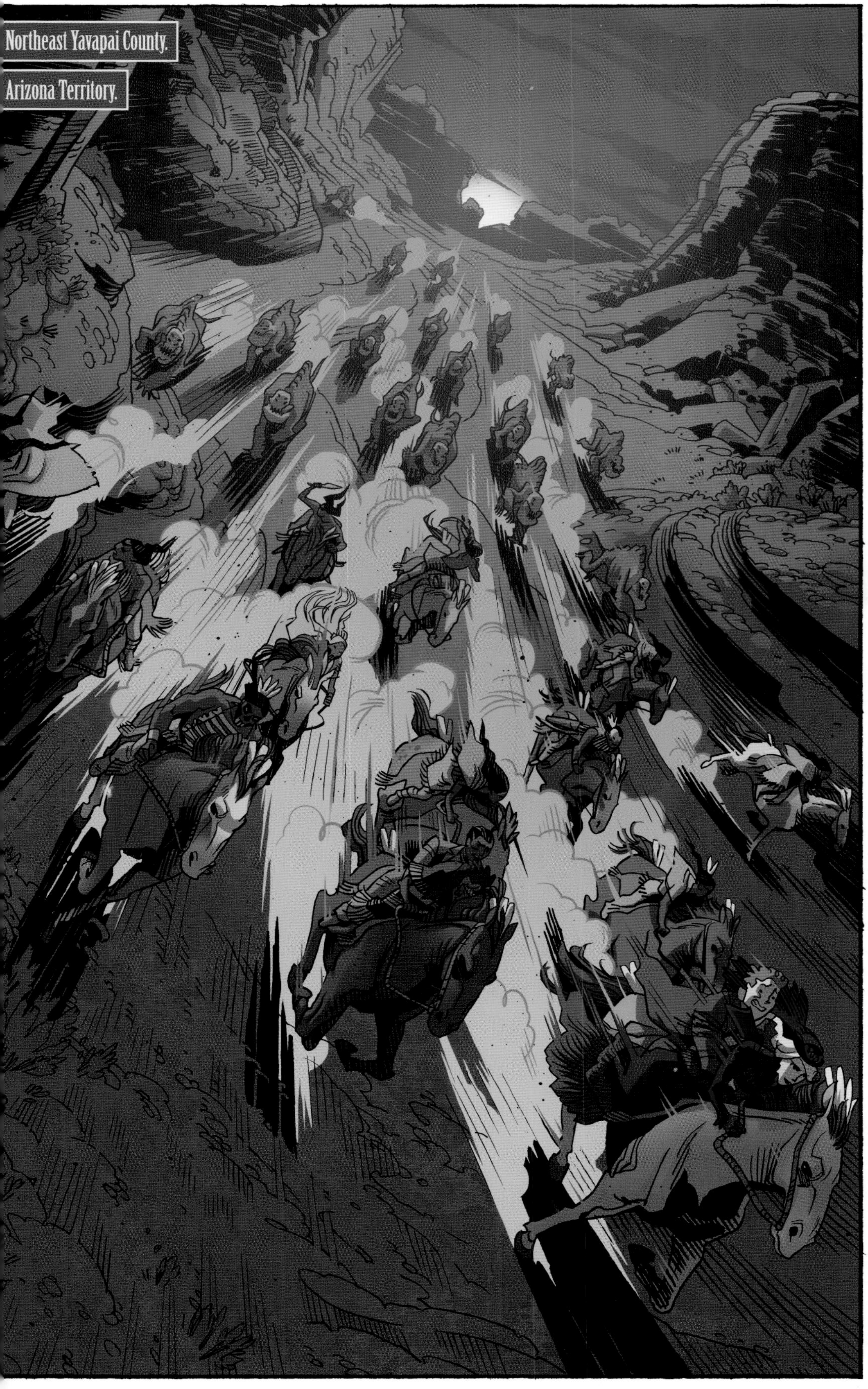
Northeast Yavapai County.
Arizona Territory.

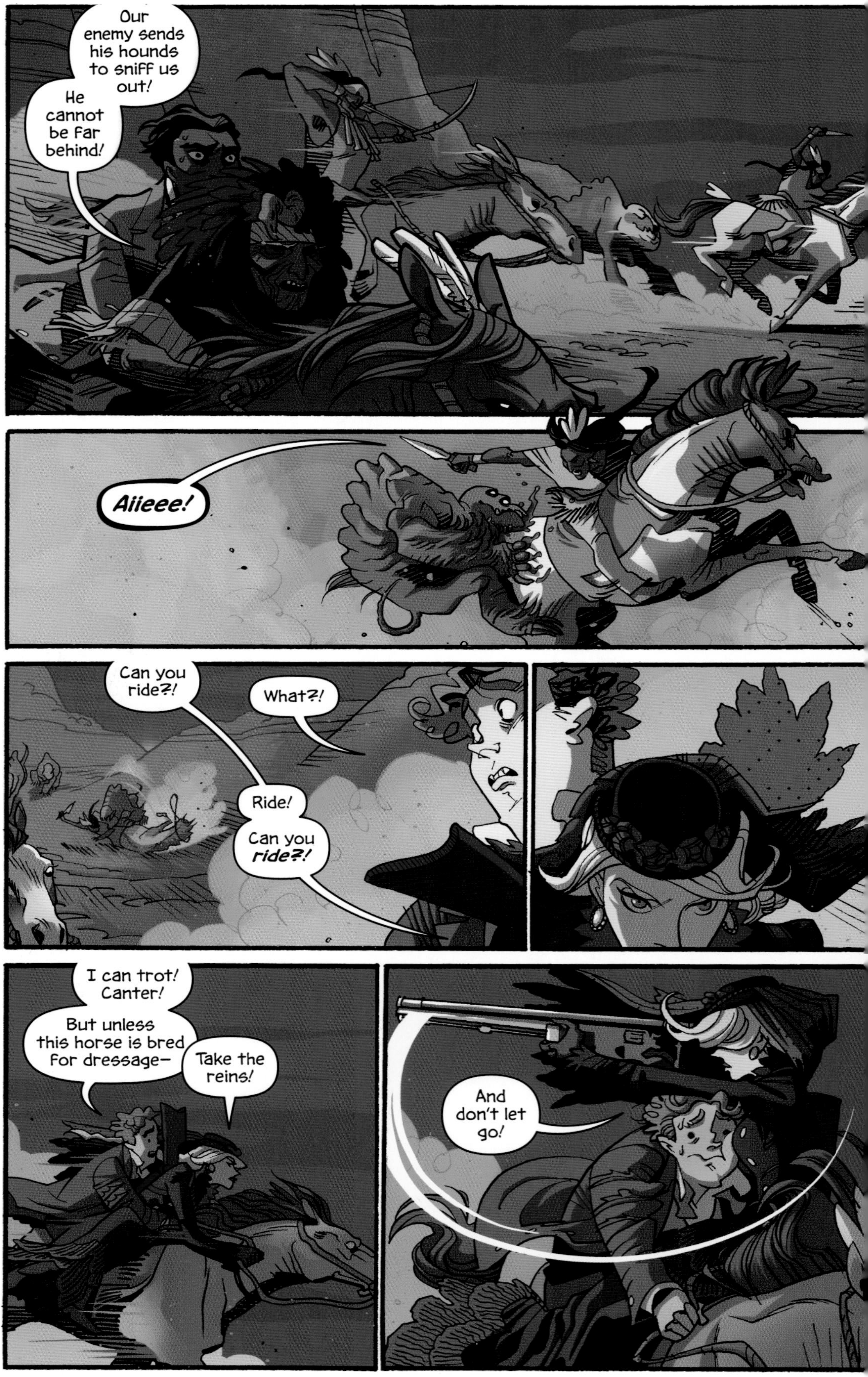
Our enemy sends his hounds to sniff us out!
He cannot be far behind!
Aiieee!
Can you ride?!
What?!
Ride!
Can you ride?!
I can trot! Canter!
But unless this horse is bred for dressage—
Take the reins!
And don't let go!

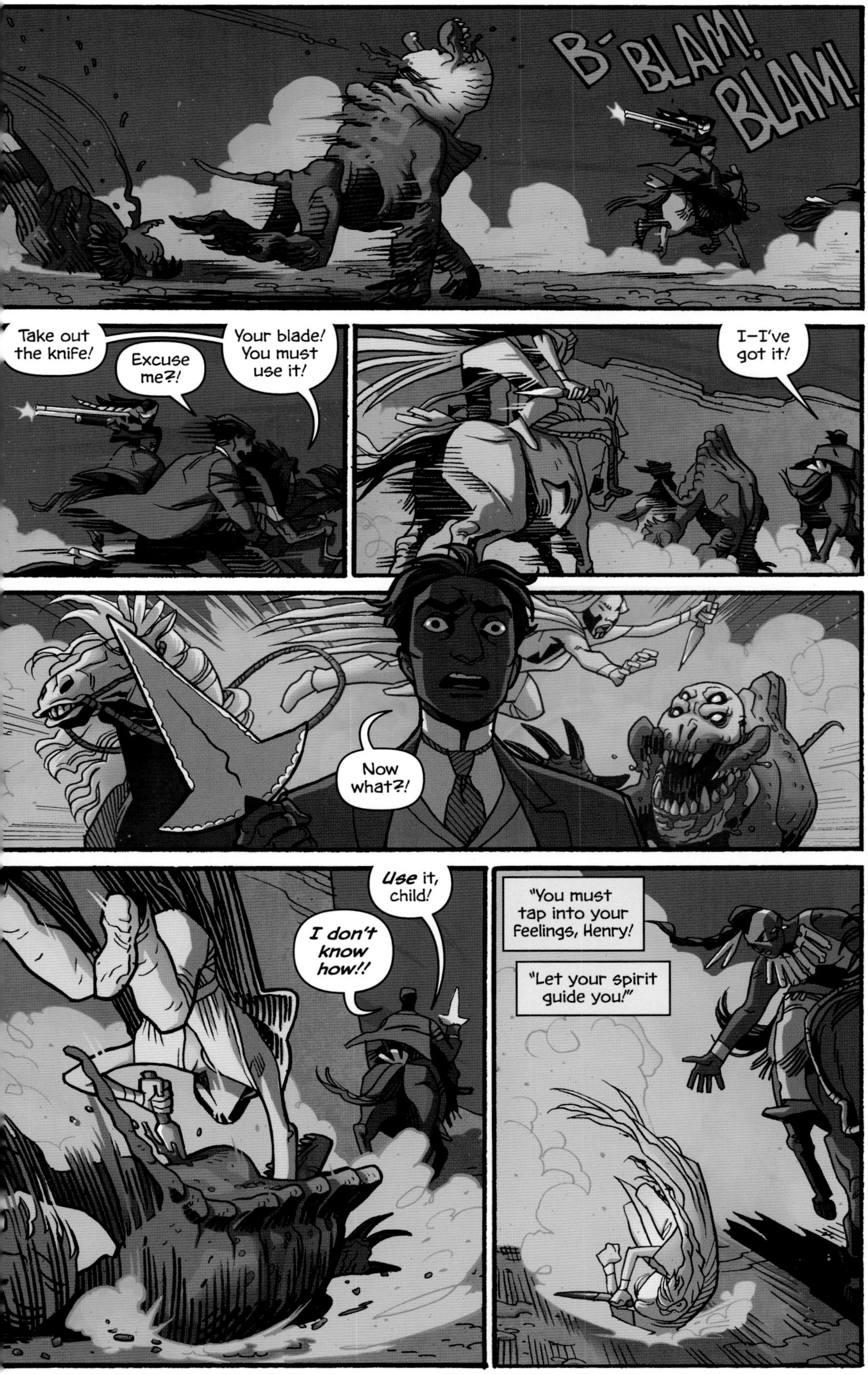
B-BLAM! BLAM!
Take out the knife!
Excuse me?!
Your blade! You must use it!
I—I've got it!
Now what?!
Use it, child!
I don't know how!!
"You must tap into your Feelings, Henry!
"Let your spirit guide you!"

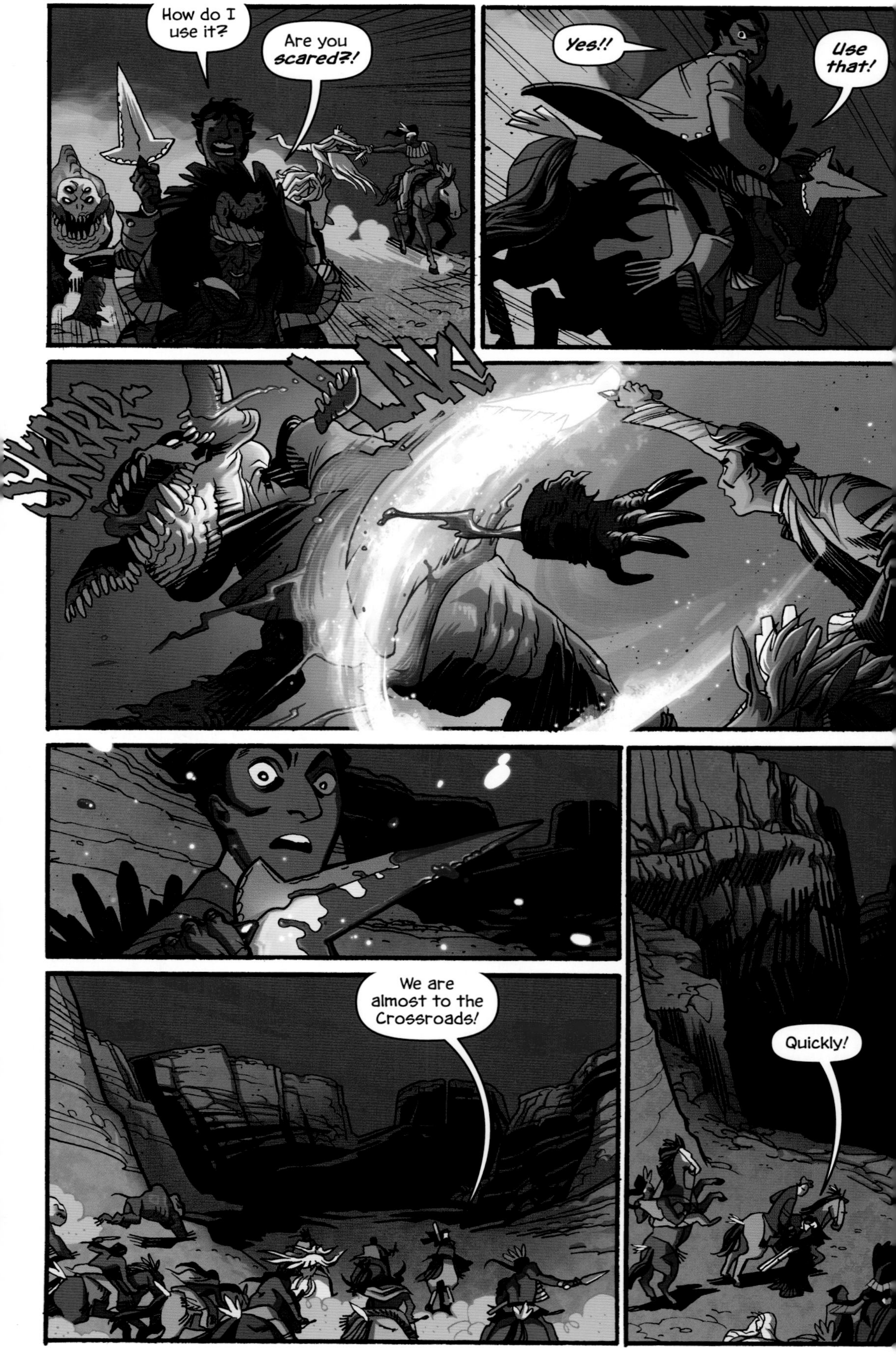

How do I use it?
Are you scared?!
Yes!!
Use that!
SHRRR-TAK!
We are almost to the Crossroads!
Quickly!

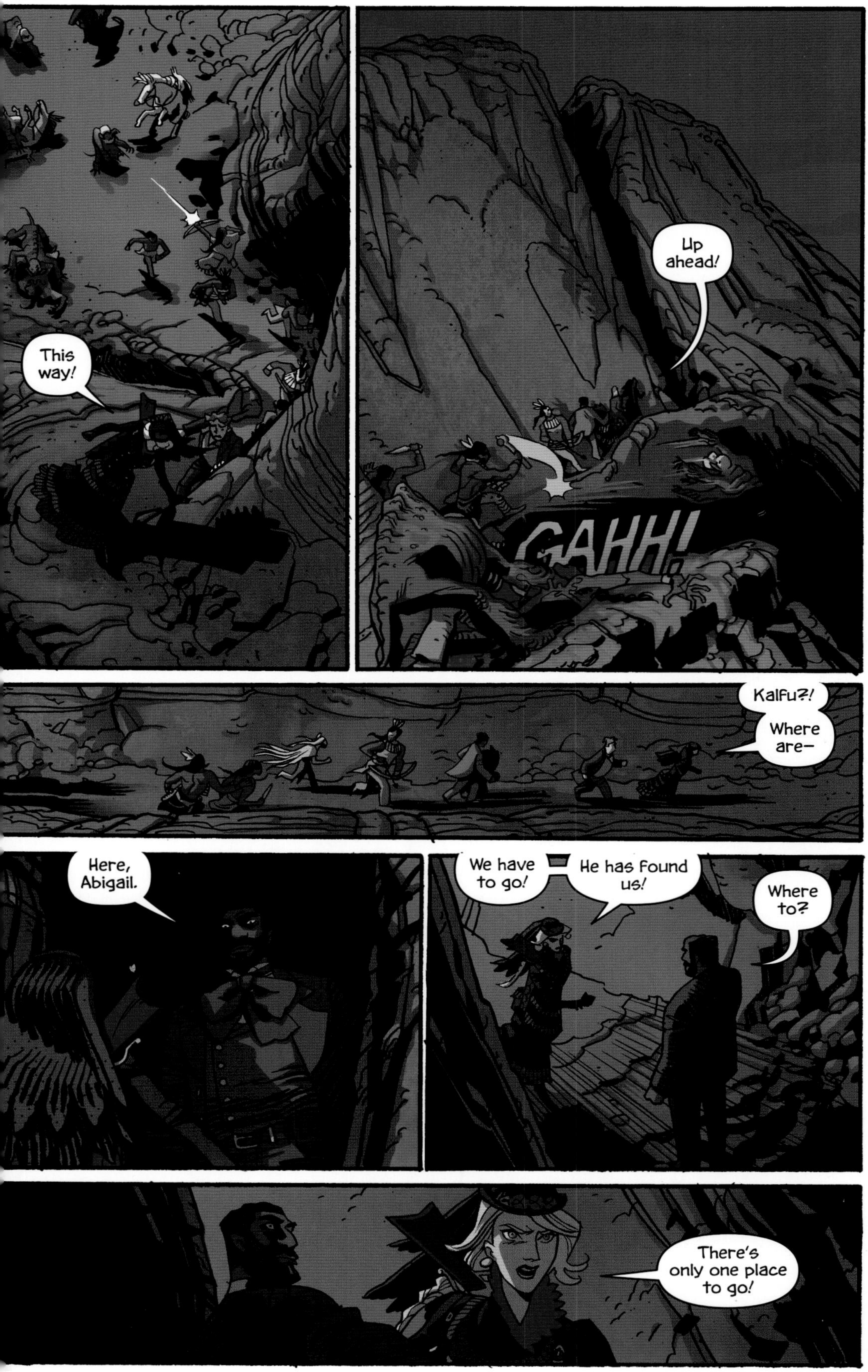
This way!
Up ahead!
GAHH!
Kalfu?!
Where are—
Here, Abigail.
We have to go!
He has found us!
Where to?
There's only one place to go!

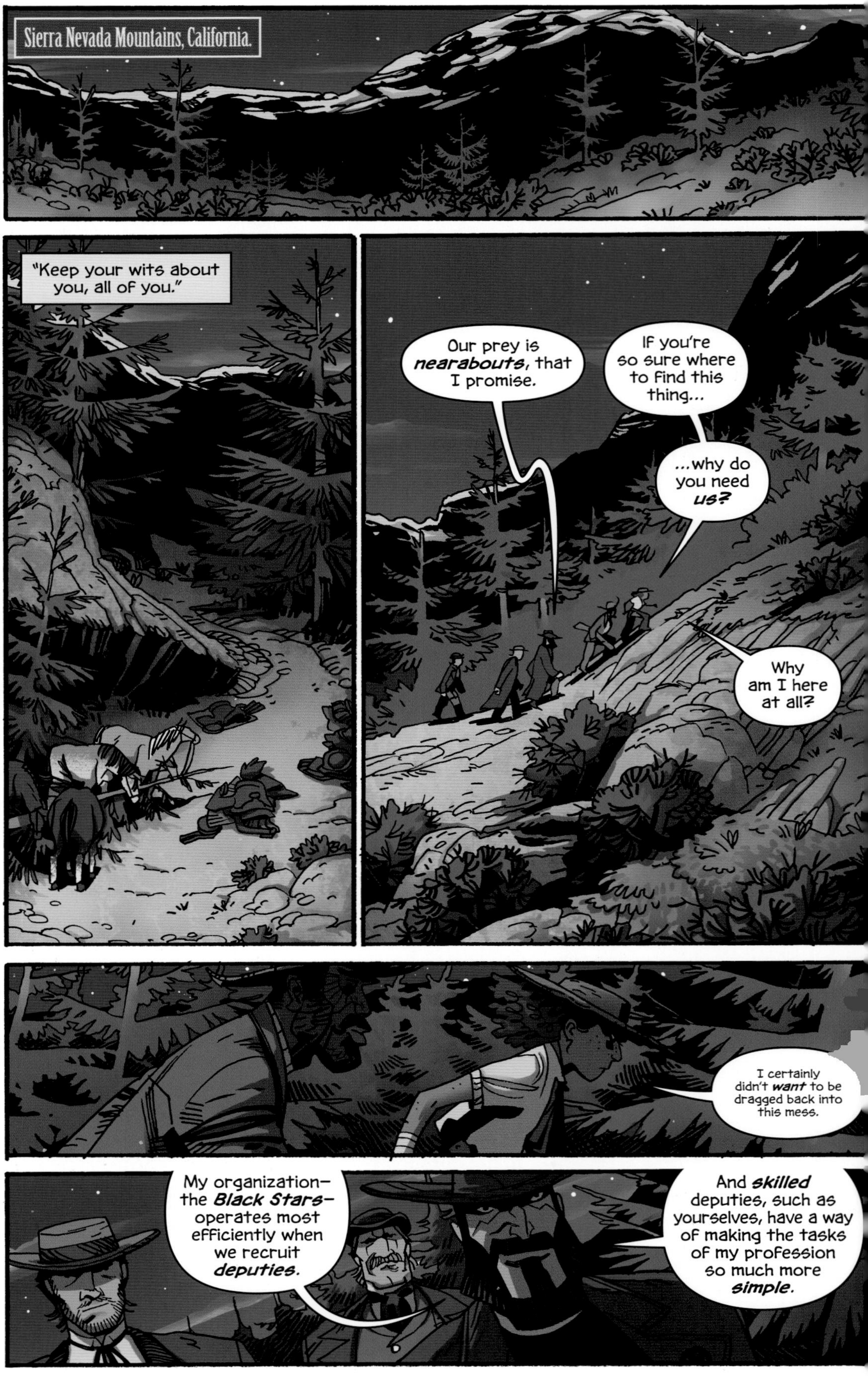
Sierra Nevada Mountains, California.
"Keep your wits about you, all of you."
Our prey is *nearabouts*, that I promise.
If you're so sure where to find this thing...
...why do you need *us?*
Why am I here at all?
I certainly didn't *want* to be dragged back into this mess.
My organization— the *Black Stars*— operates most efficiently when we recruit *deputies*.
And *skilled* deputies, such as yourselves, have a way of making the tasks of my profession so much more *simple*.

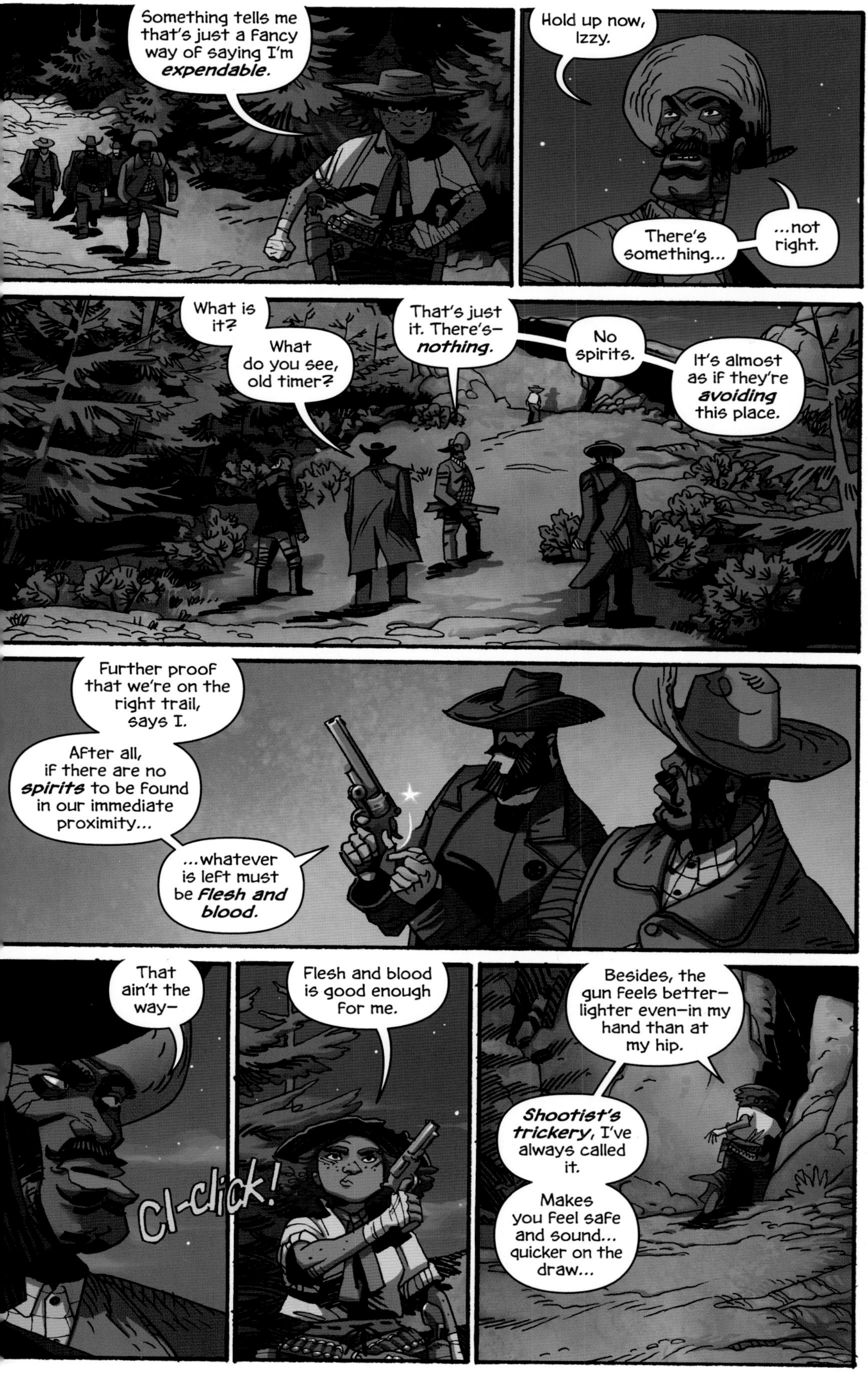
Something tells me that's just a fancy way of saying I'm *expendable.*
Hold up now, Izzy.
There's something...
...not right.
What is it?
What do you see, old timer?
That's just it. There's— *nothing.*
No spirits.
It's almost as if they're *avoiding* this place.
Further proof that we're on the right trail, says I.
After all, if there are no *spirits* to be found in our immediate proximity...
...whatever is left must be *flesh and blood.*
That ain't the way—
Cl-click!
Flesh and blood is good enough for me.
Besides, the gun feels better— lighter even—in my hand than at my hip.
Shootist's trickery, I've always called it.
Makes you feel safe and sound... quicker on the draw...

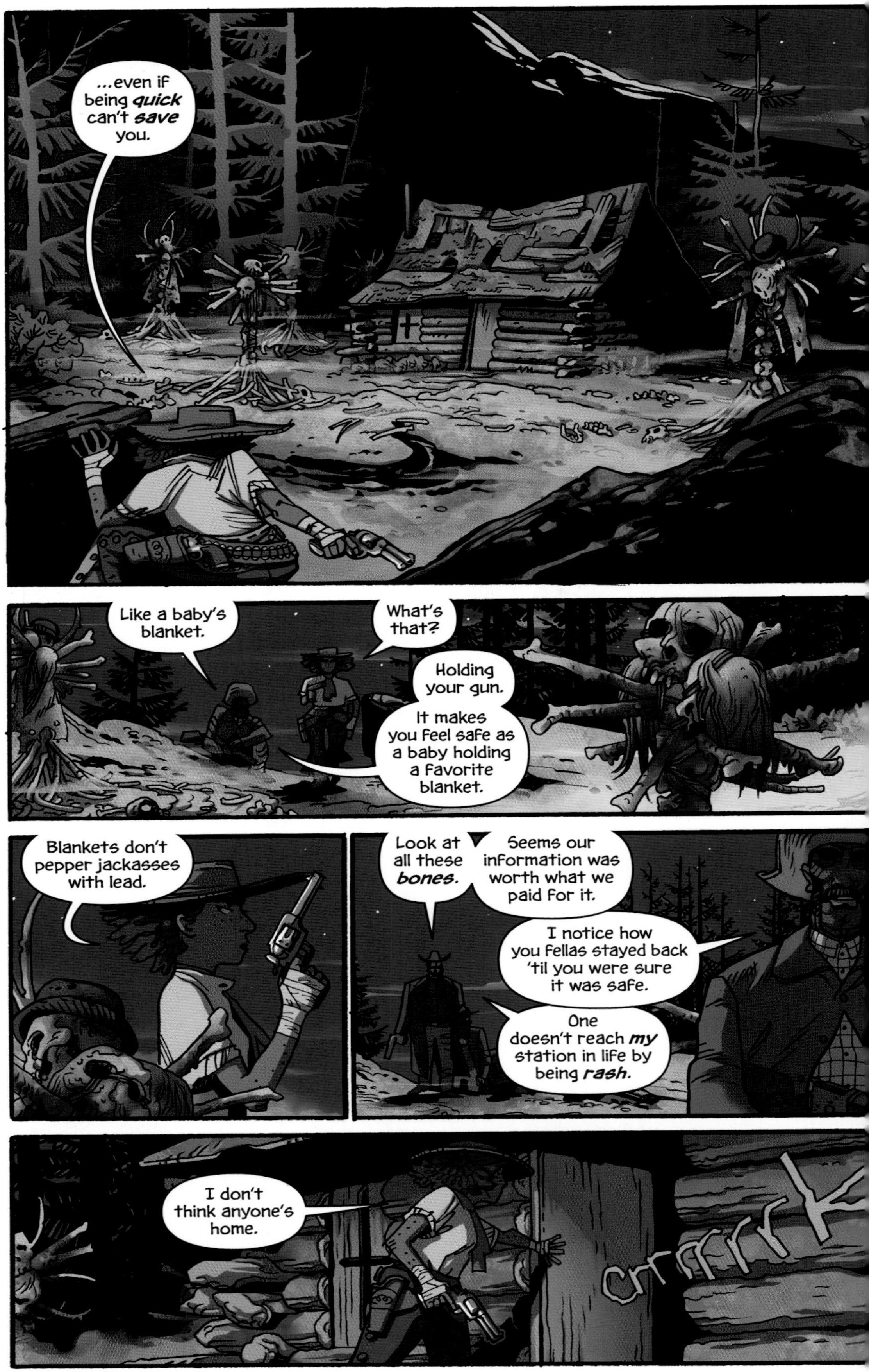
...even if being *quick* can't *save* you.
Like a baby's blanket.
What's that?
Holding your gun.
It makes you feel safe as a baby holding a favorite blanket.
Blankets don't pepper jackasses with lead.
Look at all these *bones.*
Seems our information was worth what we paid for it.
I notice how you fellas stayed back 'til you were sure it was safe.
One doesn't reach *my* station in life by being *rash.*
I don't think anyone's home.
crrrrrk

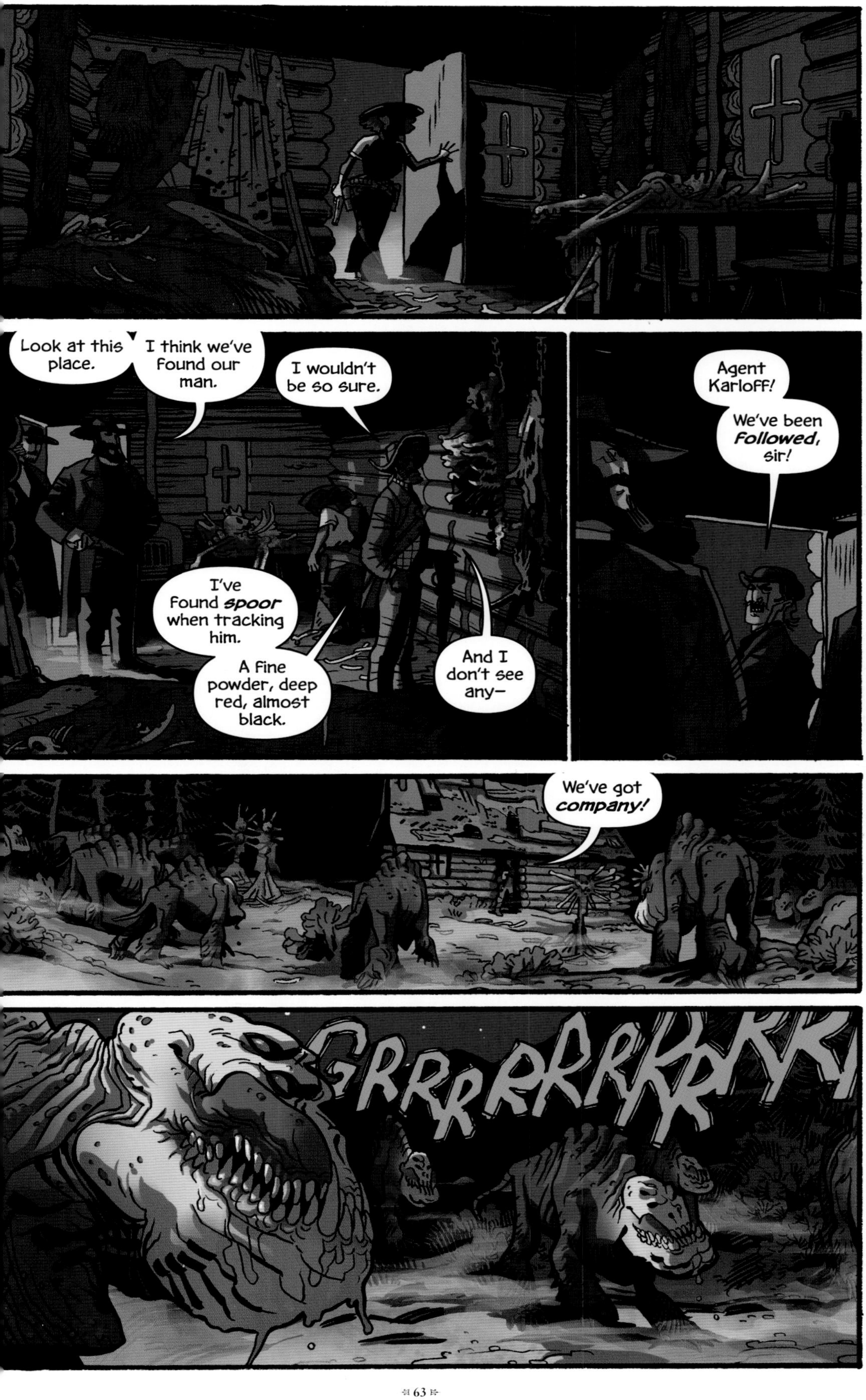
Look at this place.
I think we've found our man.
I wouldn't be so sure.
I've found spoor when tracking him.
A fine powder, deep red, almost black.
And I don't see any—
Agent Karloff!
We've been followed, sir!
We've got company!
GRRRRRRRRRRRR

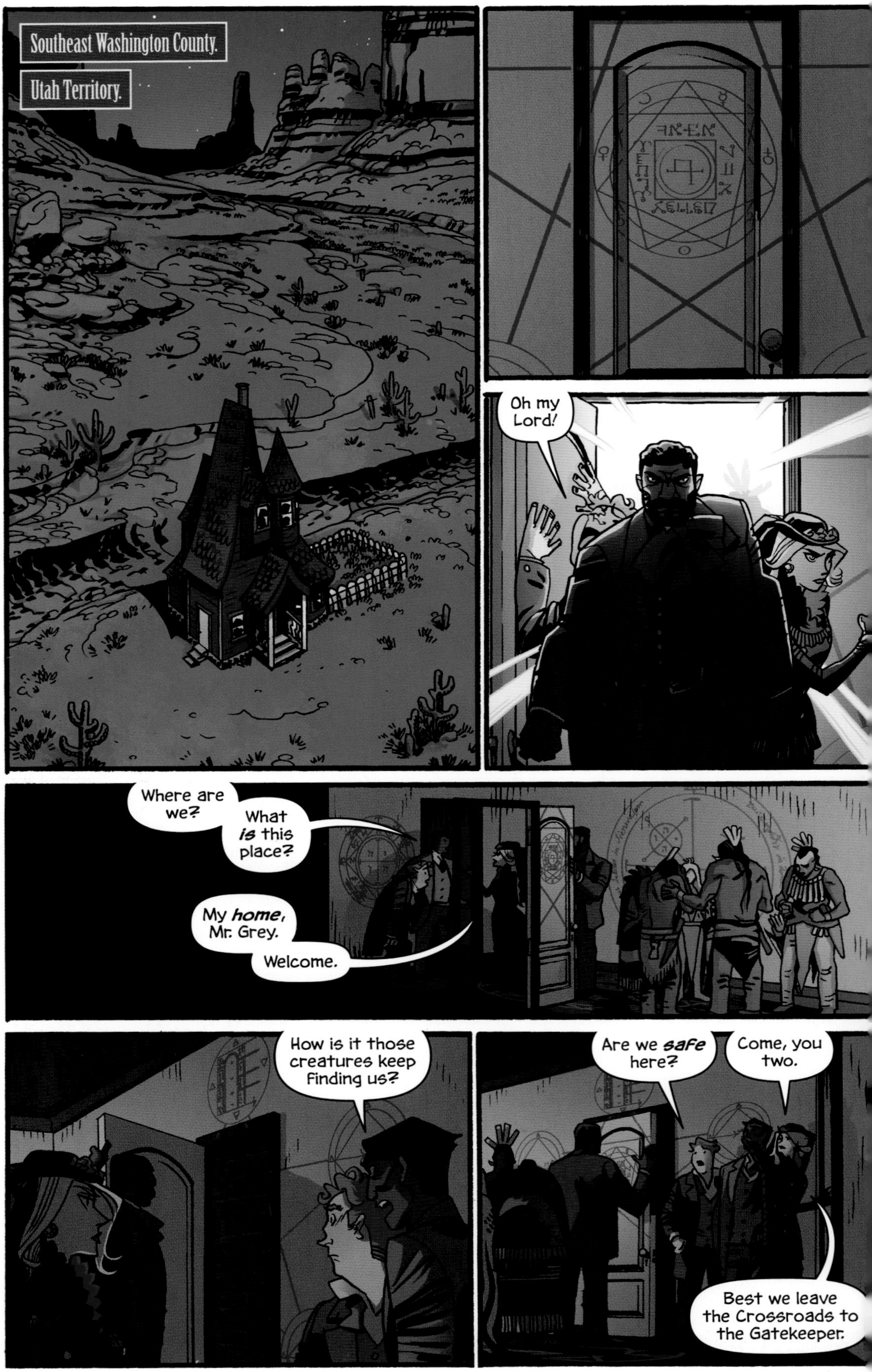
Southeast Washington County.
Utah Territory.
Oh my Lord!
Where are we?
What *is* this place?
My *home*, Mr. Grey.
Welcome.
How is it those creatures keep finding us?
Are we *safe* here?
Come, you two.
Best we leave the Crossroads to the Gatekeeper.

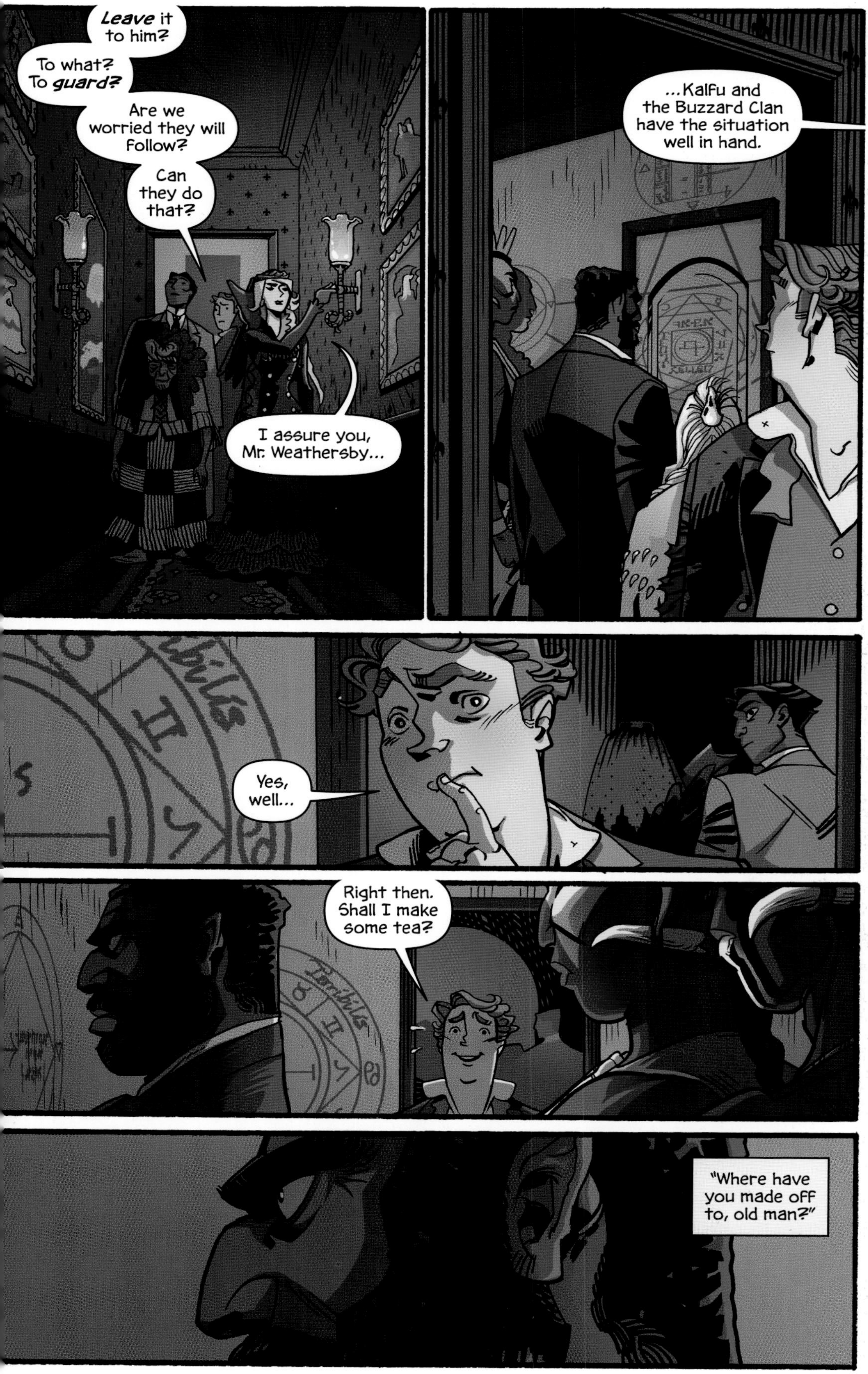
Leave it to him?
To what? To ***guard?***
Are we worried they will follow?
Can they do that?
I assure you, Mr. Weathersby...
...Kalfu and the Buzzard Clan have the situation well in hand.
Yes, well...
Right then. Shall I make some tea?
"Where have you made off to, old man?"

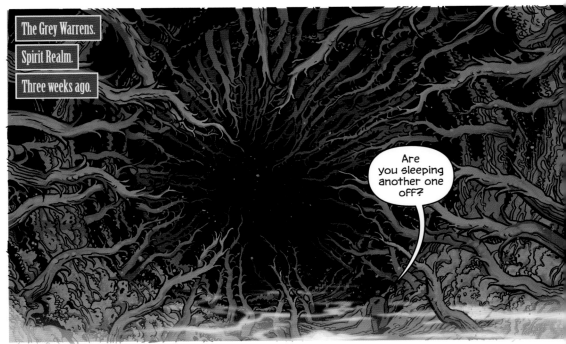

The Grey Warrens.

Spirit Realm.

Three weeks ago.

Are you sleeping another one off?

I found a door left open.

You been venturing out?

Where you got off to, you damn fool?

Old man?

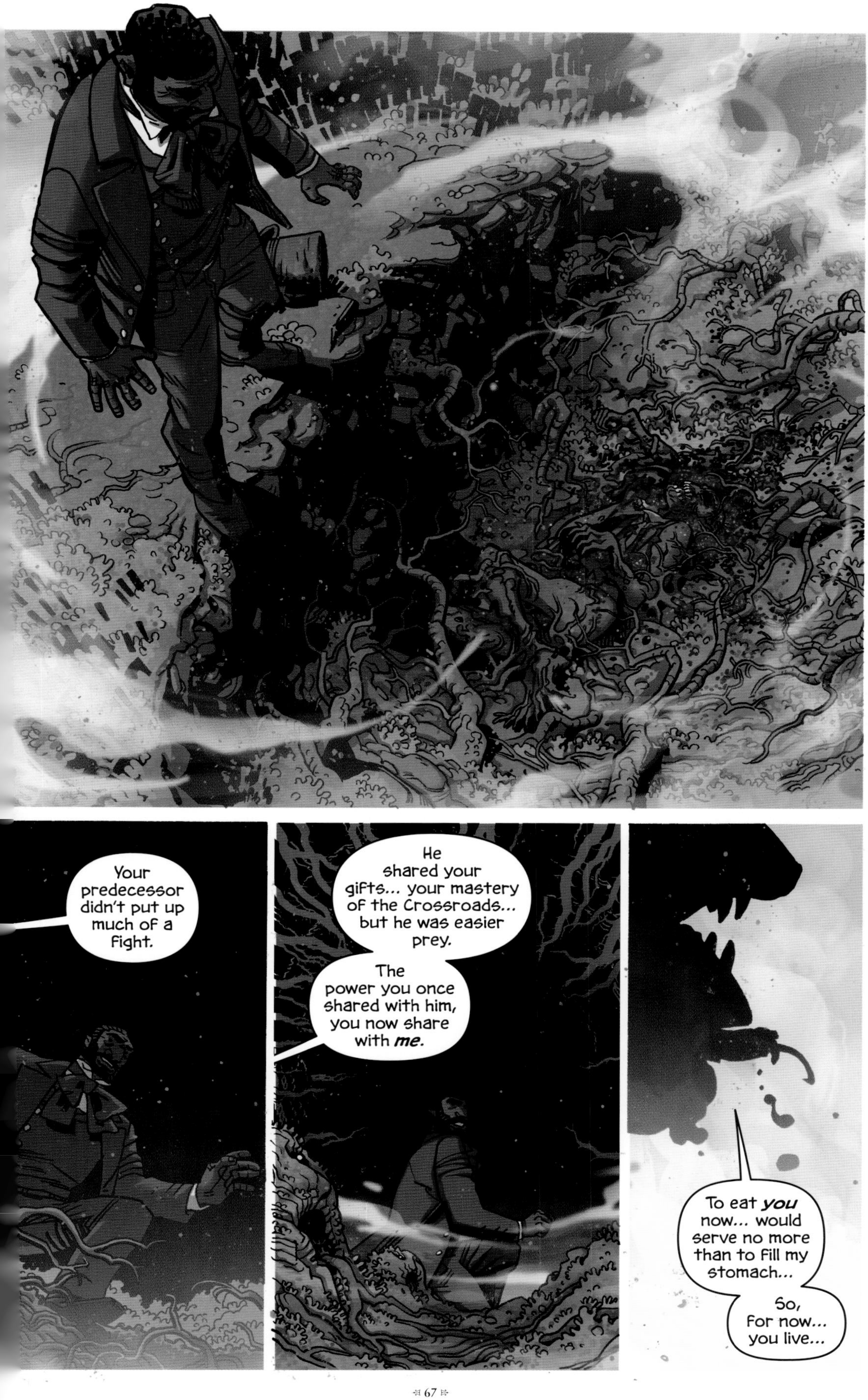
Your predecessor didn't put up much of a fight.
He shared your gifts... your mastery of the Crossroads... but he was easier prey.
The power you once shared with him, you now share with *me.*
To eat *you* now... would serve no more than to fill my stomach...
So, for now... you live...

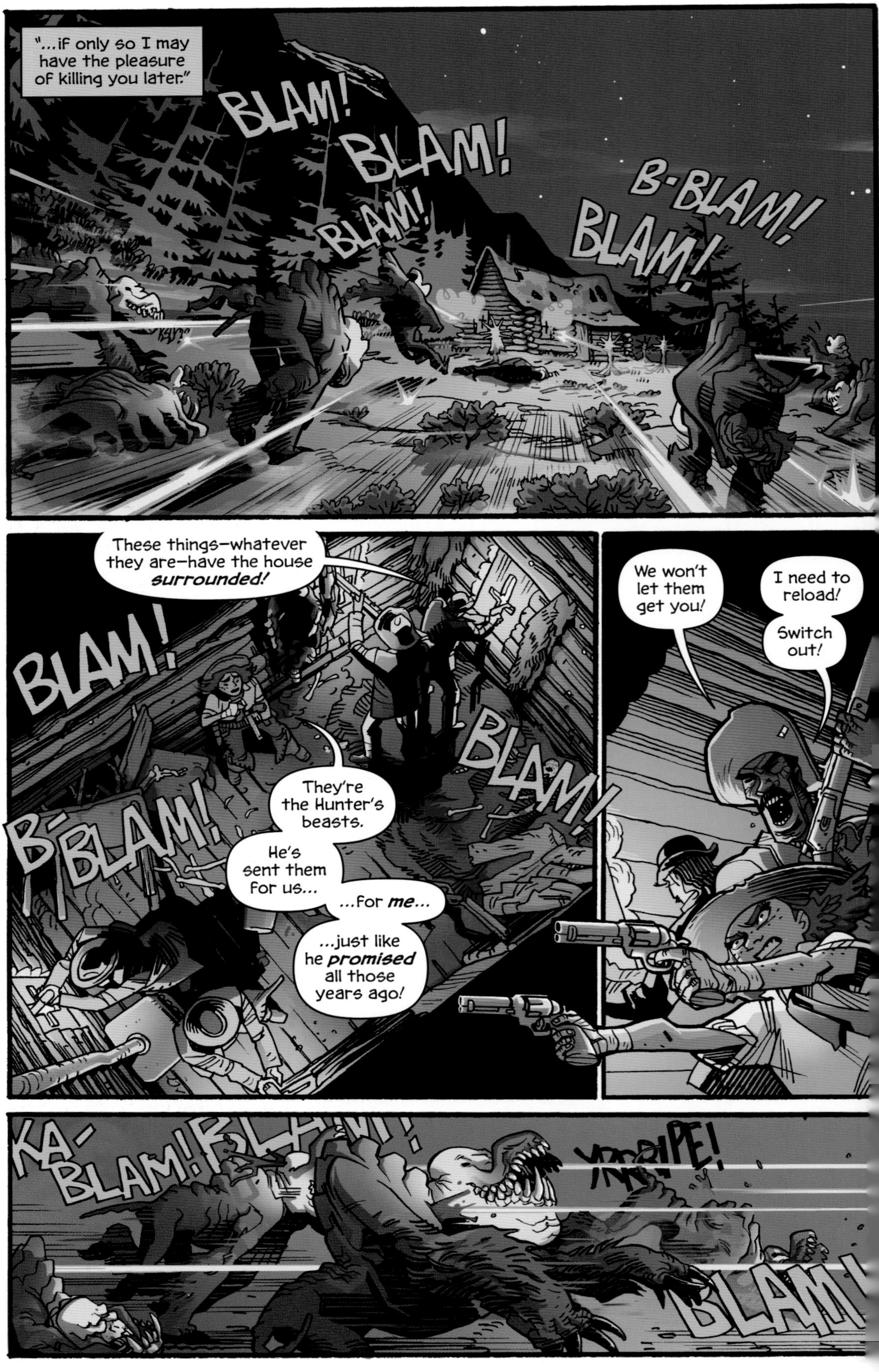
"...if only so I may have the pleasure of killing you later."
BLAM!
BLAM!
BLAM!
B-BLAM!
BLAM!
These things—whatever they are—have the house ***surrounded!***
BLAM!
BLAM!
B-BLAM!
They're the Hunter's beasts.
He's sent them for us...
...for ***me***...
...just like he ***promised*** all those years ago!
We won't let them get you!
I need to reload!
Switch out!
KA-BLAM!
BLAM!
BLAM!

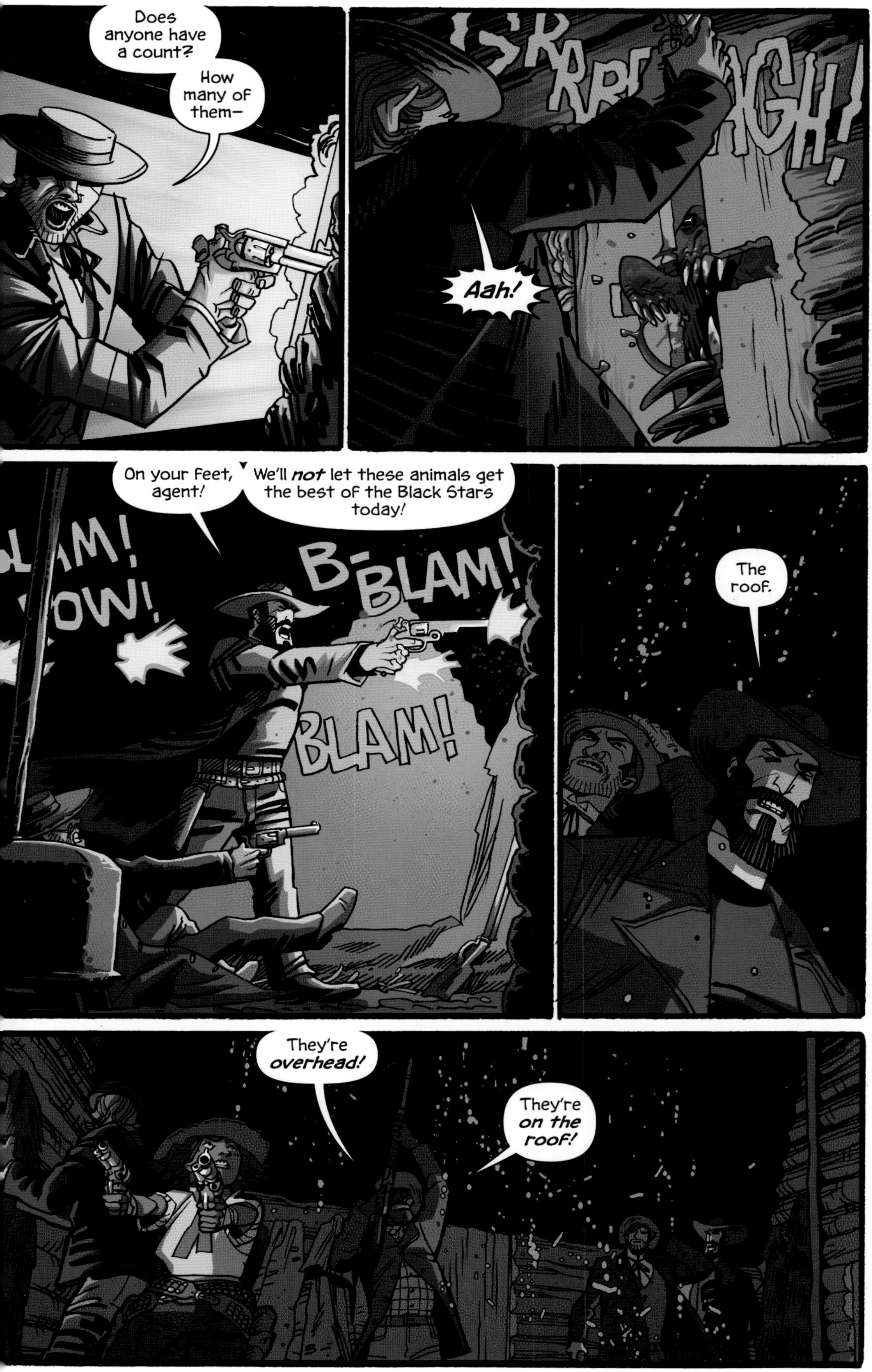
Does anyone have a count?
How many of them—
Aah!
On your feet, agent!
We'll *not* let these animals get the best of the Black Stars today!
B-BLAM!
BLAM!
The roof.
They're *overhead!*
They're *on the roof!*

I feel like Alice... passed through the looking-glass.

Everything has gone all *topsy-turvy.*

You say there is... magic in me? *Magic?!*

Like some *wizard* in a fairy tale?

And this so-called Hunter wants to what? Take it from me? Kill me?!

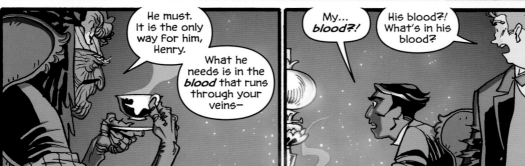

He must. It is the only way for him, Henry.

What he needs is in the *blood* that runs through your veins—

My... *blood?!*

His blood?! What's in his blood?

Power. The power of his *parents.*

You knew... my parents?

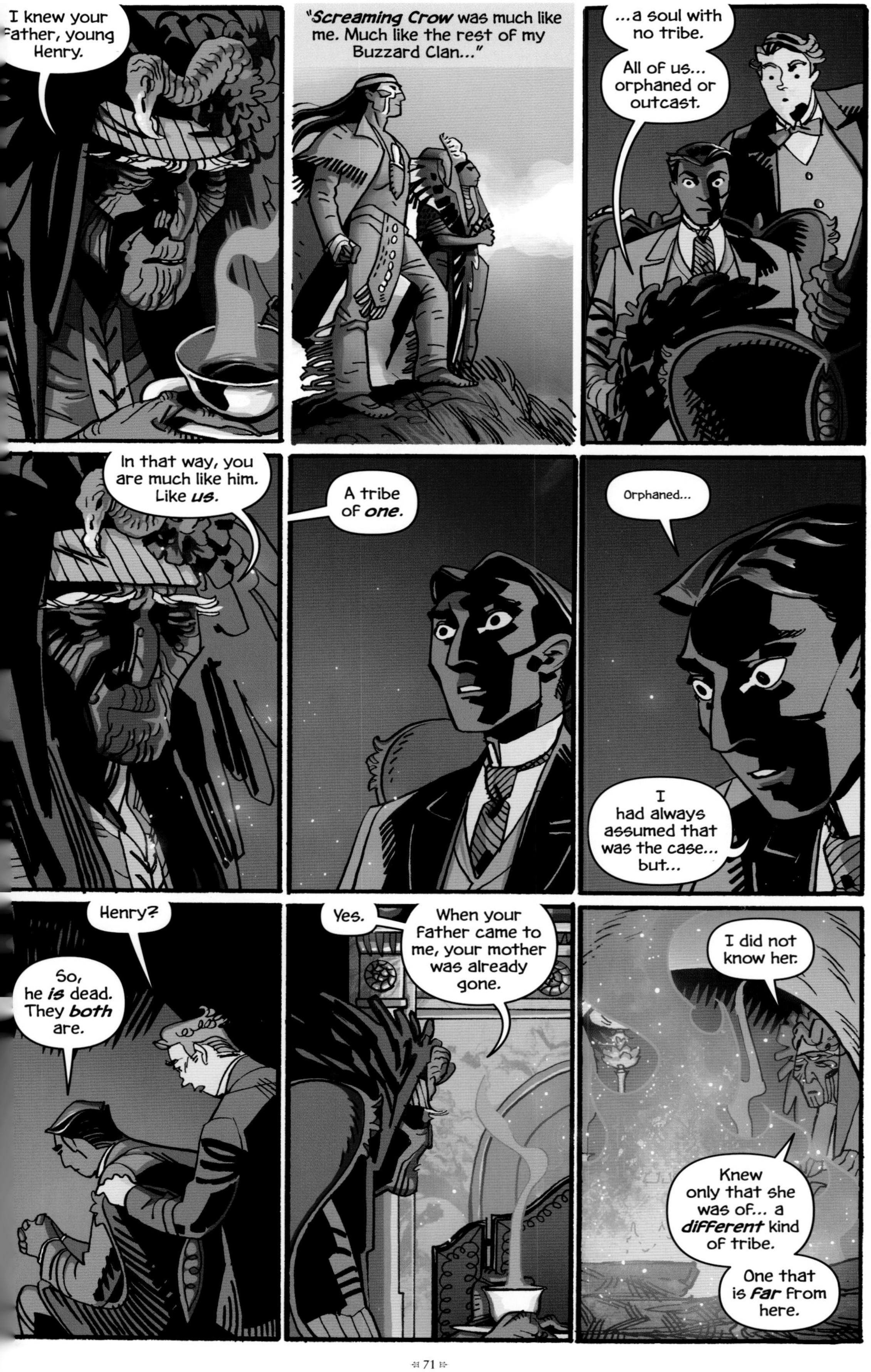
I knew your father, young Henry.
"Screaming Crow was much like me. Much like the rest of my Buzzard Clan..."
...a soul with no tribe.
All of us... orphaned or outcast.
In that way, you are much like him. Like us.
A tribe of one.
Orphaned...
I had always assumed that was the case... but...
Henry?
So, he is dead. They both are.
Yes.
When your father came to me, your mother was already gone.
I did not know her.
Knew only that she was of... a different kind of tribe.
One that is far from here.

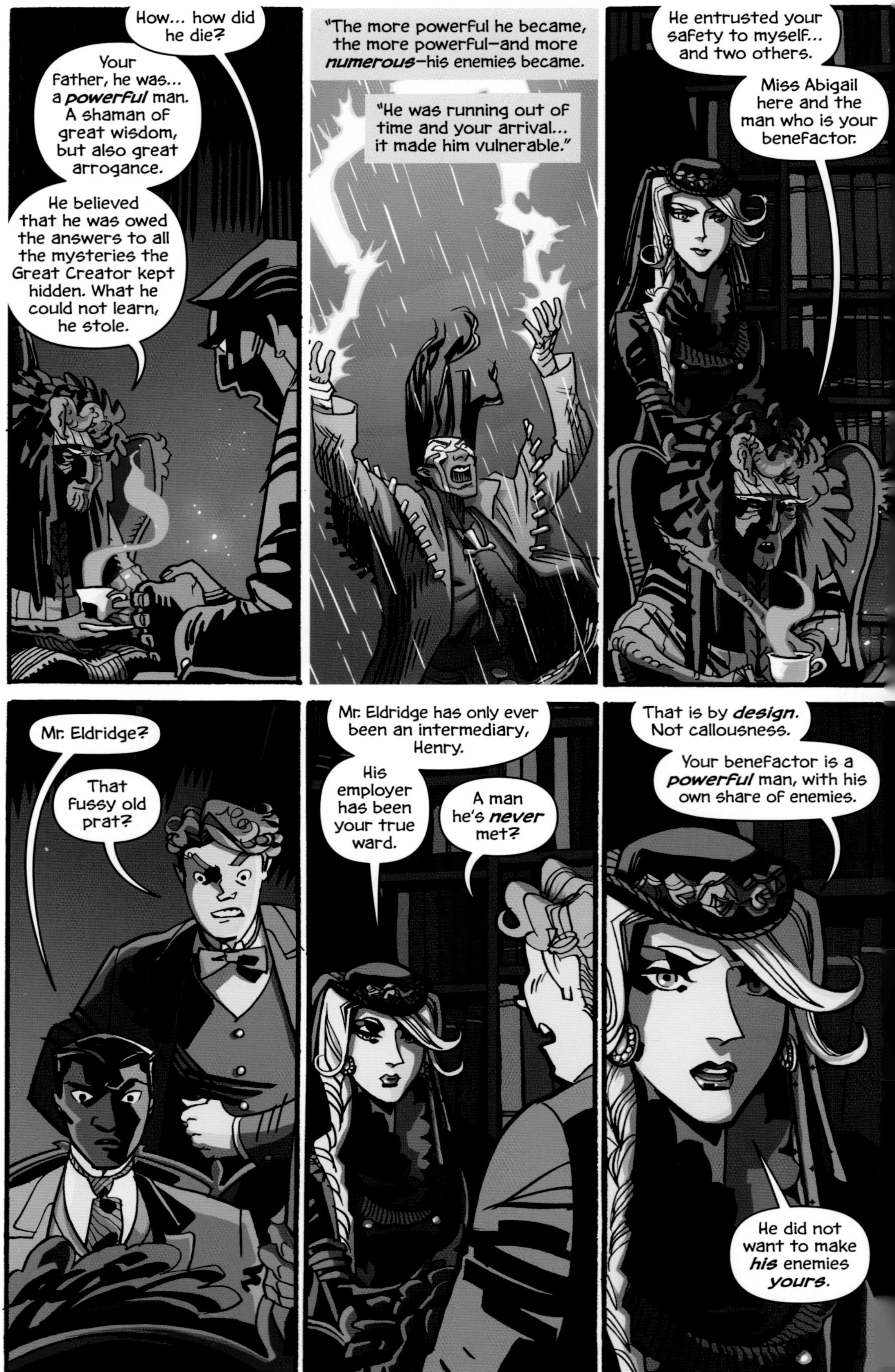
How... how did he die?
Your father, he was... a *powerful* man. A shaman of great wisdom, but also great arrogance.
He believed that he was owed the answers to all the mysteries the Great Creator kept hidden. What he could not learn, he stole.
"The more powerful he became, the more powerful—and more *numerous*—his enemies became.
"He was running out of time and your arrival... it made him vulnerable."
He entrusted your safety to myself... and two others.
Miss Abigail here and the man who is your benefactor.
Mr. Eldridge?
That fussy old prat?
Mr. Eldridge has only ever been an intermediary, Henry.
His employer has been your true ward.
A man he's *never* met?
That is by *design*. Not callousness.
Your benefactor is a *powerful* man, with his own share of enemies.
He did not want to make *his* enemies *yours*.

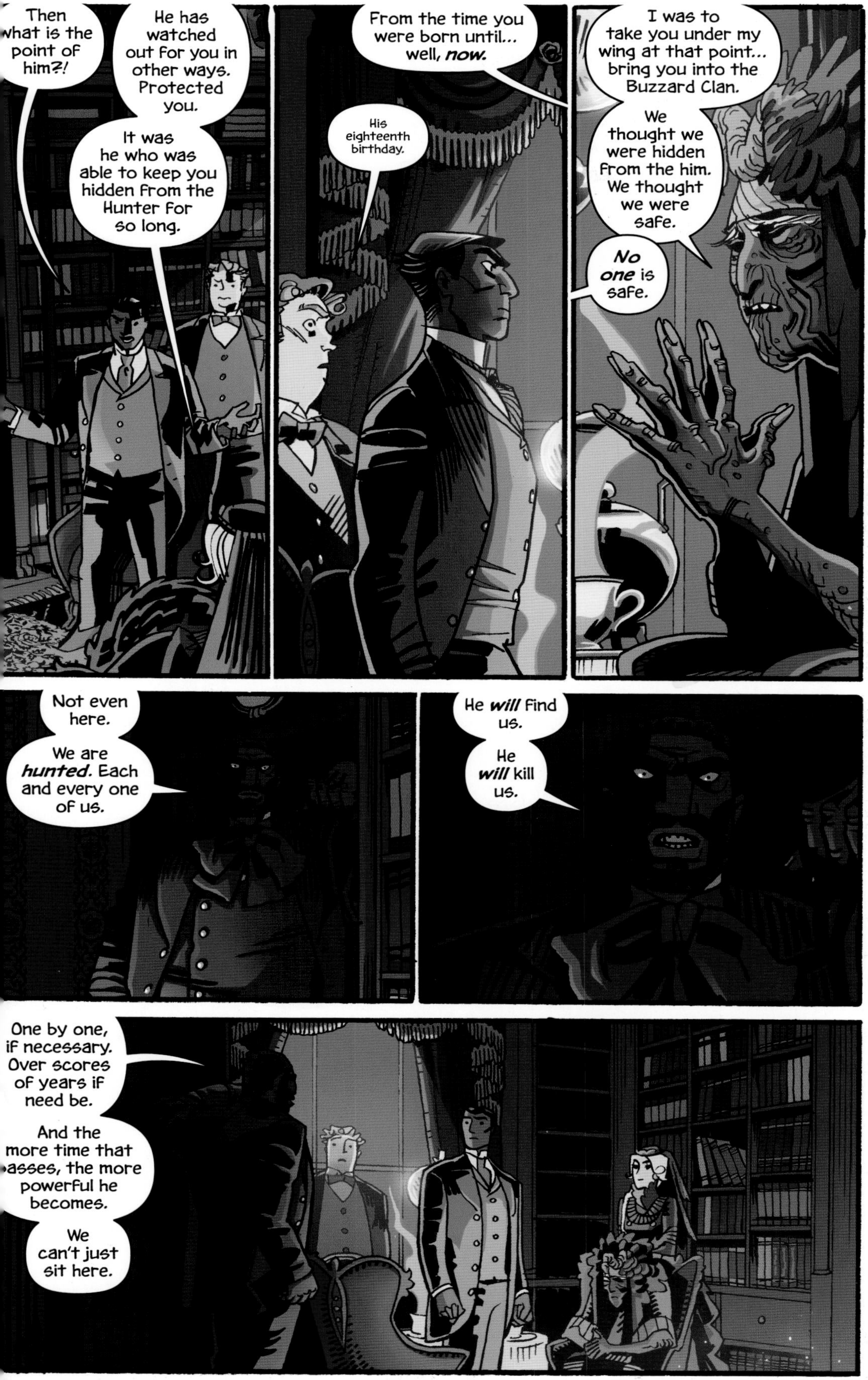
Then what is the point of him?!
He has watched out for you in other ways. Protected you.
It was he who was able to keep you hidden from the Hunter for so long.
From the time you were born until... well, now.
His eighteenth birthday.
I was to take you under my wing at that point... bring you into the Buzzard Clan.
We thought we were hidden from the him. We thought we were safe.
No one is safe.
Not even here.
We are hunted. Each and every one of us.
He will find us.
He will kill us.
One by one, if necessary. Over scores of years if need be.
And the more time that asses, the more powerful he becomes.
We can't just sit here.

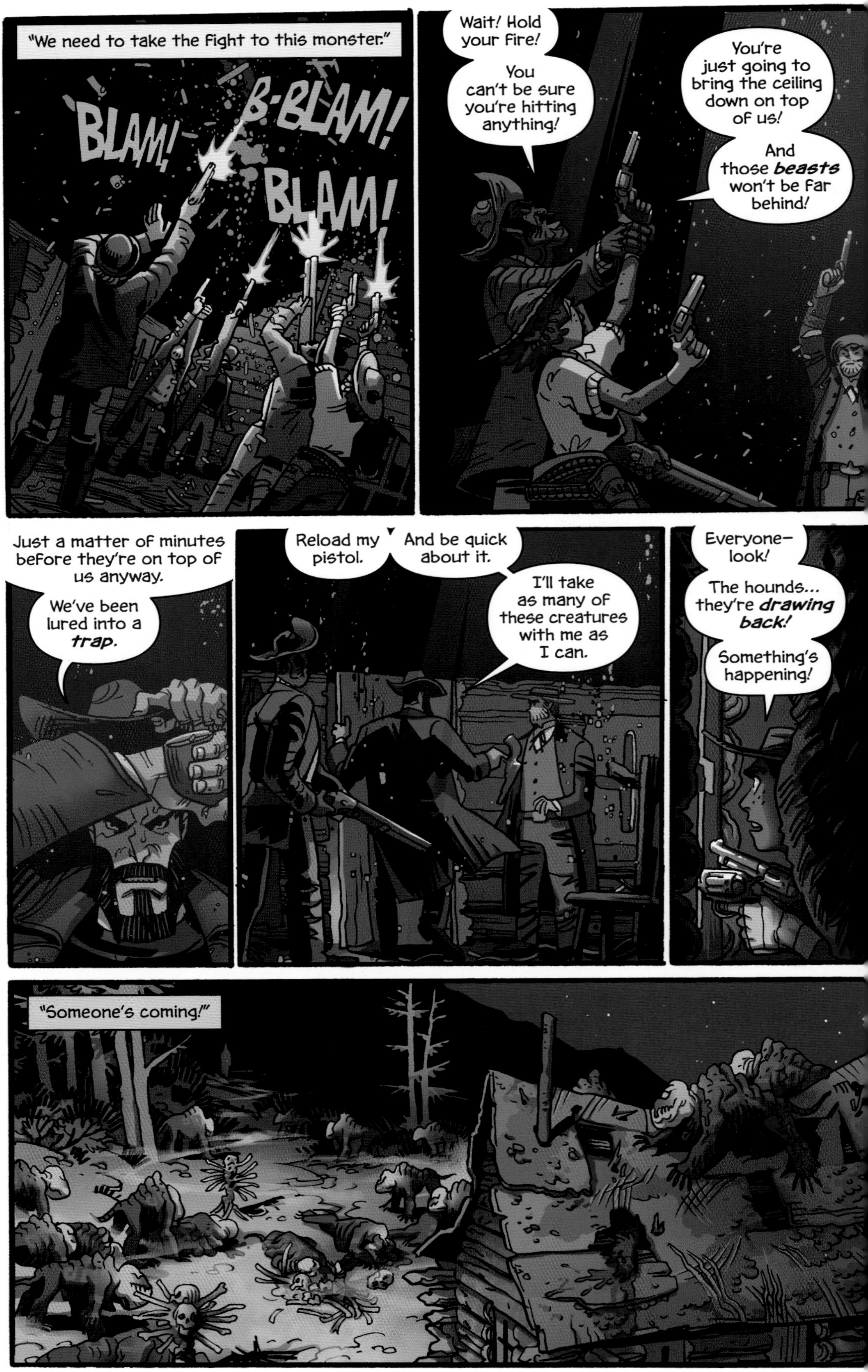
"We need to take the fight to this monster."
BLAM!
B-BLAM!
BLAM!
Wait! Hold your fire!
You can't be sure you're hitting anything!
You're just going to bring the ceiling down on top of us!
And those ***beasts*** won't be far behind!
Just a matter of minutes before they're on top of us anyway.
We've been lured into a ***trap***.
Reload my pistol.
And be quick about it.
I'll take as many of these creatures with me as I can.
Everyone—look!
The hounds... they're ***drawing back!***
Something's happening!
"Someone's coming!"

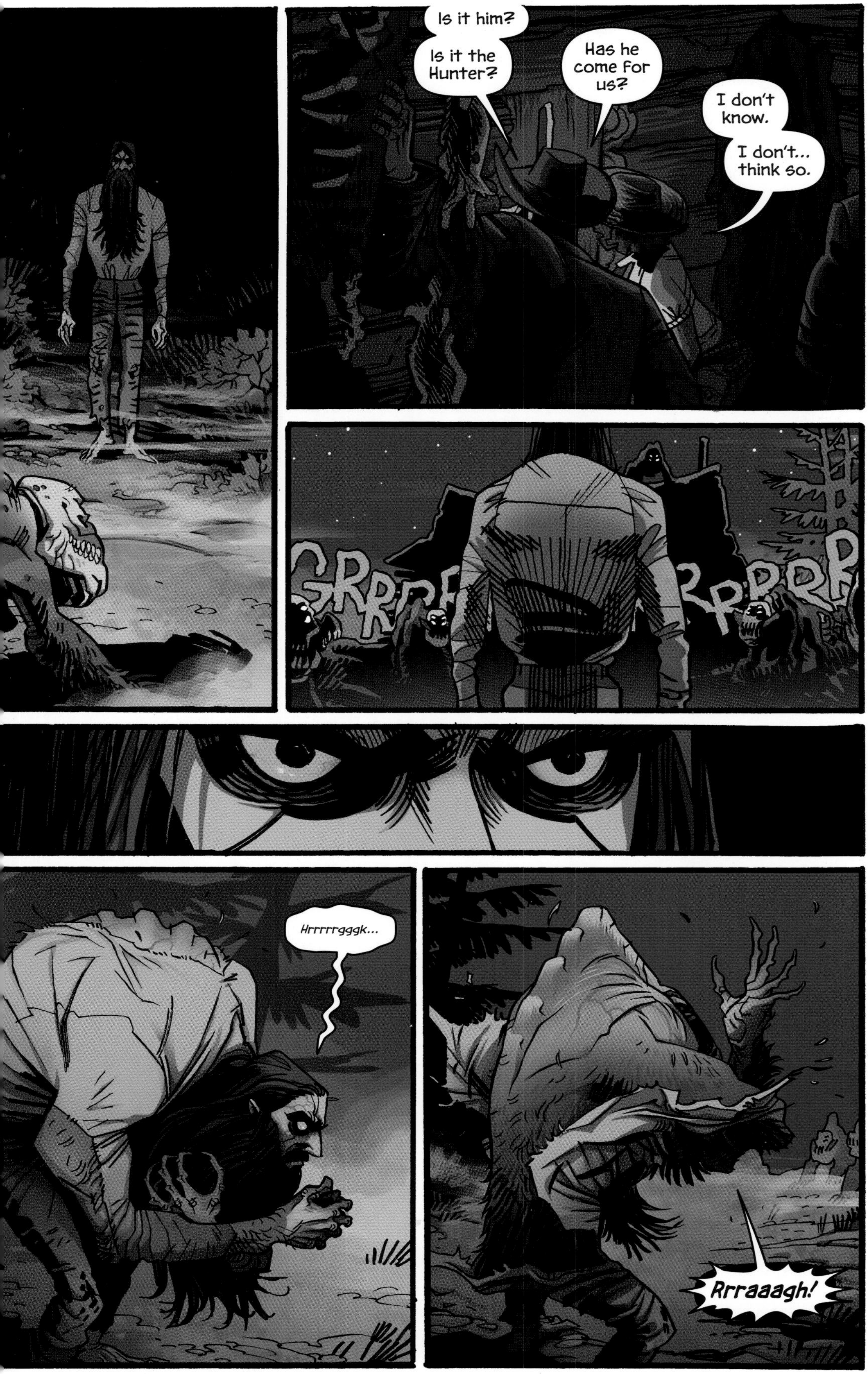
Is it him?
Is it the Hunter?
Has he come for us?
I don't know.
I don't... think so.
GRRRR
RRRR
Hrrrrrgggk...
Rrraaagh!

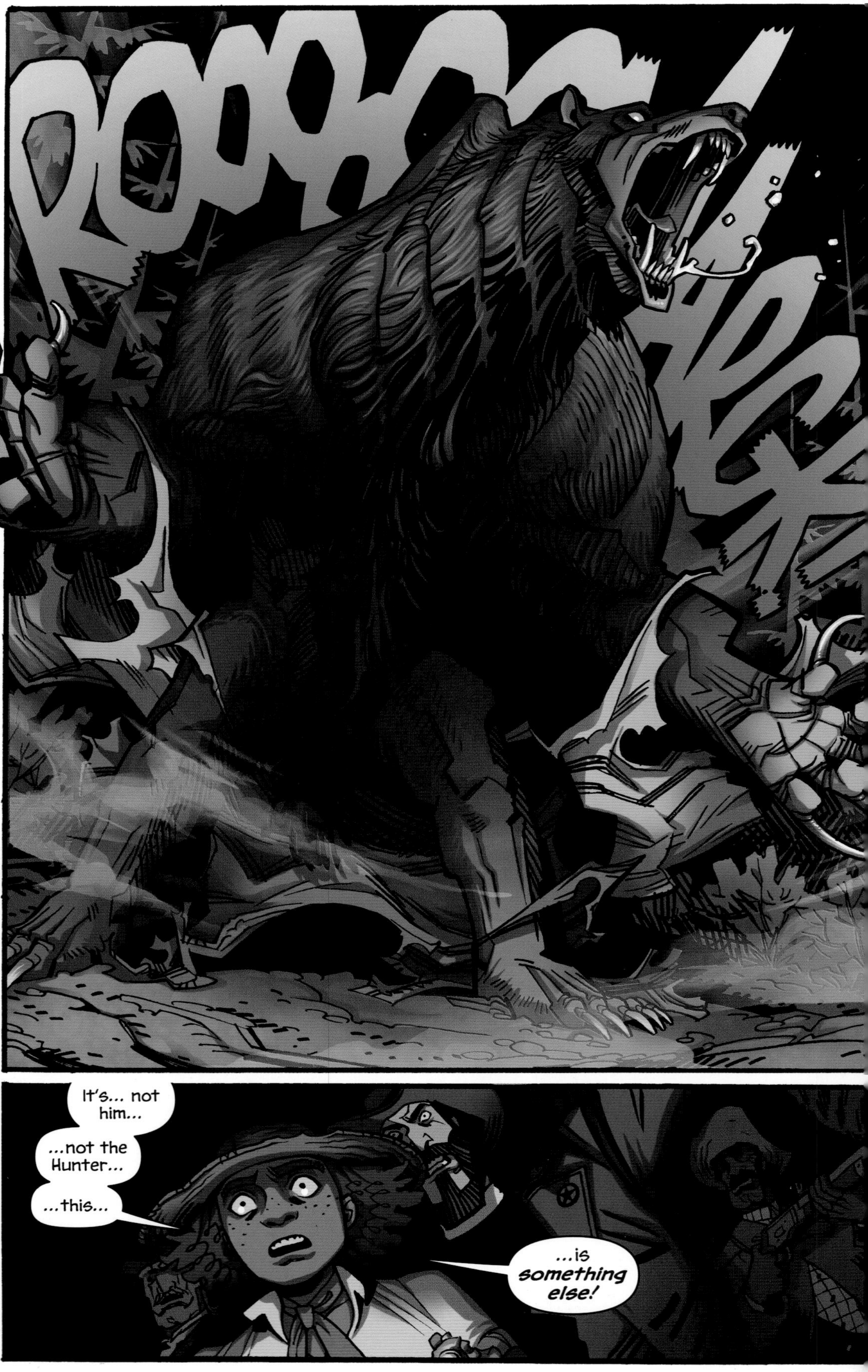
It's... not him...
...not the Hunter...
...this...
...is *something else!*

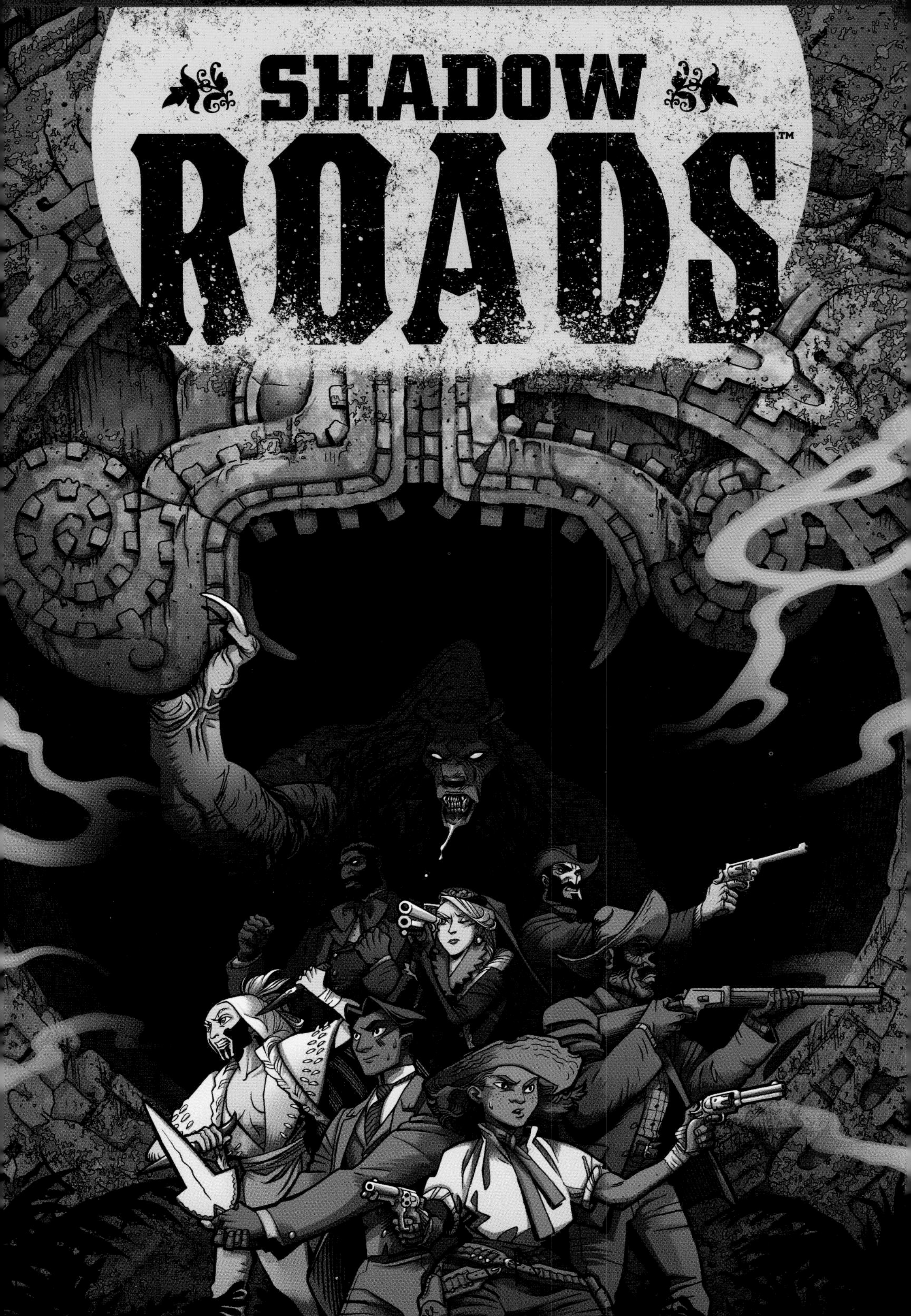
SHADOW
ROADS™

CHAPTER 4

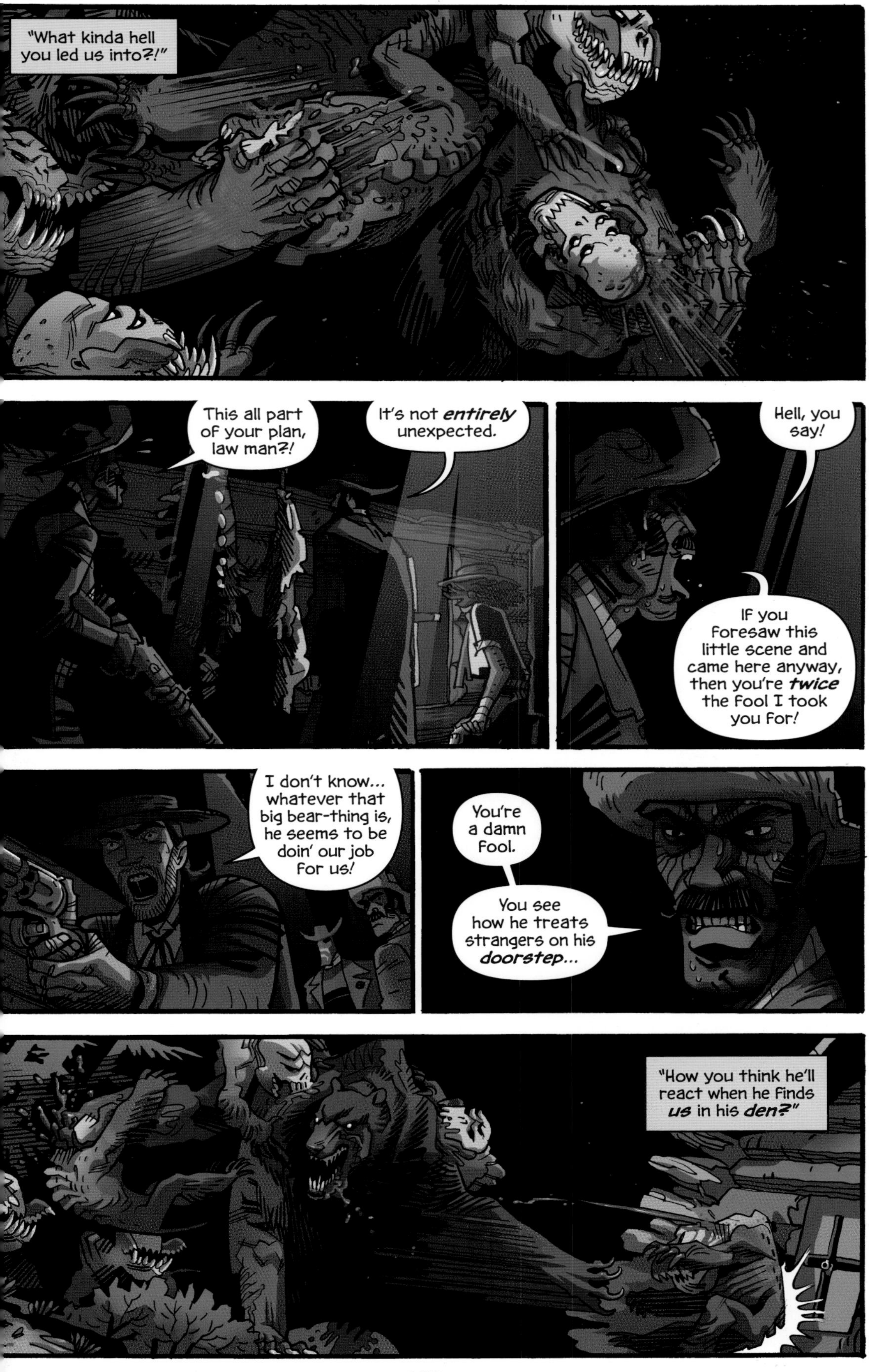
"What kinda hell you led us into?!"
This all part of your plan, law man?!
It's not *entirely* unexpected.
Hell, you say!
If you foresaw this little scene and came here anyway, then you're *twice* the fool I took you for!
I don't know... whatever that big bear-thing is, he seems to be doin' our job for us!
You're a damn fool.
You see how he treats strangers on his *doorstep*...
"How you think he'll react when he finds *us* in his *den?*"

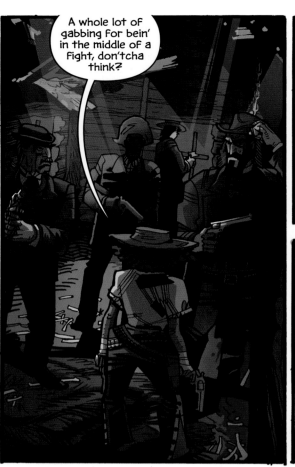

A whole lot of gabbing for bein' in the middle of a fight, don'tcha think?

Way I see it, we don't got much of a *choice*, boys.

Best we take what time we might have left—

—and try to make a good first impression with our host.

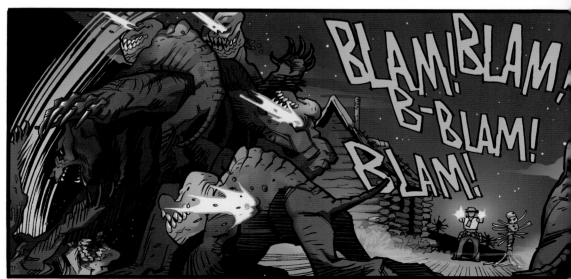

BLAM! BLAM! B-BLAM! BLAM!

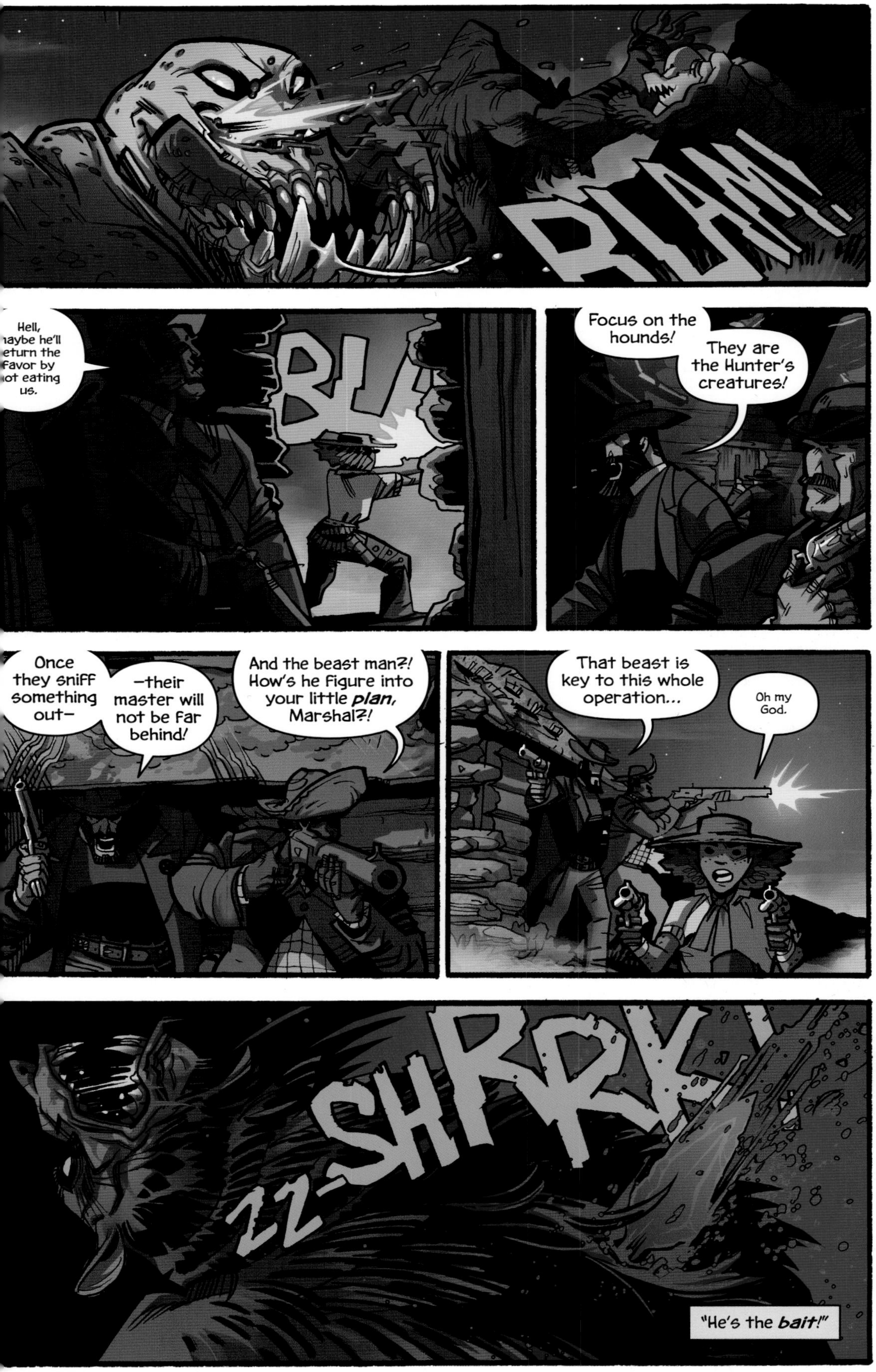

BLAM!
Hell, aybe he'll eturn the favor by ot eating us.
BL
Focus on the hounds!
They are the Hunter's creatures!
Once they sniff something out–
–their master will not be far behind!
And the beast man?! How's he figure into your little *plan*, Marshal?!
That beast is key to this whole operation...
Oh my God.
ZZ-SHRRK!
"He's the *bait!*"

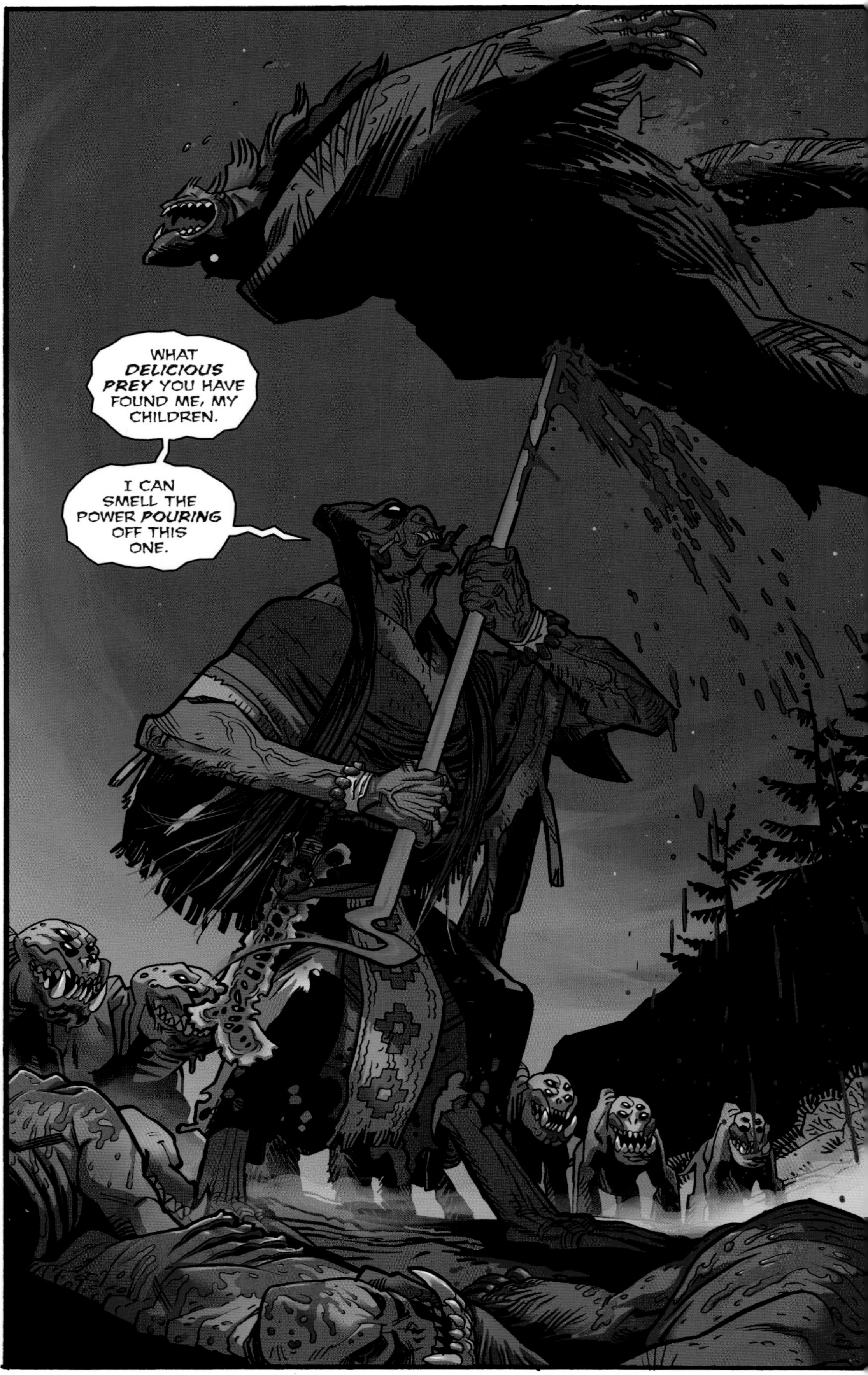
WHAT *DELICIOUS PREY* YOU HAVE FOUND ME, MY CHILDREN.
I CAN SMELL THE POWER *POURING* OFF THIS ONE.

A TRAGEDY...

...POWER OF THIS NATURE...

...*WASTED* ON SUCH A WORTHLESS, FRAGILE VESSEL.

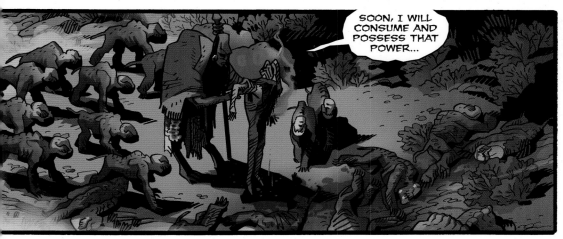

SOON, I WILL CONSUME AND POSSESS THAT POWER...

BUT THERE ARE OTHER MATTERS HERE THAT I MUST ATTEND TO.

ENOUGH!

THERE IS PLENTY MEAT TO GO AROUND!

THE NIGHT-SKINNED MAN AND THE *RIPE* GIRL... THEY ARE *MINE.*

FEED ON THE REST.

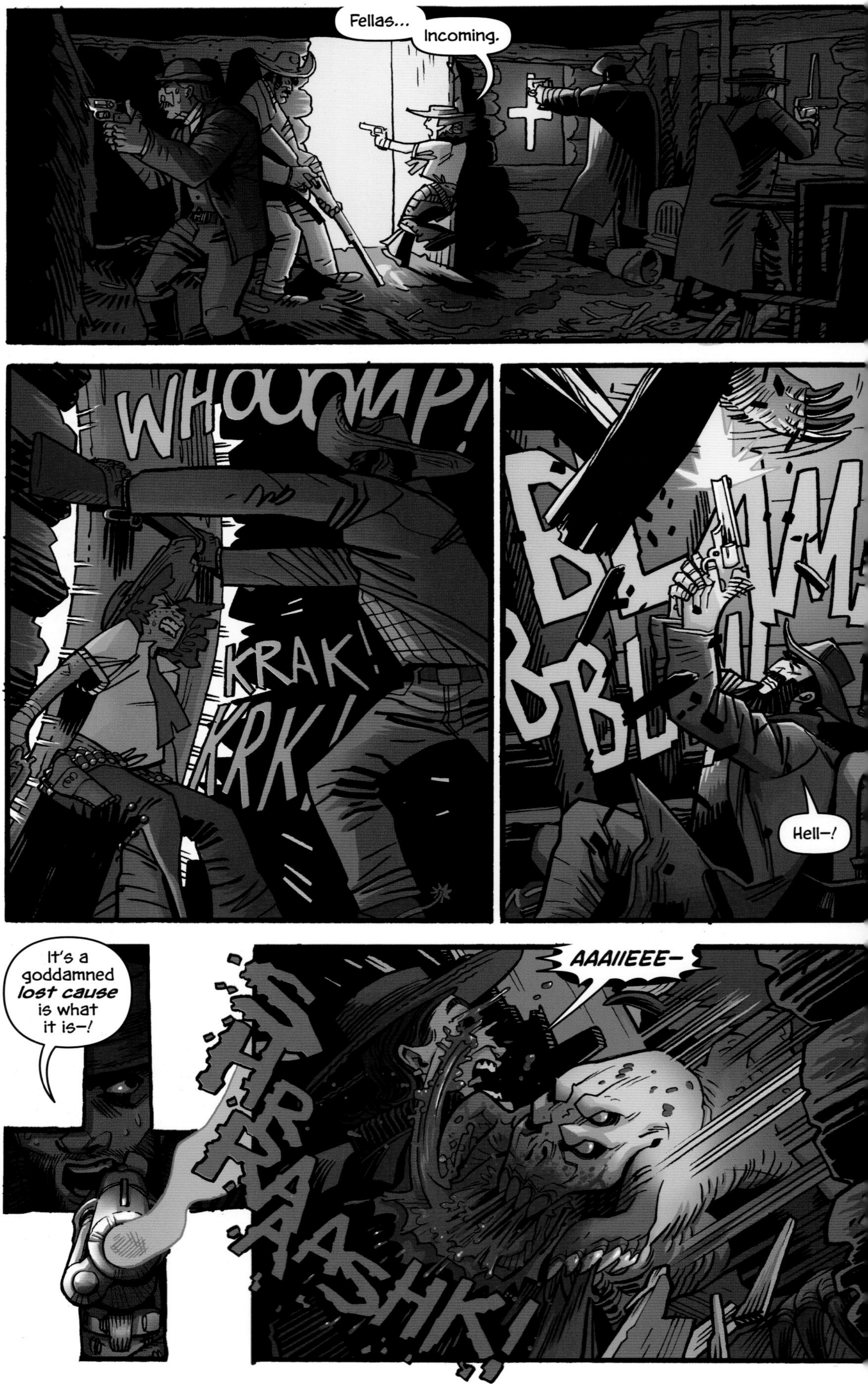
Fellas...
Incoming.
WHOOOMP!
KRAK!
KRK!
Hell—!
It's a goddamned *lost cause* is what it is—!
AAAIIEEE—
SHRAASHK!

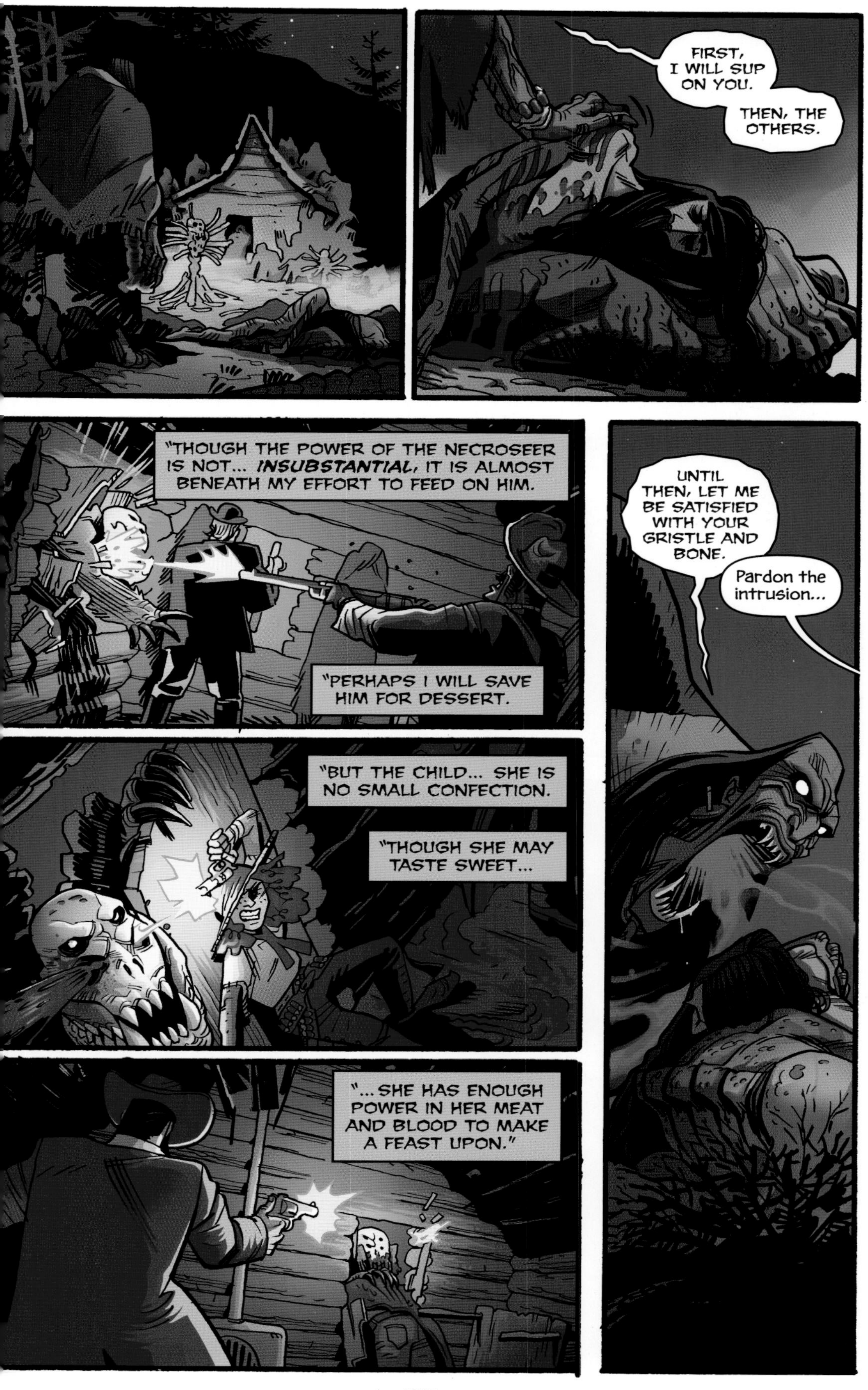
FIRST, I WILL SUP ON YOU.
THEN, THE OTHERS.
"THOUGH THE POWER OF THE NECROSEER IS NOT... *INSUBSTANTIAL,* IT IS ALMOST BENEATH MY EFFORT TO FEED ON HIM.
"PERHAPS I WILL SAVE HIM FOR DESSERT.
"BUT THE CHILD... SHE IS NO SMALL CONFECTION.
"THOUGH SHE MAY TASTE SWEET...
"...SHE HAS ENOUGH POWER IN HER MEAT AND BLOOD TO MAKE A FEAST UPON."
UNTIL THEN, LET ME BE SATISFIED WITH YOUR GRISTLE AND BONE.
Pardon the intrusion...

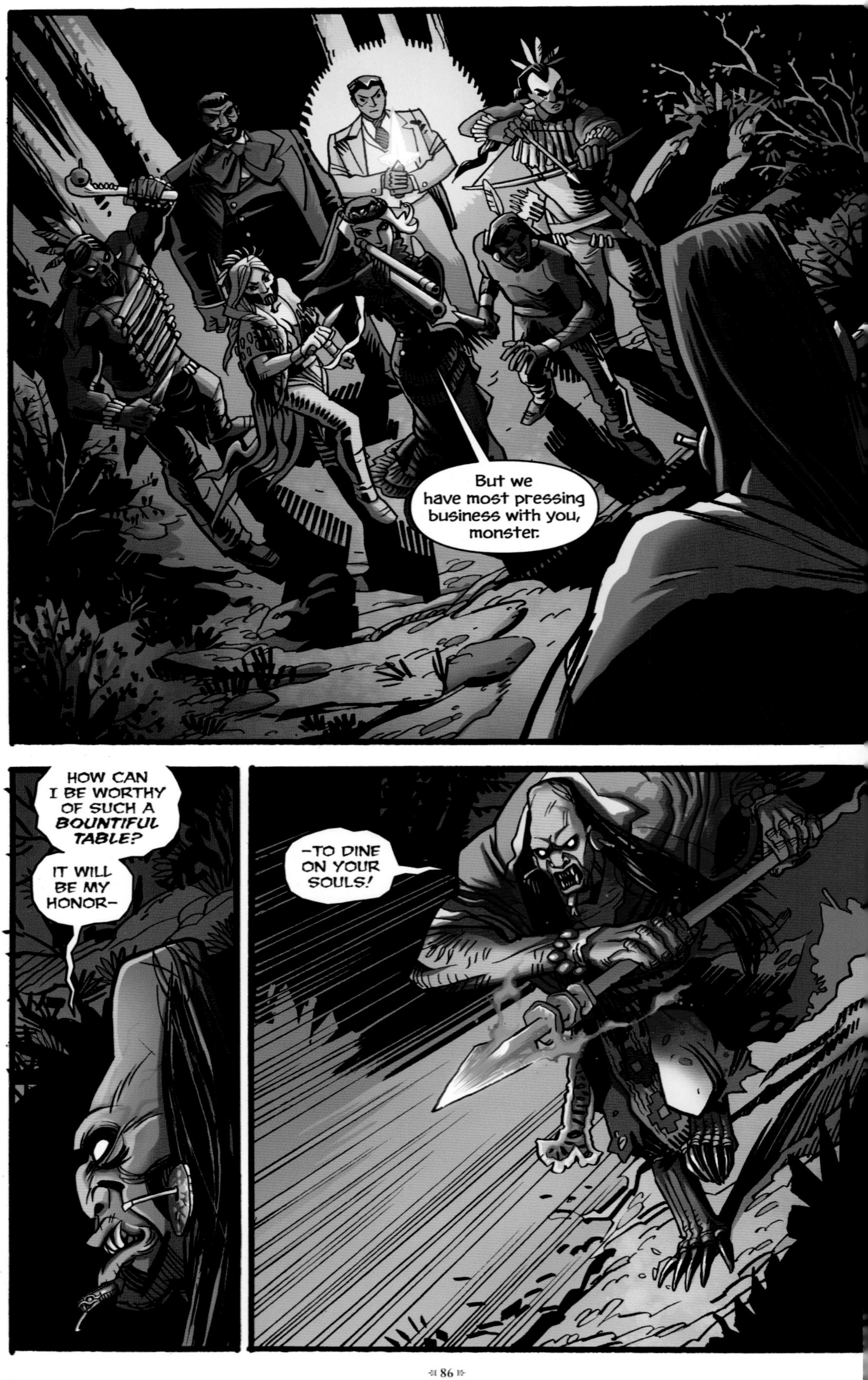
But we have most pressing business with you, monster.
HOW CAN I BE WORTHY OF SUCH A BOUNTIFUL TABLE?
IT WILL BE MY HONOR-
-TO DINE ON YOUR SOULS!

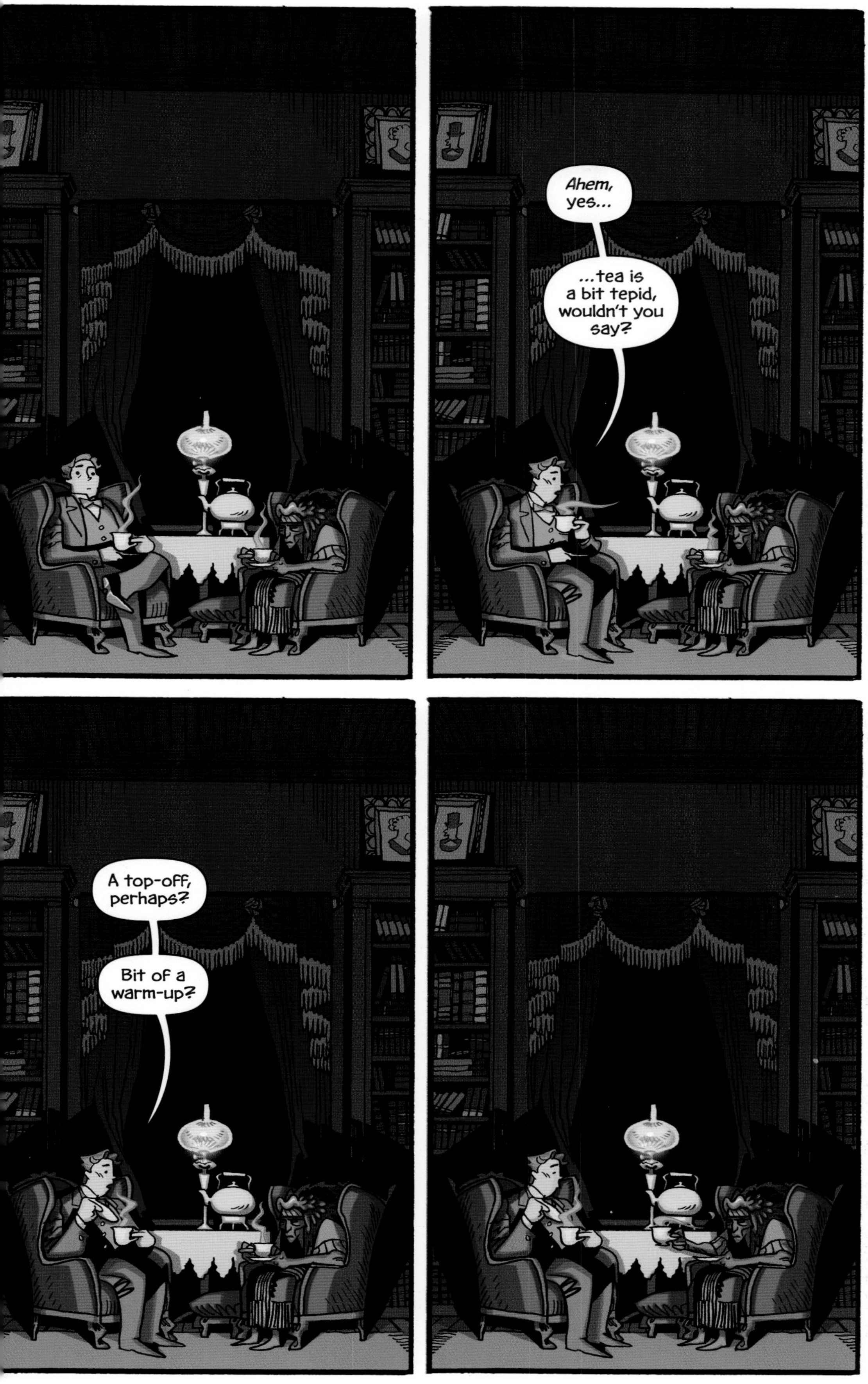
Ahem, yes...
...tea is a bit tepid, wouldn't you say?
A top-off, perhaps?
Bit of a warm-up?

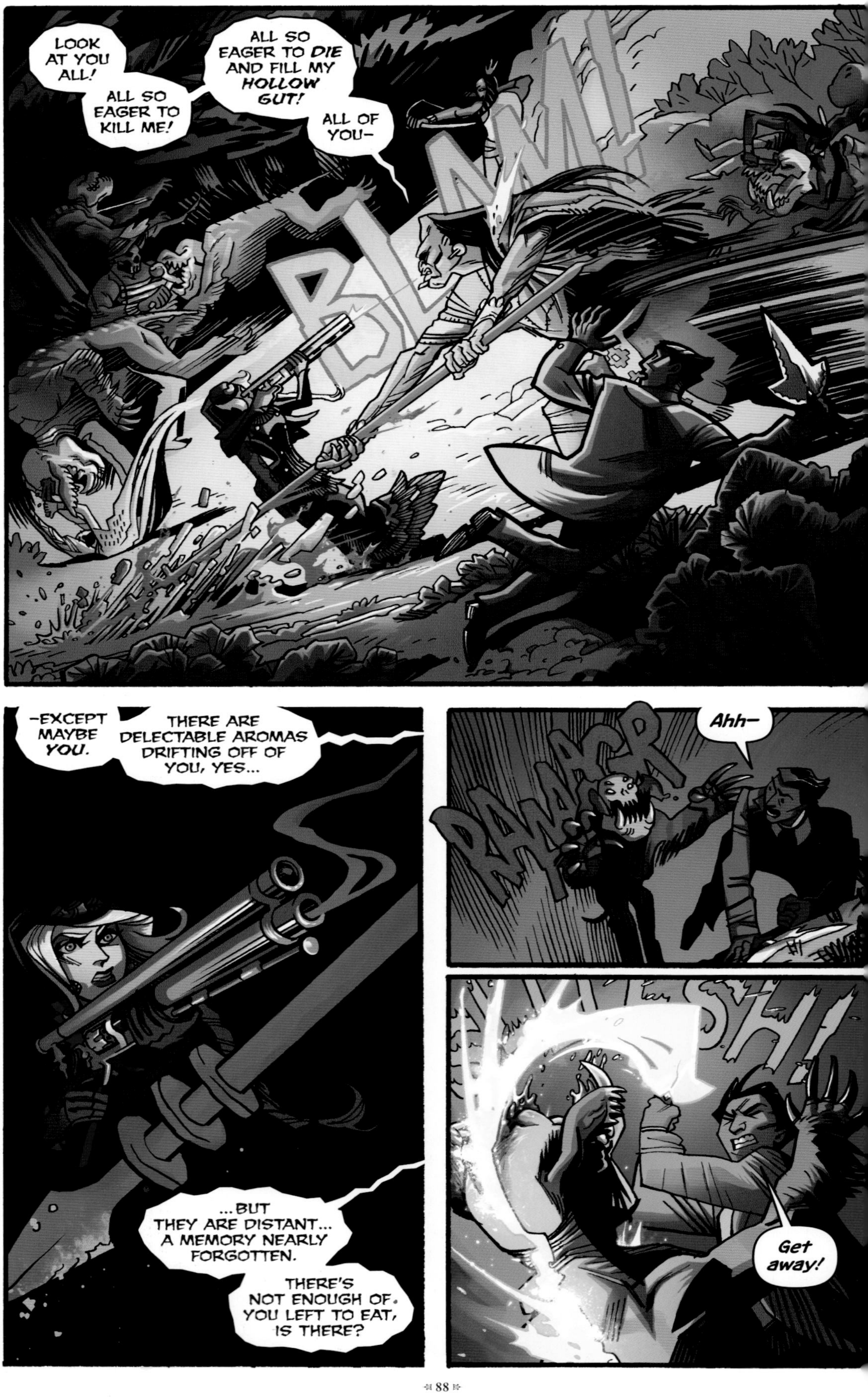
LOOK AT YOU ALL!
ALL SO EAGER TO KILL ME!
ALL SO EAGER TO *DIE* AND FILL MY *HOLLOW GUT!*
ALL OF YOU–
BLAM!
–EXCEPT MAYBE *YOU*.
THERE ARE DELECTABLE AROMAS DRIFTING OFF OF YOU, YES...
...BUT THEY ARE DISTANT... A MEMORY NEARLY FORGOTTEN.
THERE'S NOT ENOUGH OF YOU LEFT TO EAT, IS THERE?
Ahh–
RAAACR
Get away!

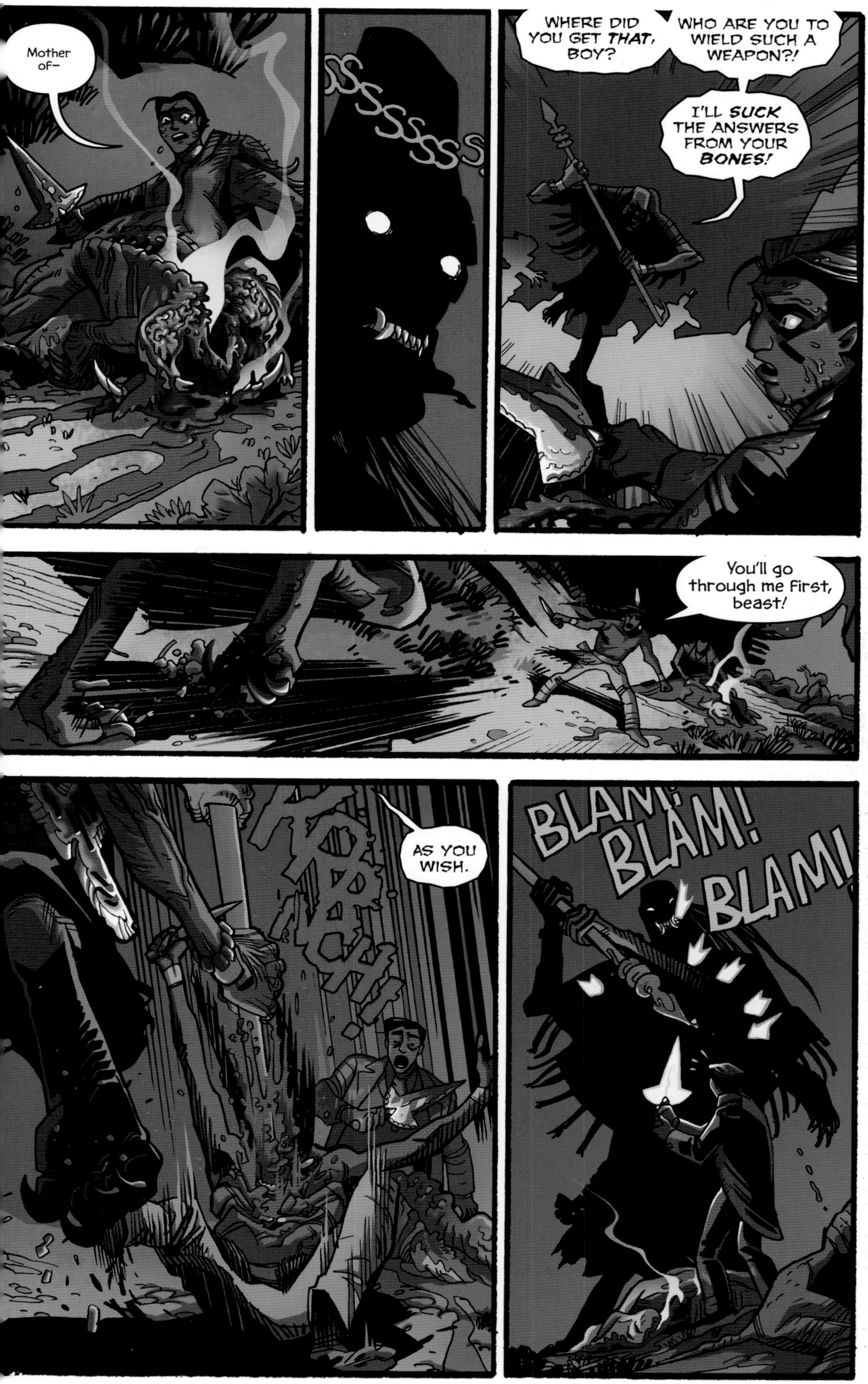
Mother of–
SSSSSSSS
WHERE DID YOU GET *THAT*, BOY?
WHO ARE YOU TO WIELD SUCH A WEAPON?!
I'LL *SUCK* THE ANSWERS FROM YOUR *BONES!*
You'll go through me first, beast!
AS YOU WISH.
BLAM! BLAM! BLAM!

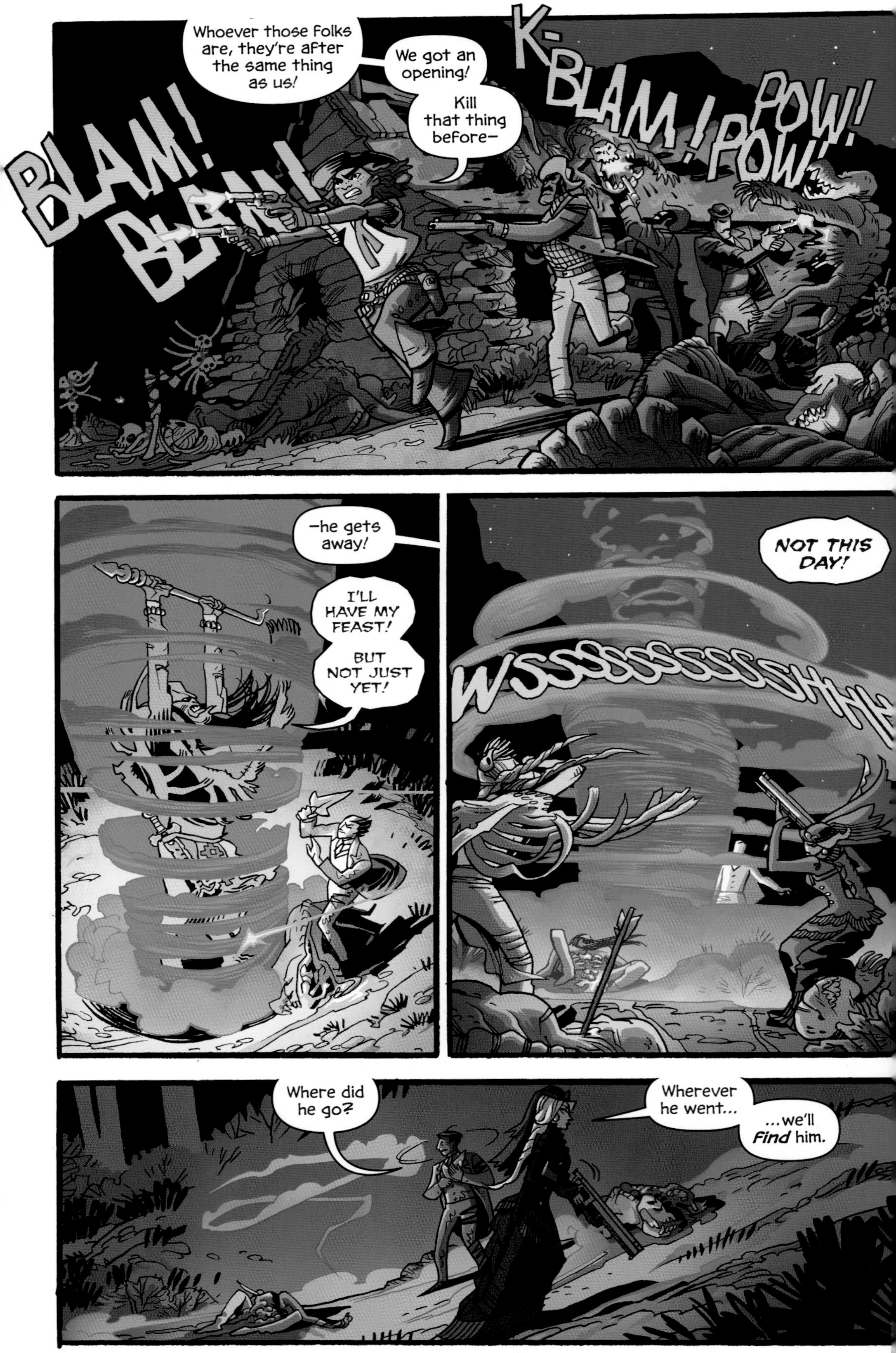
Whoever those folks are, they're after the same thing as us!
We got an opening!
Kill that thing before—
BLAM!
K-BLAM!
POW! POW!
—he gets away!
I'LL HAVE MY FEAST!
BUT NOT JUST YET!
NOT THIS DAY!
WSSSSSSSSSSHHH
Where did he go?
Wherever he went...
...we'll *Find* him.

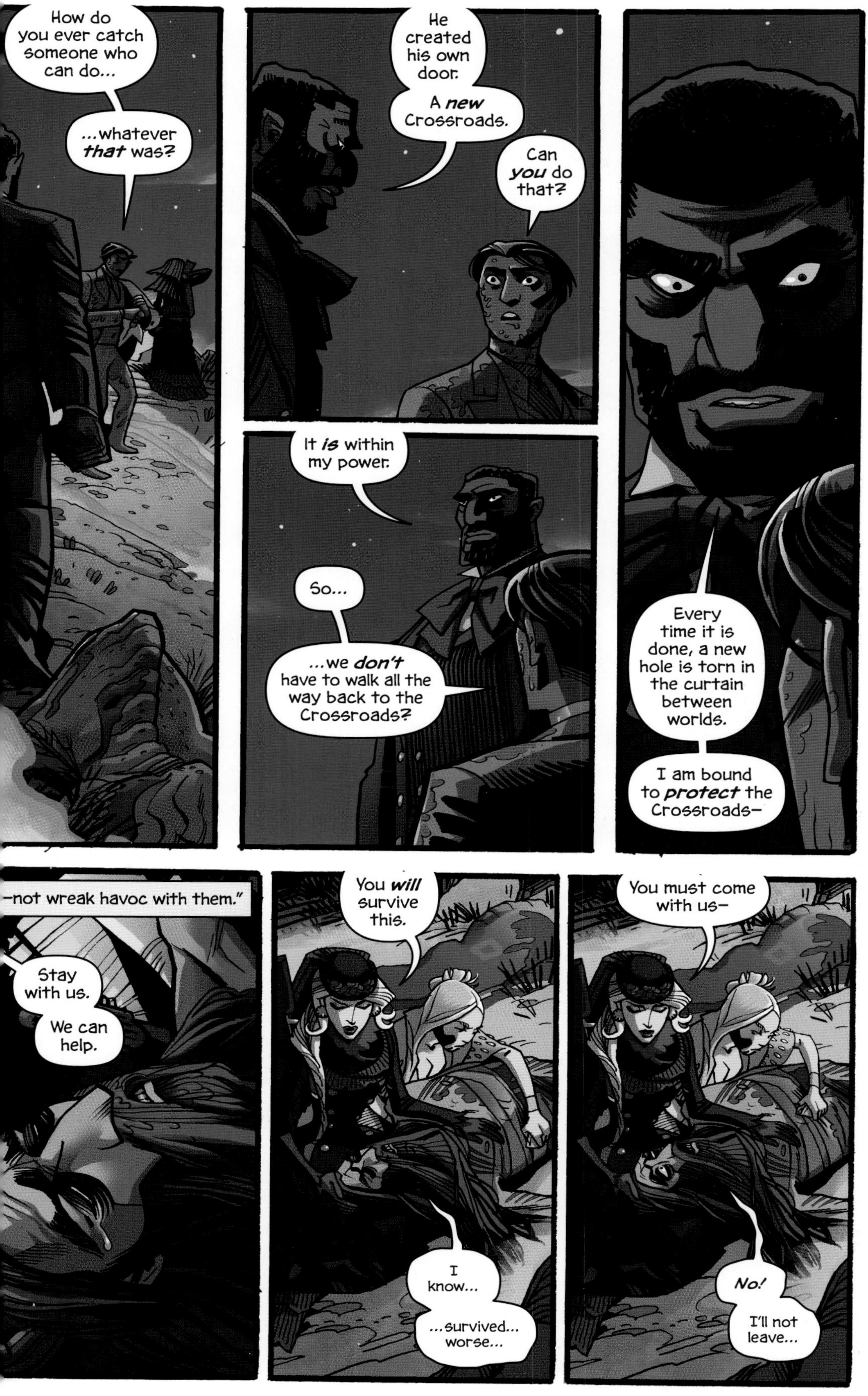
How do you ever catch someone who can do...
...whatever *that* was?
He created his own door.
A *new* Crossroads.
Can *you* do that?
It *is* within my power.
So...
...we *don't* have to walk all the way back to the Crossroads?
Every time it is done, a new hole is torn in the curtain between worlds.
I am bound to *protect* the Crossroads—
—not wreak havoc with them."
Stay with us.
We can help.
You *will* survive this.
I know...
...survived... worse...
You must come with us—
No!
I'll not leave...

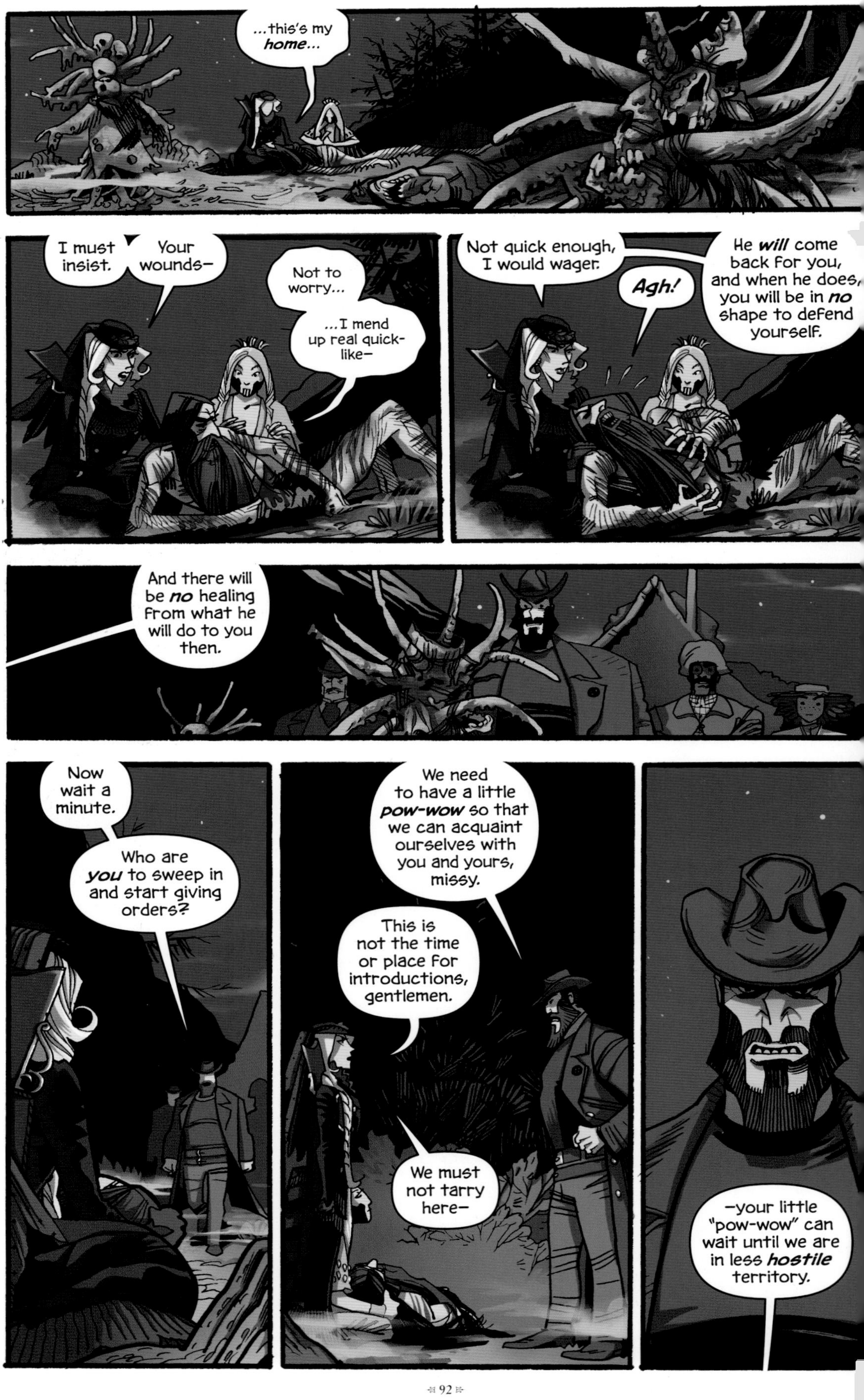
...this's my *home*...
I must insist.
Your wounds–
Not to worry...
...I mend up real quick-like–
Not quick enough, I would wager.
Agh!
He *will* come back for you, and when he does, you will be in *no* shape to defend yourself.
And there will be *no* healing from what he will do to you then.
Now wait a minute.
Who are *you* to sweep in and start giving orders?
We need to have a little *pow-wow* so that we can acquaint ourselves with you and yours, missy.
This is not the time or place for introductions, gentlemen.
We must not tarry here–
–your little "pow-wow" can wait until we are in less *hostile* territory.

Odd little gang you guys have here.

What's with the **princess?**

Oh! *Um...* actually, I believe she is a... **duchess?**

Hmph!

And what're you, then?

King of India?

Heh... not quite, I'm afraid.

I am just a student at—

What kind of fancy-pants **tribe** you a party to?

Uh... E-English?

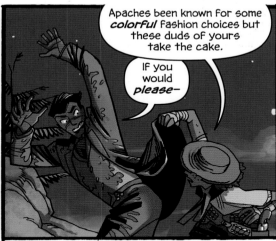

Apaches been known for some **colorful** fashion choices but these duds of yours take the cake.

If you would **please—**

Enough with the **hanky-panky**, children—

We must make haste.

It is time we take our leave of this place.

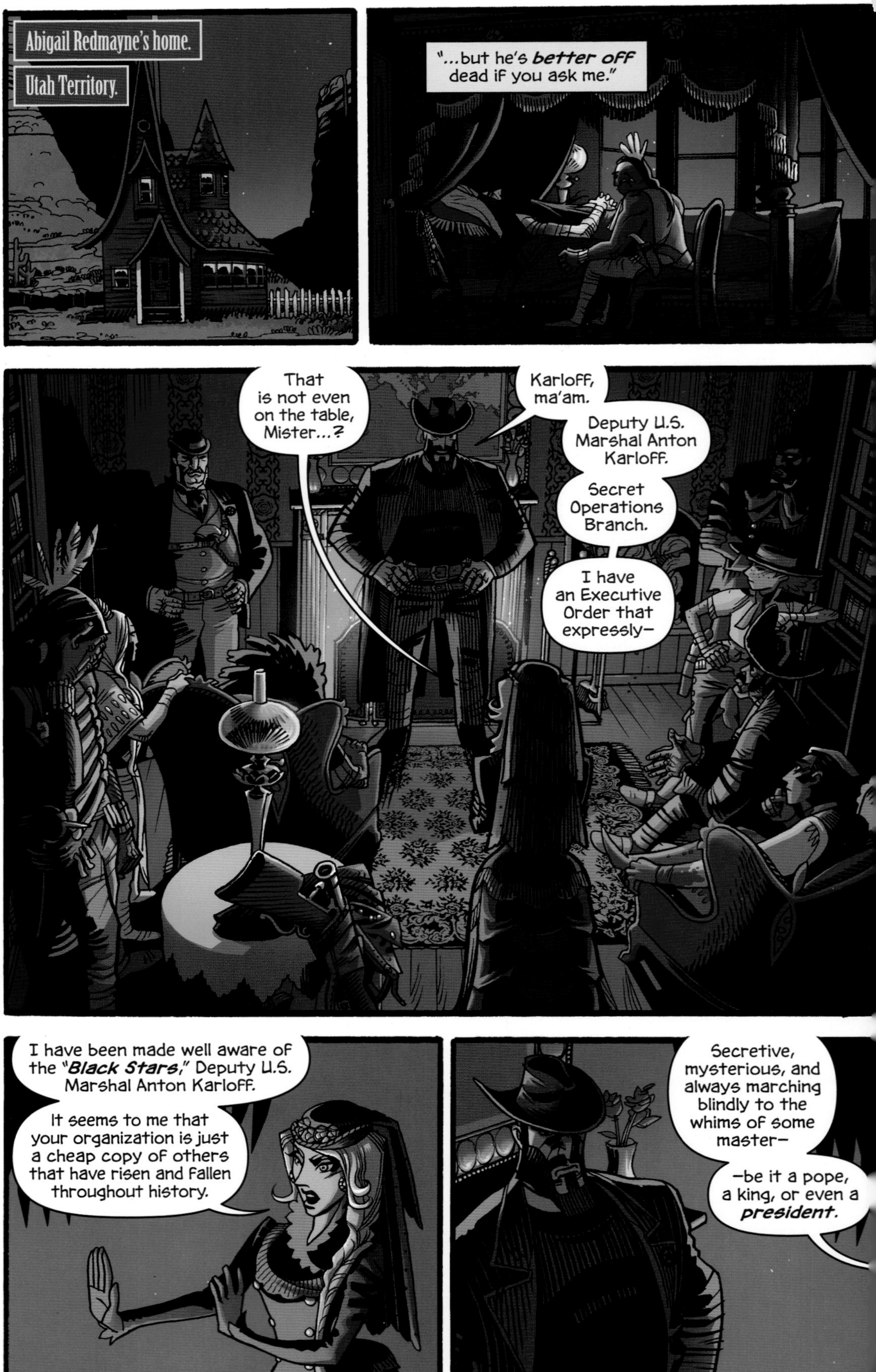
Abigail Redmayne's home.
Utah Territory.
"...but he's *better off* dead if you ask me."
That is not even on the table, Mister...?
Karloff, ma'am.
Deputy U.S. Marshal Anton Karloff.
Secret Operations Branch.
I have an Executive Order that expressly—
I have been made well aware of the "*Black Stars*," Deputy U.S. Marshal Anton Karloff.
It seems to me that your organization is just a cheap copy of others that have risen and fallen throughout history.
Secretive, mysterious, and always marching blindly to the whims of some master—
—be it a pope, a king, or even a *president*.

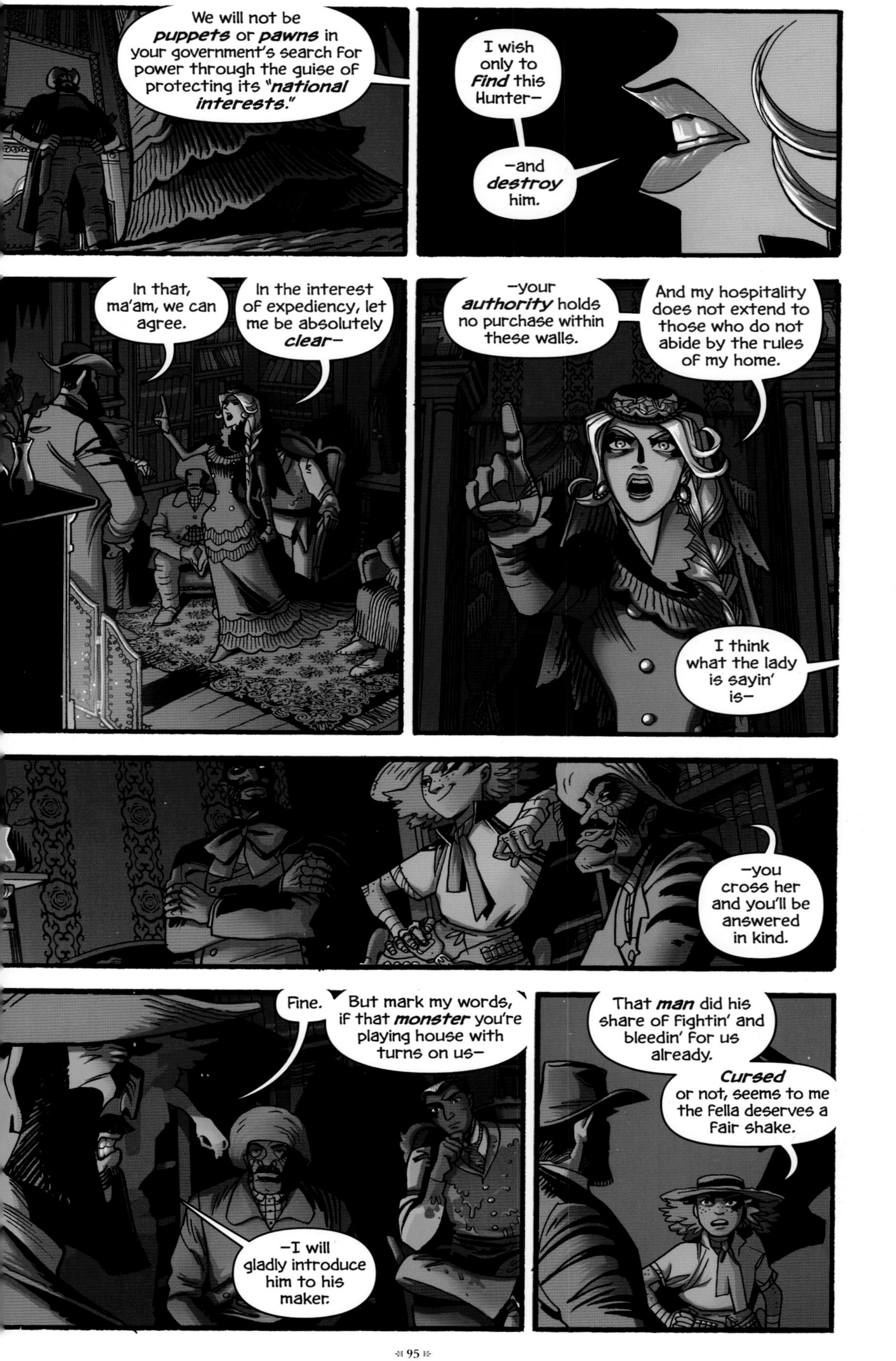
We will not be puppets or pawns in your government's search for power through the guise of protecting its "national interests."
I wish only to find this Hunter–
–and destroy him.
In that, ma'am, we can agree.
In the interest of expediency, let me be absolutely clear–
–your authority holds no purchase within these walls.
And my hospitality does not extend to those who do not abide by the rules of my home.
I think what the lady is sayin' is–
–you cross her and you'll be answered in kind.
Fine.
But mark my words, if that monster you're playing house with turns on us–
–I will gladly introduce him to his maker.
That man did his share of fightin' and bleedin' for us already.
Cursed or not, seems to me the fella deserves a fair shake.

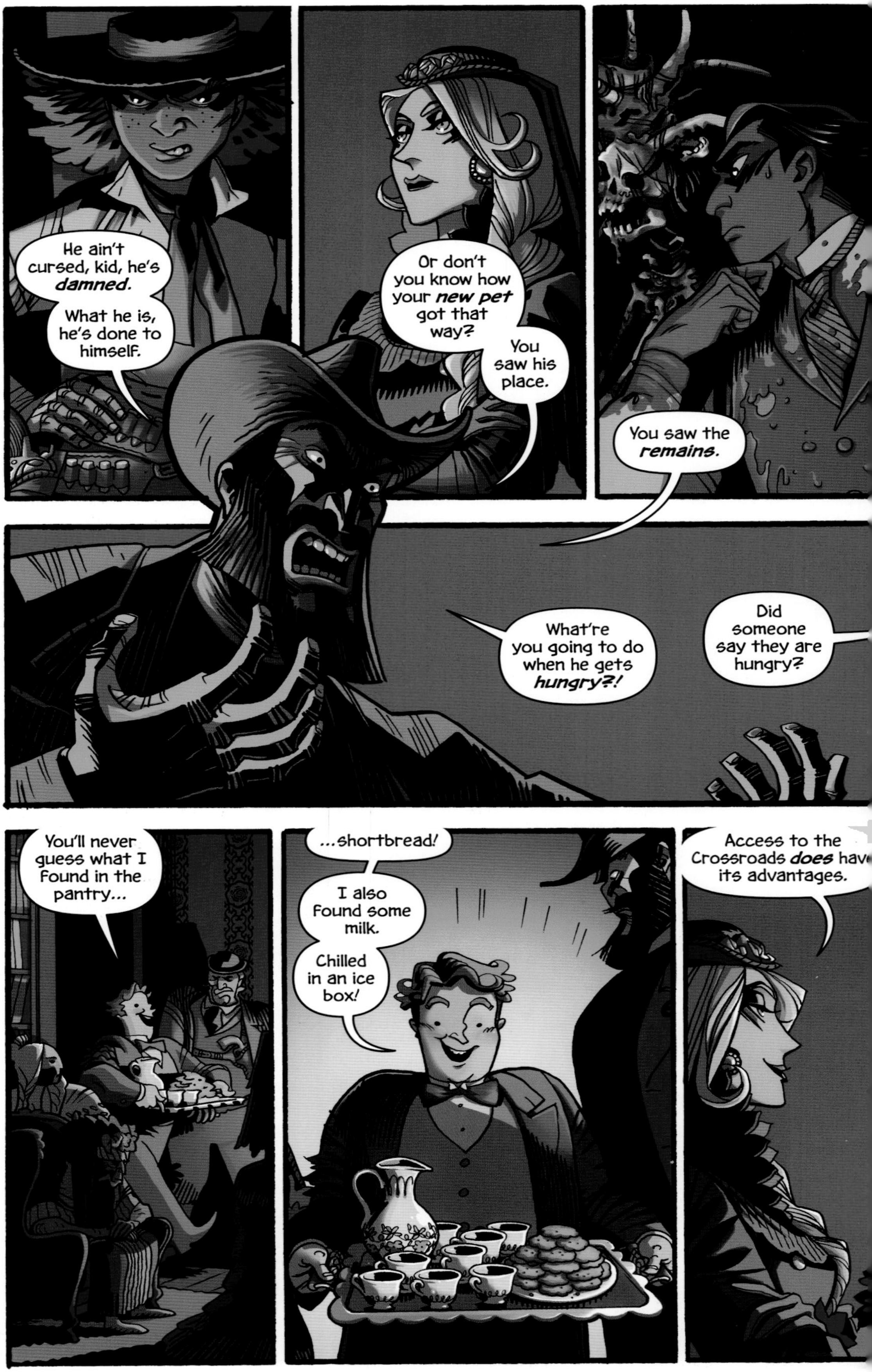
He ain't cursed, kid, he's *damned.*
What he is, he's done to himself.
Or don't you know how your ***new pet*** got that way?
You saw his place.
You saw the ***remains.***
What're you going to do when he gets ***hungry?!***
Did someone say they are hungry?
You'll never guess what I found in the pantry...
...shortbread!
I also found some milk.
Chilled in an ice box!
Access to the Crossroads ***does*** have its advantages.

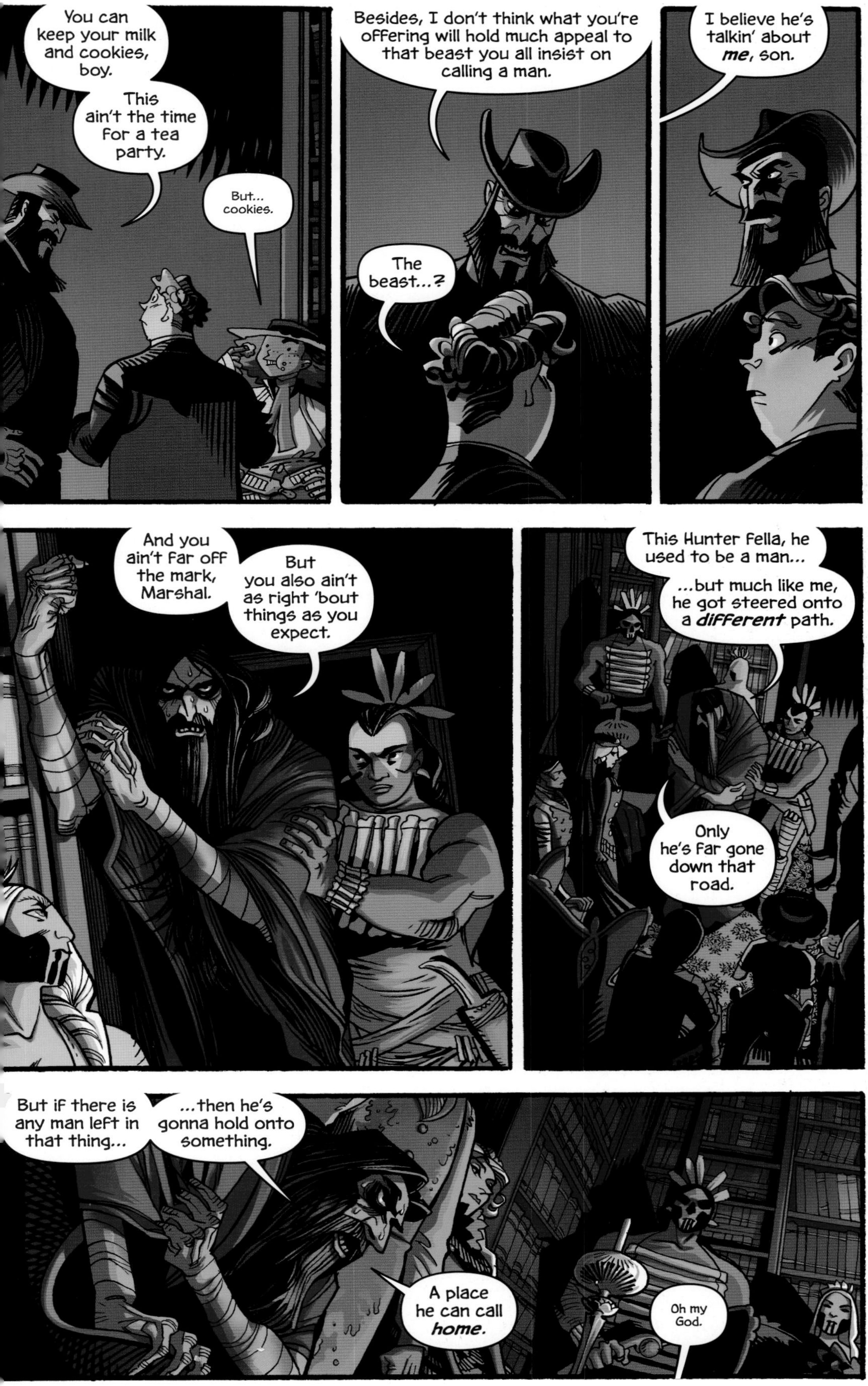
You can keep your milk and cookies, boy.
This ain't the time for a tea party.
But... cookies.
Besides, I don't think what you're offering will hold much appeal to that beast you all insist on calling a man.
The beast...?
I believe he's talkin' about *me*, son.
And you ain't far off the mark, Marshal.
But you also ain't as right 'bout things as you expect.
This Hunter fella, he used to be a man...
...but much like me, he got steered onto a *different* path.
Only he's far gone down that road.
But if there is any man left in that thing...
...then he's gonna hold onto something.
A place he can call *home*.
Oh my God.

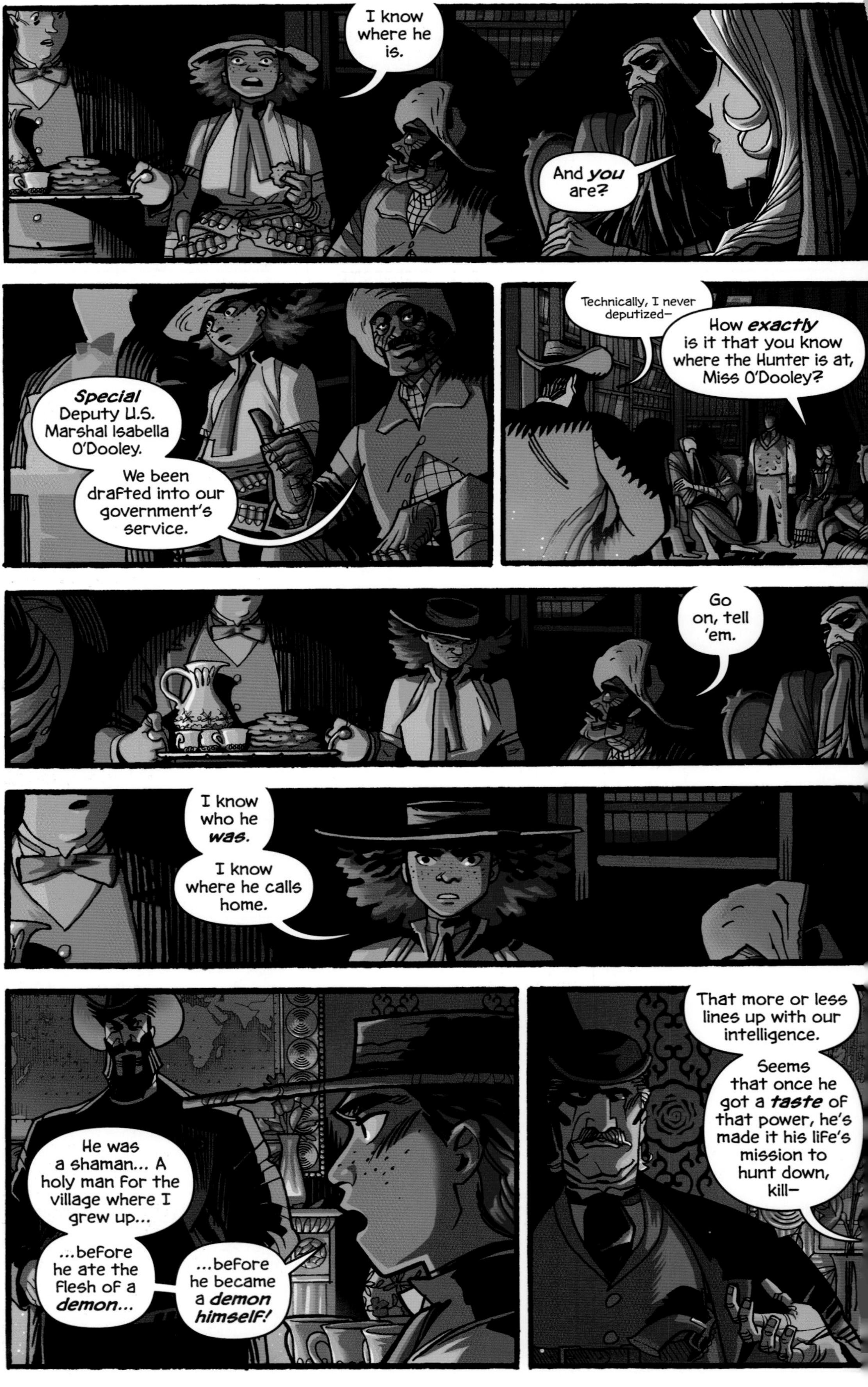

I know where he is.
And *you* are?
Special Deputy U.S. Marshal Isabella O'Dooley.
We been drafted into our government's service.
Technically, I never deputized—
How *exactly* is it that you know where the Hunter is at, Miss O'Dooley?
Go on, tell 'em.
I know who he *was.*
I know where he calls home.
He was a shaman... A holy man for the village where I grew up...
...before he ate the flesh of a *demon*...
...before he became a *demon himself!*
That more or less lines up with our intelligence.
Seems that once he got a *taste* of that power, he's made it his life's mission to hunt down, kill—

—and *devour* his prey.

By consuming their flesh he is able to absorb whatever power his prey got...

Magical beings, and the like.

Whether they are gods, spirits... or some kind of voodoo psychopomp like your big friend over there.

We've been tracking the Hunter for years as he's cut a slow and bloody path up from Mexico and places south.

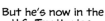

But he's now in the U.S. Territories.

And it's the Black Stars' duty to make sure he regrets setting foot *here*.

And how you plan on doin' *that*, Marshal?

How do you intend to hunt a man can disappear with a snap of the fingers?

snap

Obviously, we need to adjust our tactics—

The rules have *changed*.

You've seen it, haven't you?

The sudden escalation.

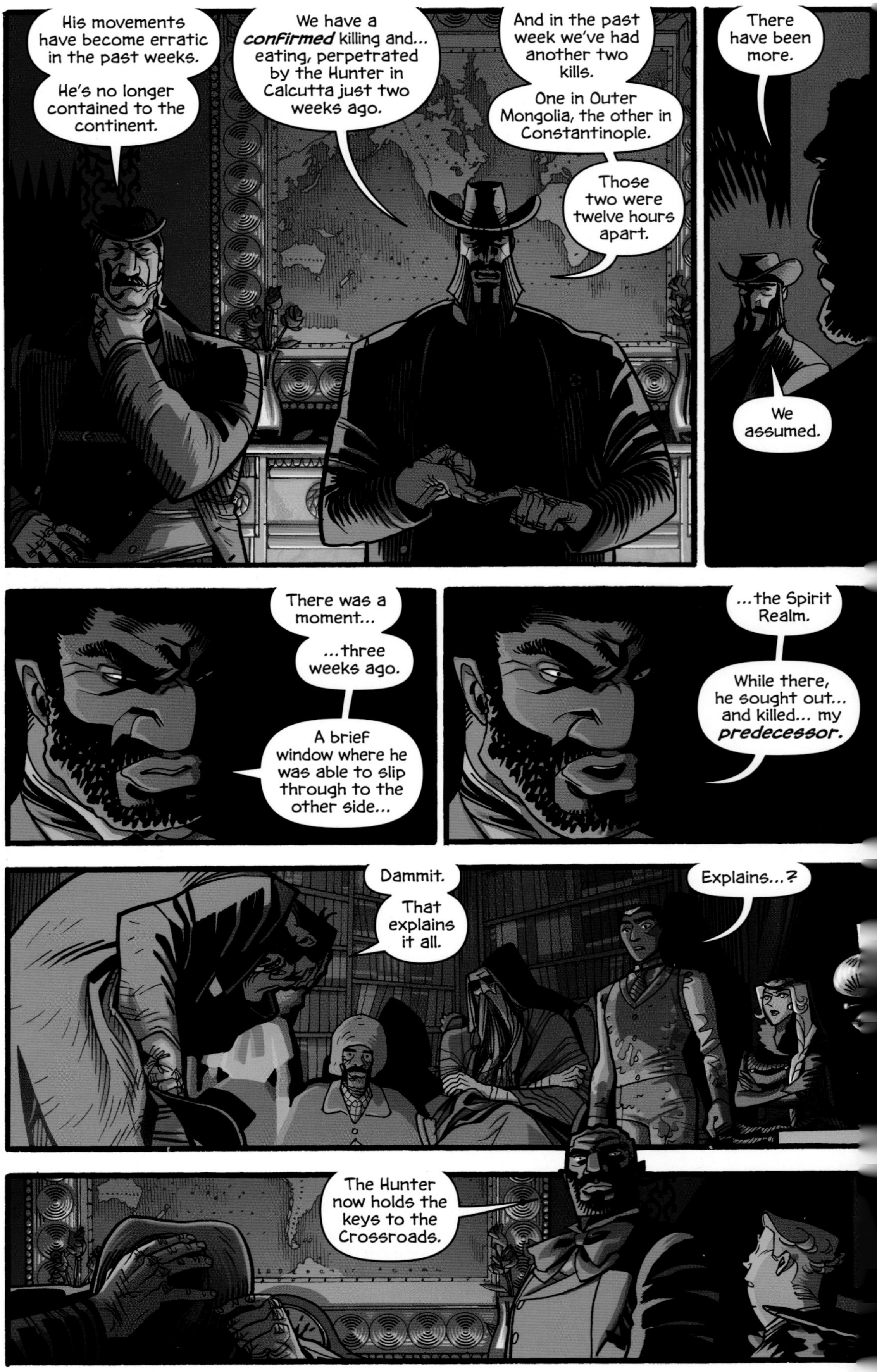
His movements have become erratic in the past weeks.
He's no longer contained to the continent.
We have a ***confirmed*** killing and... eating, perpetrated by the Hunter in Calcutta just two weeks ago.
And in the past week we've had another two kills.
One in Outer Mongolia, the other in Constantinople.
Those two were twelve hours apart.
There have been more.
We assumed.
There was a moment...
...three weeks ago.
A brief window where he was able to slip through to the other side...
...the Spirit Realm.
While there, he sought out... and killed... my ***predecessor.***
Dammit.
That explains it all.
Explains...?
The Hunter now holds the keys to the Crossroads.

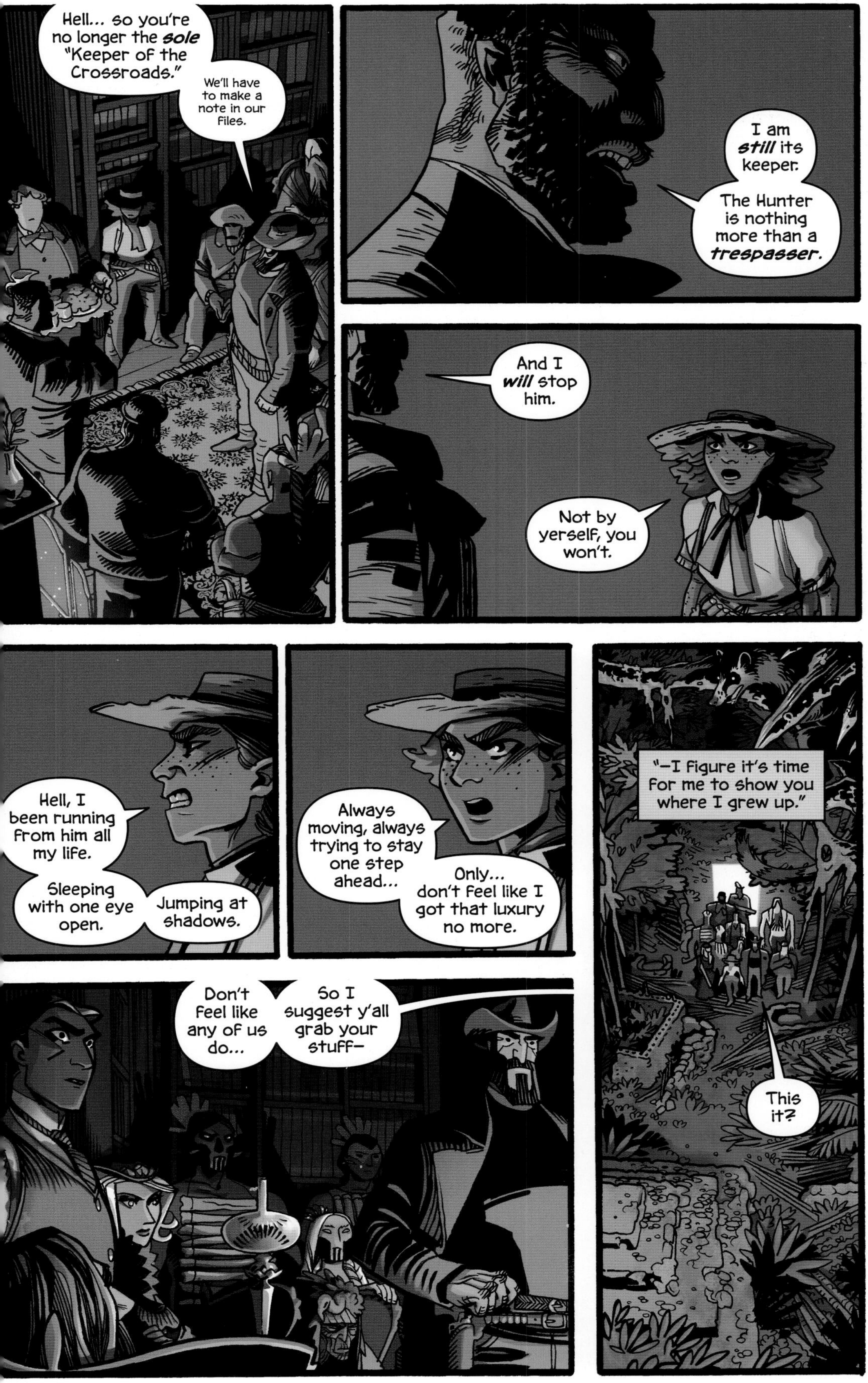
Hell... so you're no longer the *sole* "Keeper of the Crossroads."
We'll have to make a note in our files.
I am *still* its keeper.
The Hunter is nothing more than a *trespasser*.
And I *will* stop him.
Not by yerself, you won't.
Hell, I been running from him all my life.
Sleeping with one eye open.
Jumping at shadows.
Always moving, always trying to stay one step ahead...
Only... don't feel like I got that luxury no more.
Don't feel like any of us do...
So I suggest y'all grab your stuff–
"–I figure it's time for me to show you where I grew up."
This it?

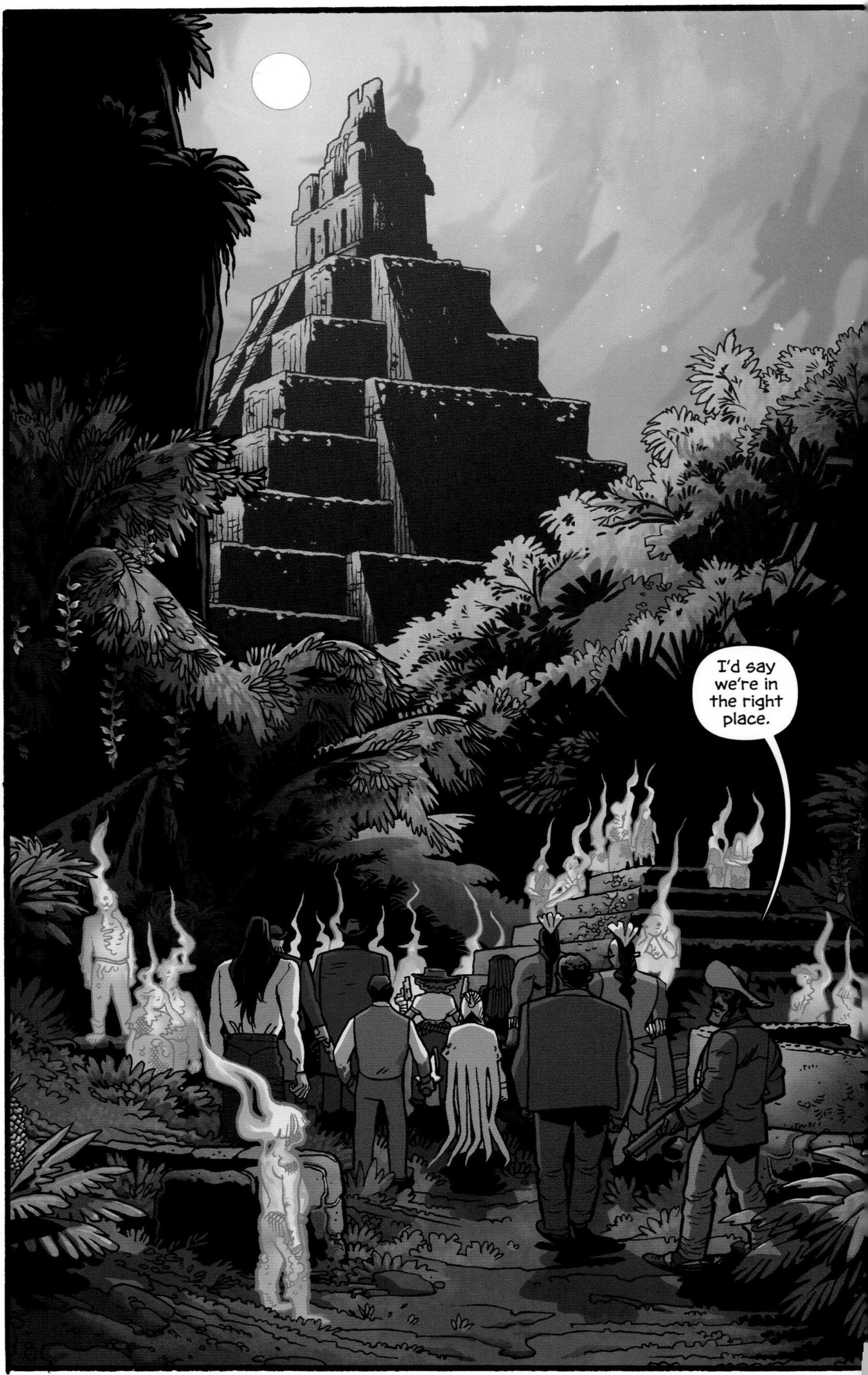
I'd say we're in the right place.

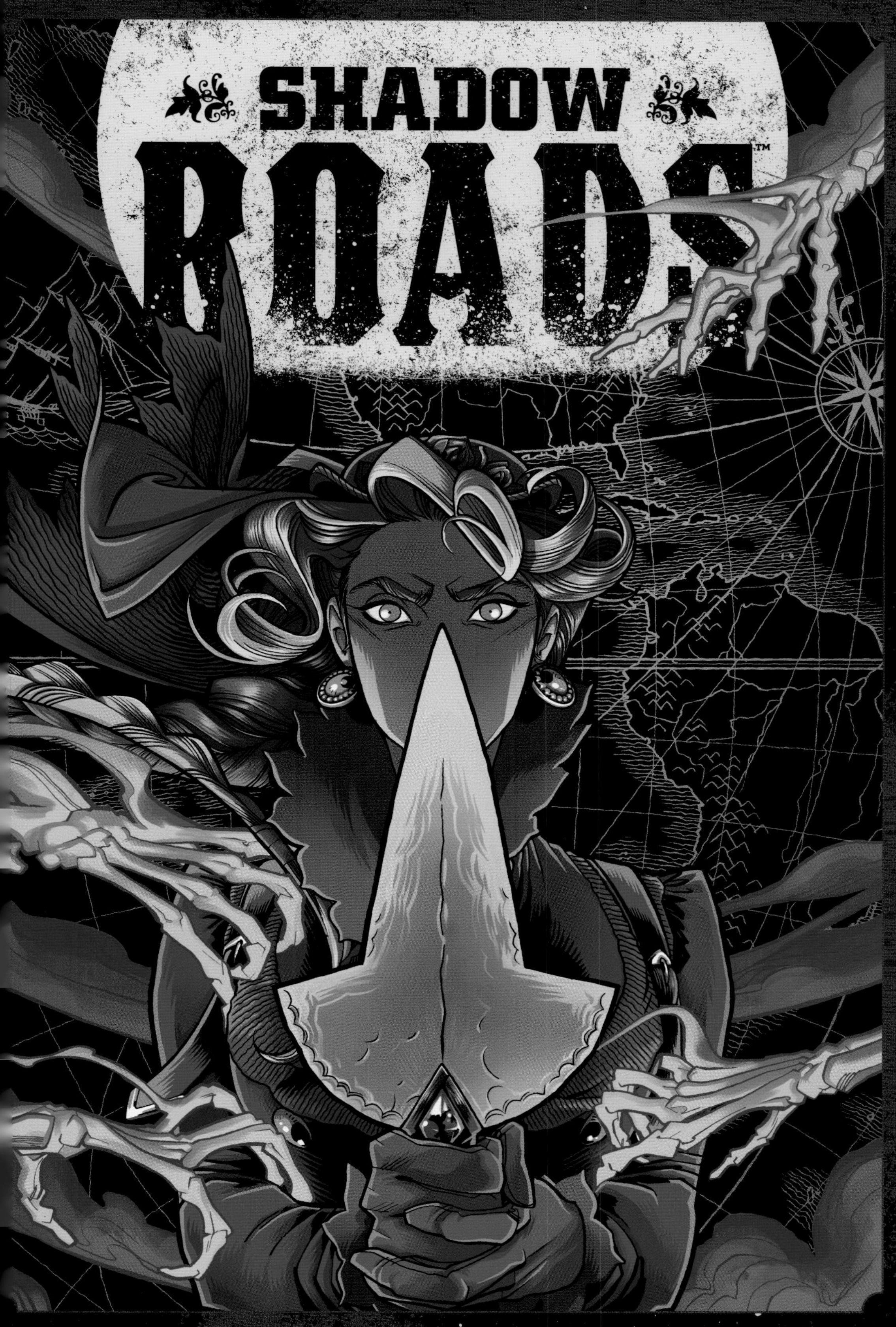
SHADOW
ROADS™

CHAPTER 5

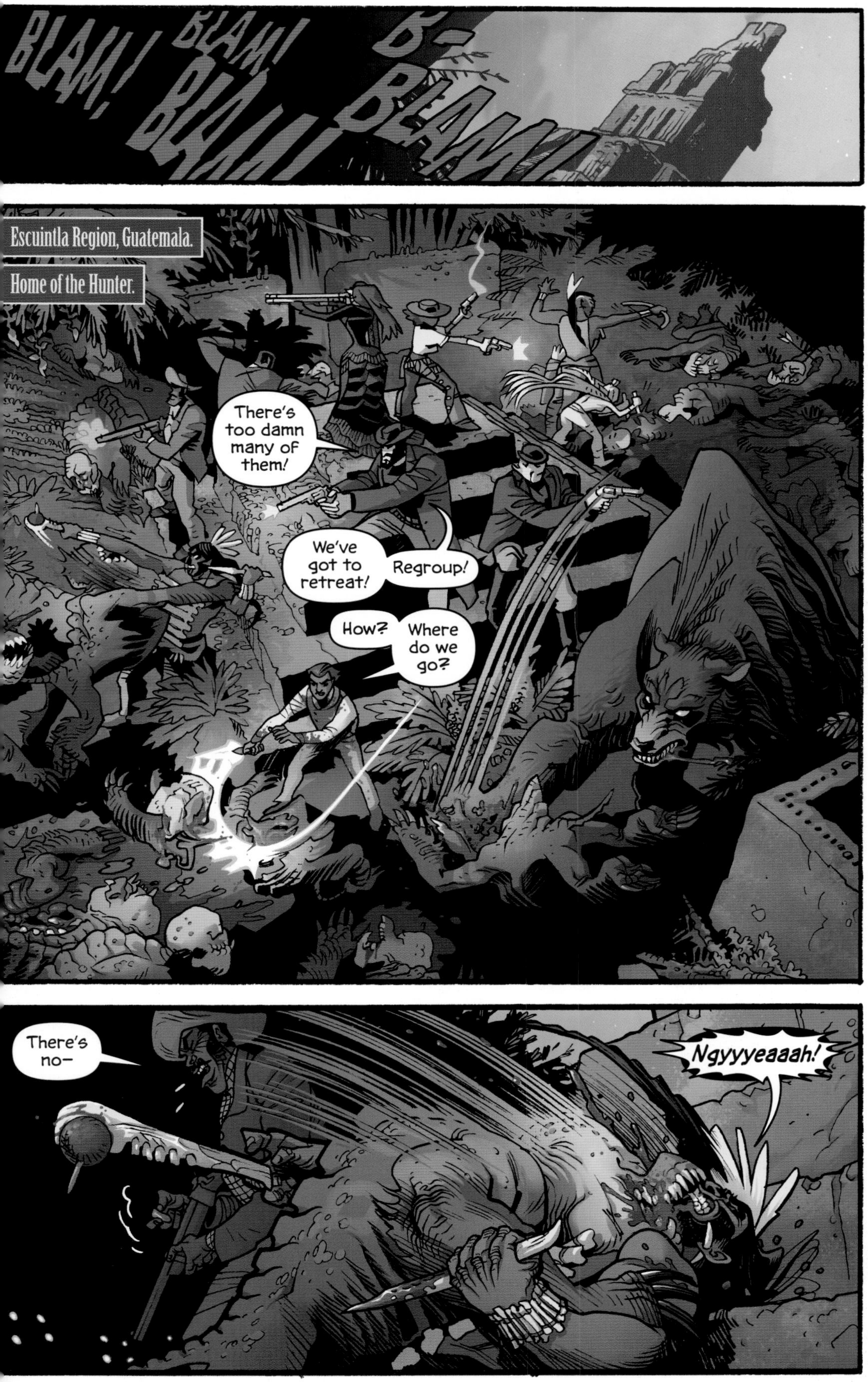

BLAM! BLAM! BLAM! BLAM!
B-BLAM!!
Escuintla Region, Guatemala.
Home of the Hunter.
There's too damn many of them!
We've got to retreat!
Regroup!
How?
Where do we go?
There's no—
Ngyyyeaaah!

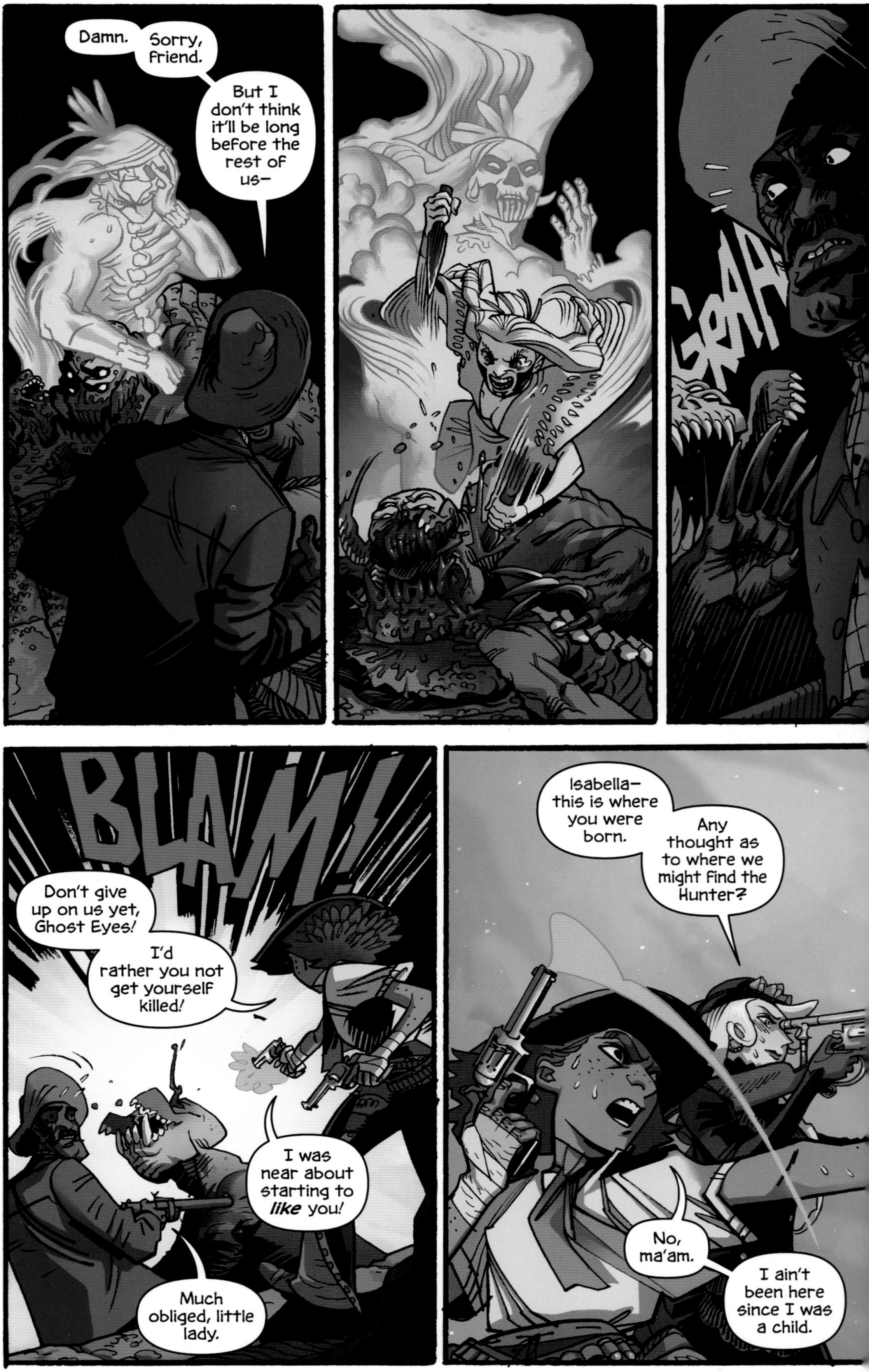

Damn.
Sorry, friend.
But I don't think it'll be long before the rest of us–
GRAA
BLAM!
Don't give up on us yet, Ghost Eyes!
I'd rather you not get yourself killed!
I was near about starting to *like* you!
Much obliged, little lady.
Isabella– this is where you were born.
Any thought as to where we might find the Hunter?
No, ma'am.
I ain't been here since I was a child.

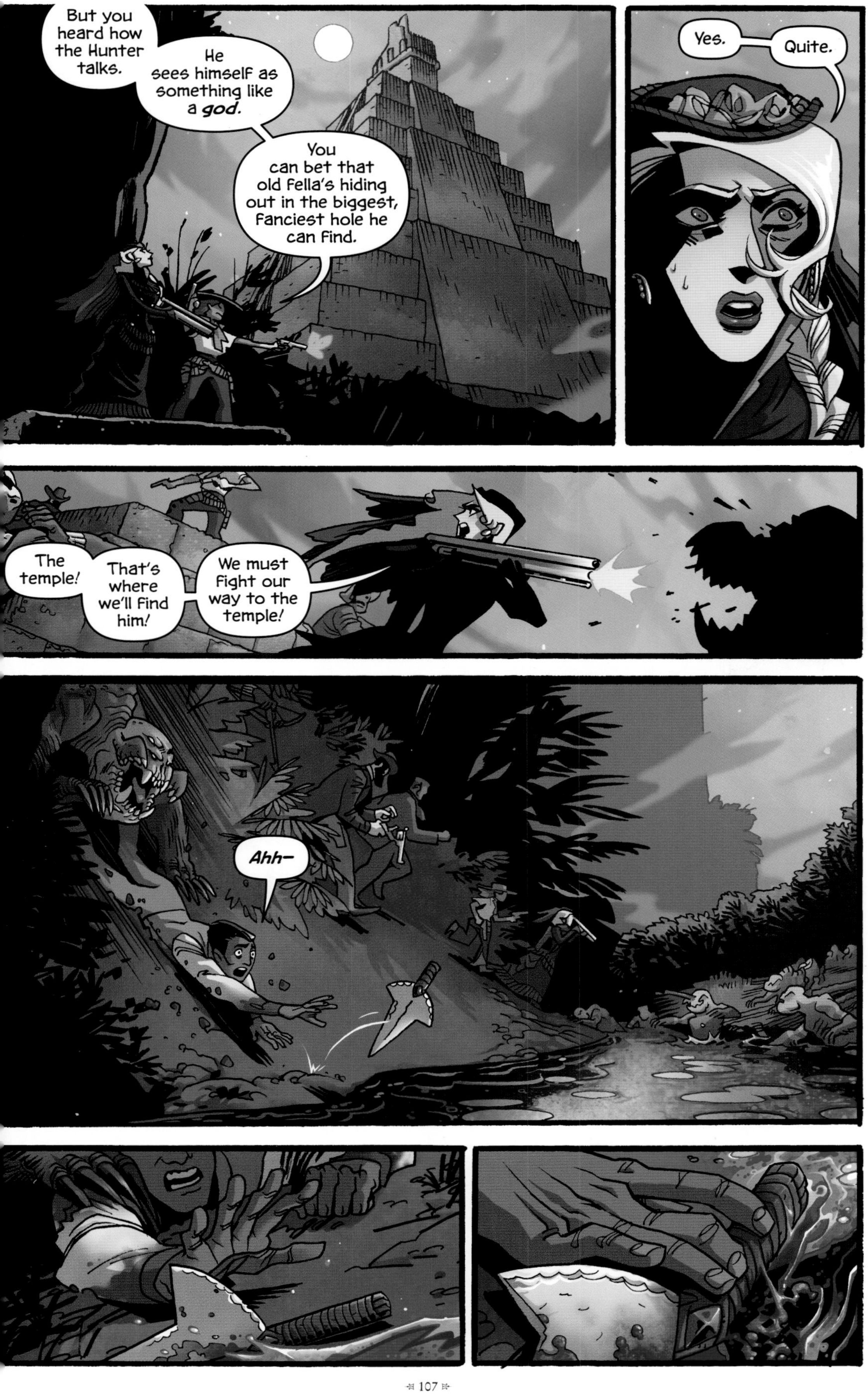
But you heard how the Hunter talks.
He sees himself as something like a *god.*
You can bet that old fella's hiding out in the biggest, fanciest hole he can find.
Yes.
Quite.
The temple!
That's where we'll find him!
We must fight our way to the temple!
Ahh—

Get back!
I...
I hope you've learned your lesson.
No!
Noooo!
Th-thank you.
I thought I–

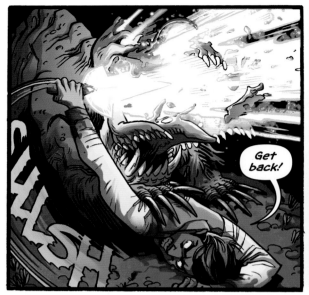

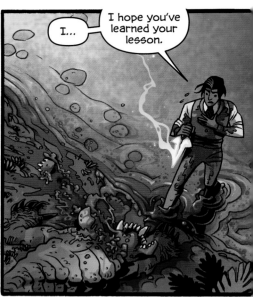

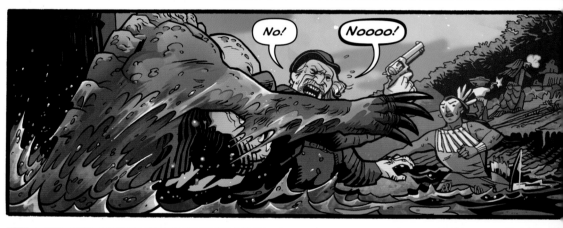

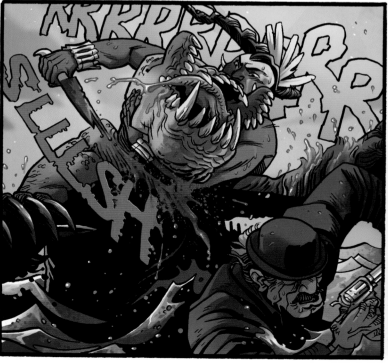

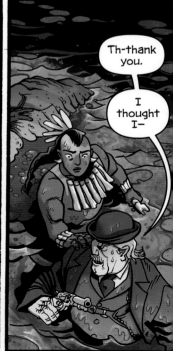

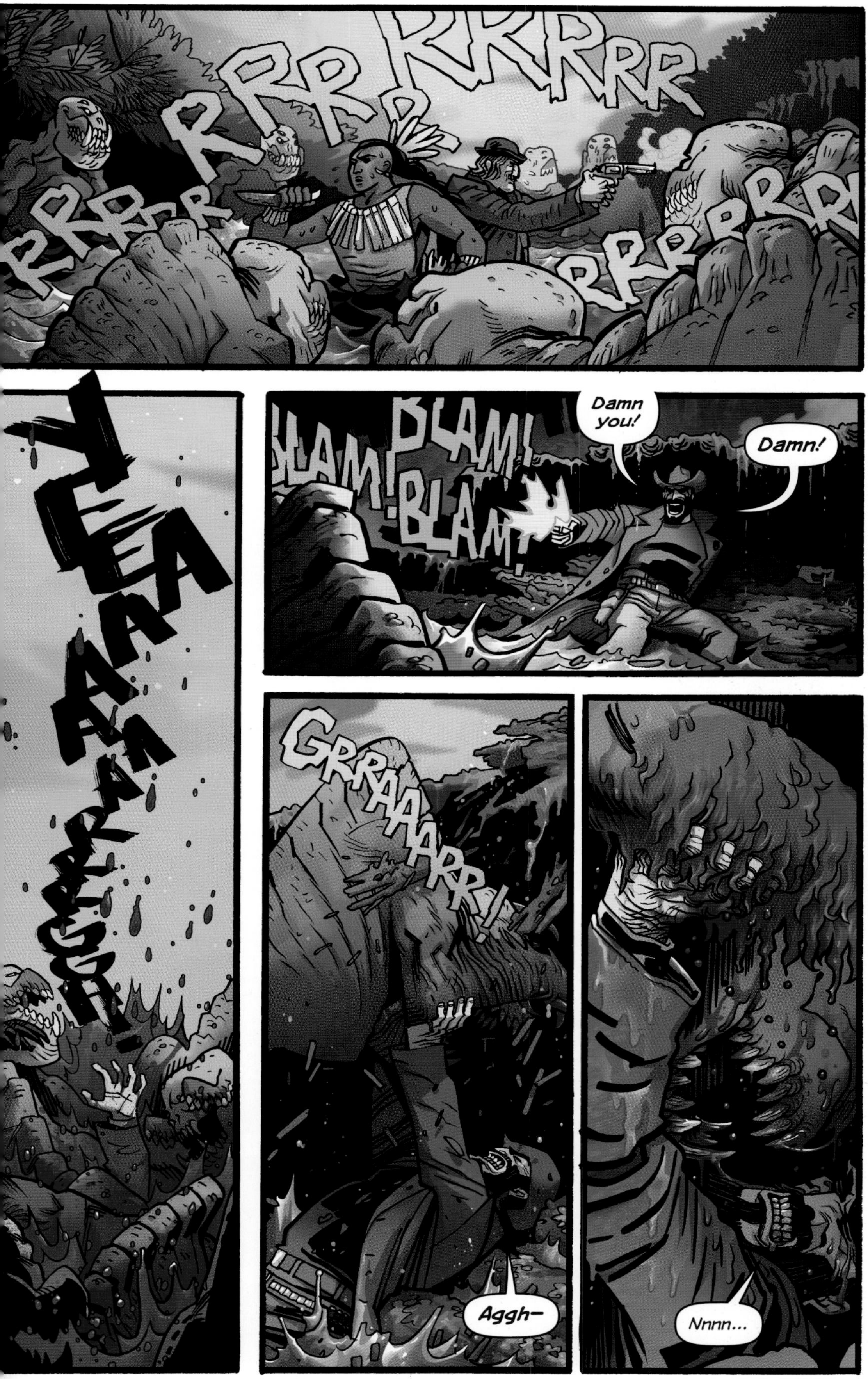
BLAM! BLAM!
BLAM! BLAM!
Damn you!
Damn!
GRRAAAARRR!
Aggh—
Nnnn...

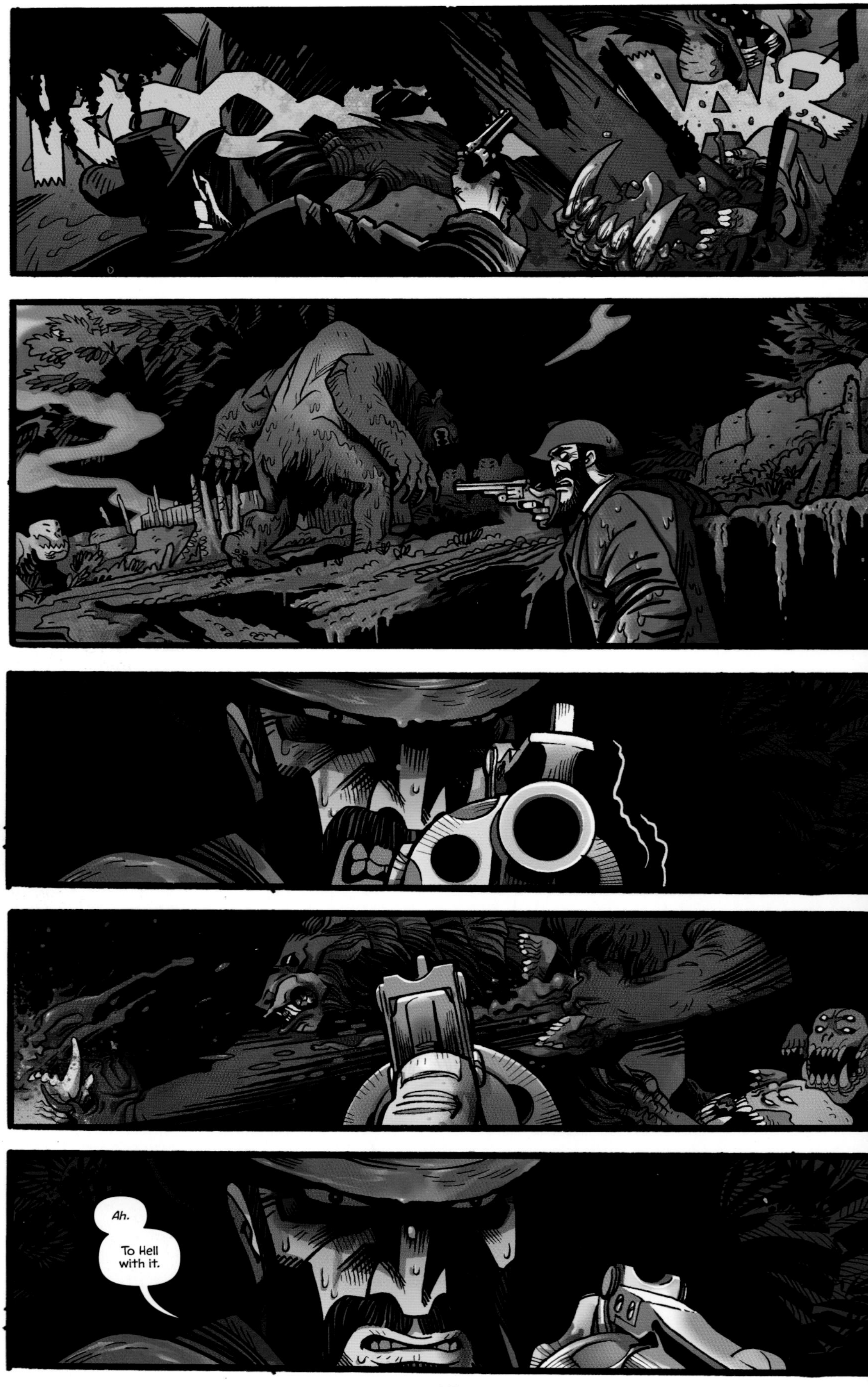
Ah.
To Hell with it.

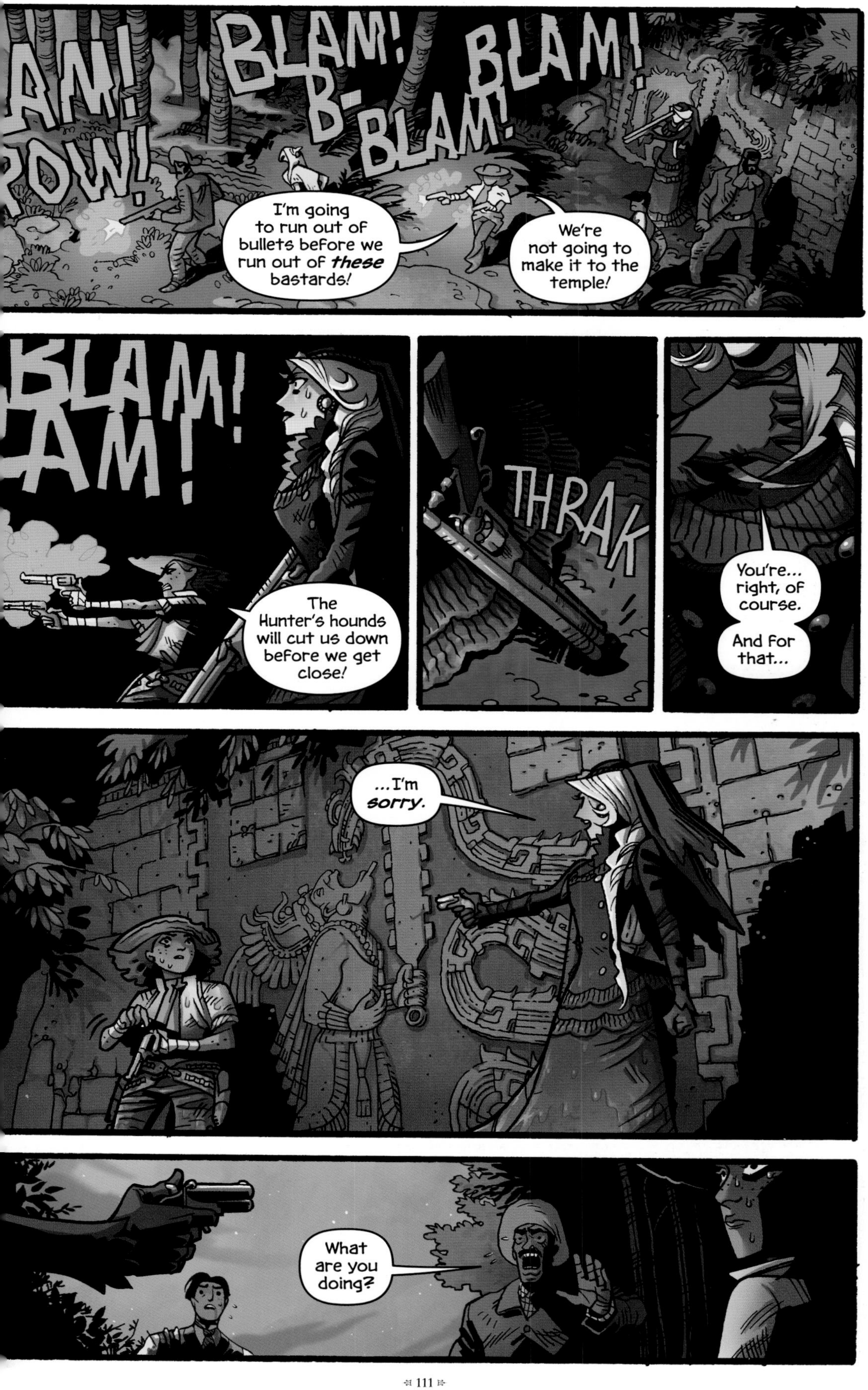

BLAM!
POW!
BLAM!
B-BLAM!
BLAM!
I'm going to run out of bullets before we run out of ***these*** bastards!
We're not going to make it to the temple!
BLAM!
AM!
The Hunter's hounds will cut us down before we get close!
THRAK
You're... right, of course.
And for that...
...I'm ***sorry.***
What are you doing?

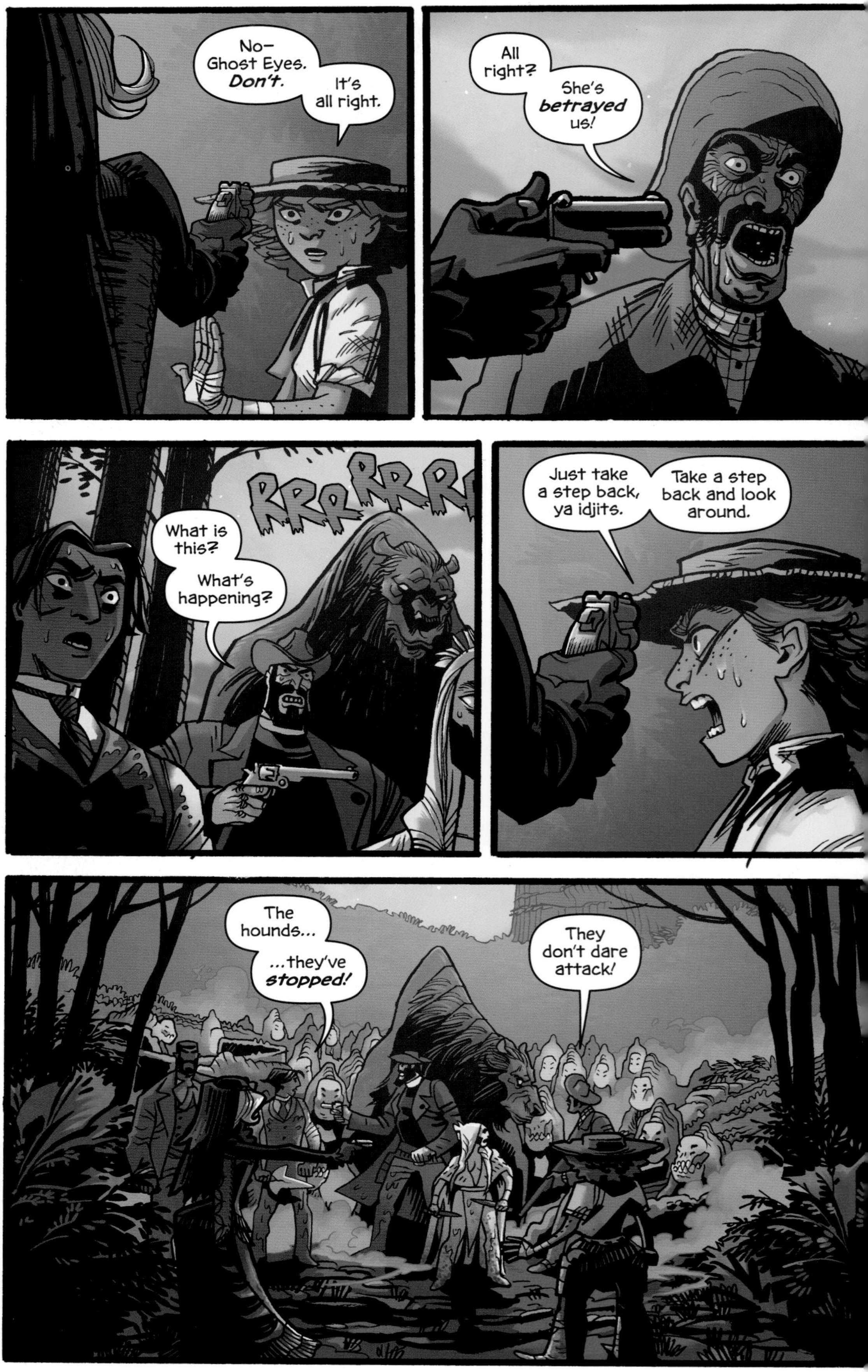
No— Ghost Eyes. Don't.
It's all right.
All right?
She's betrayed us!
RRRRRRR
What is this?
What's happening?
Just take a step back, ya idjits.
Take a step back and look around.
The hounds...
...they've stopped!
They don't dare attack!

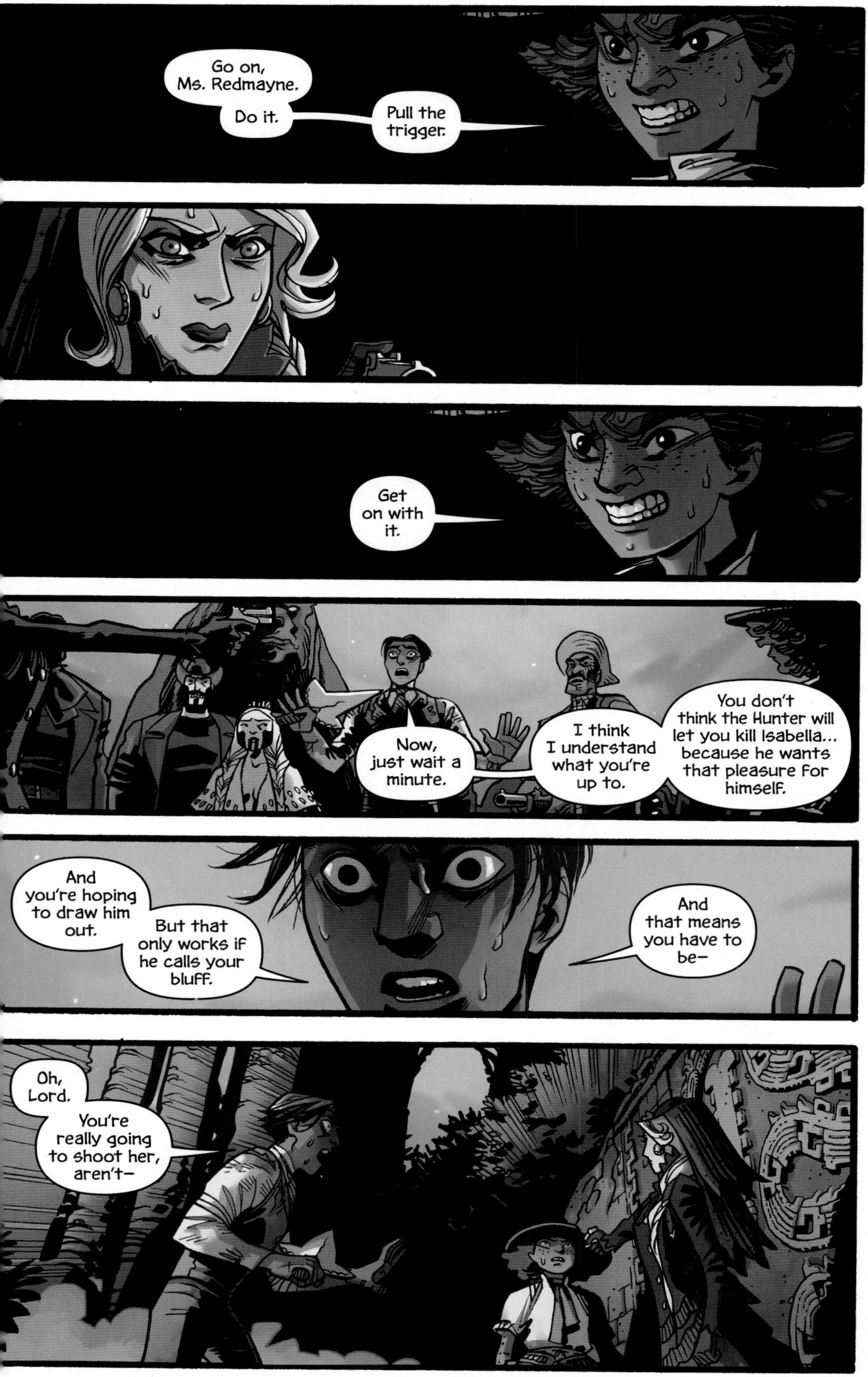
Go on, Ms. Redmayne.
Do it.
Pull the trigger.
Get on with it.
Now, just wait a minute.
I think I understand what you're up to.
You don't think the Hunter will let you kill Isabella... because he wants that pleasure for himself.
And you're hoping to draw him out.
But that only works if he calls your bluff.
And that means you have to be—
Oh, Lord.
You're really going to shoot her, aren't—

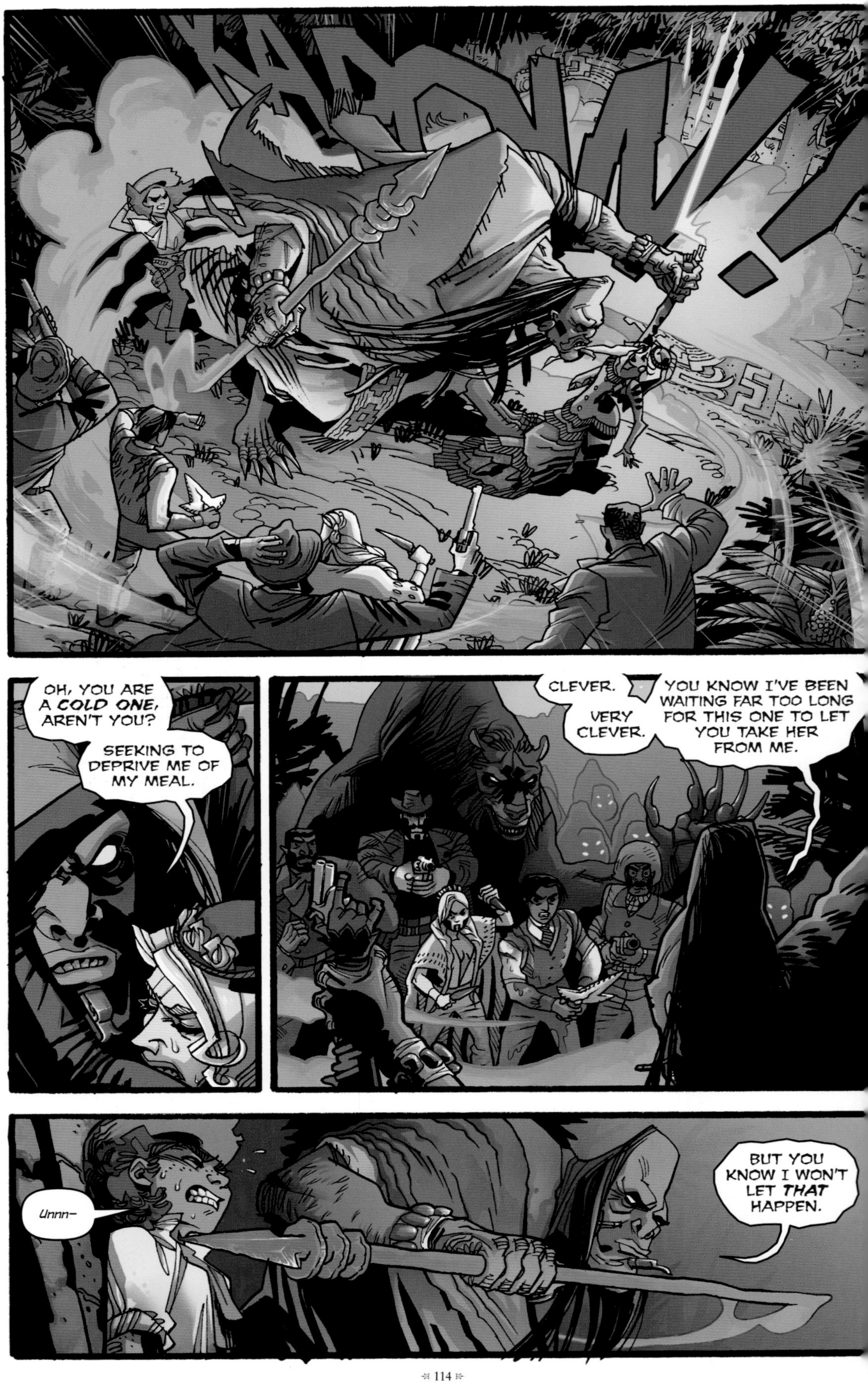
KA-BOOM!!
OH, YOU ARE A COLD ONE, AREN'T YOU?
SEEKING TO DEPRIVE ME OF MY MEAL.
CLEVER.
VERY CLEVER.
YOU KNOW I'VE BEEN WAITING FAR TOO LONG FOR THIS ONE TO LET YOU TAKE HER FROM ME.
Unnn–
BUT YOU KNOW I WON'T LET THAT HAPPEN.

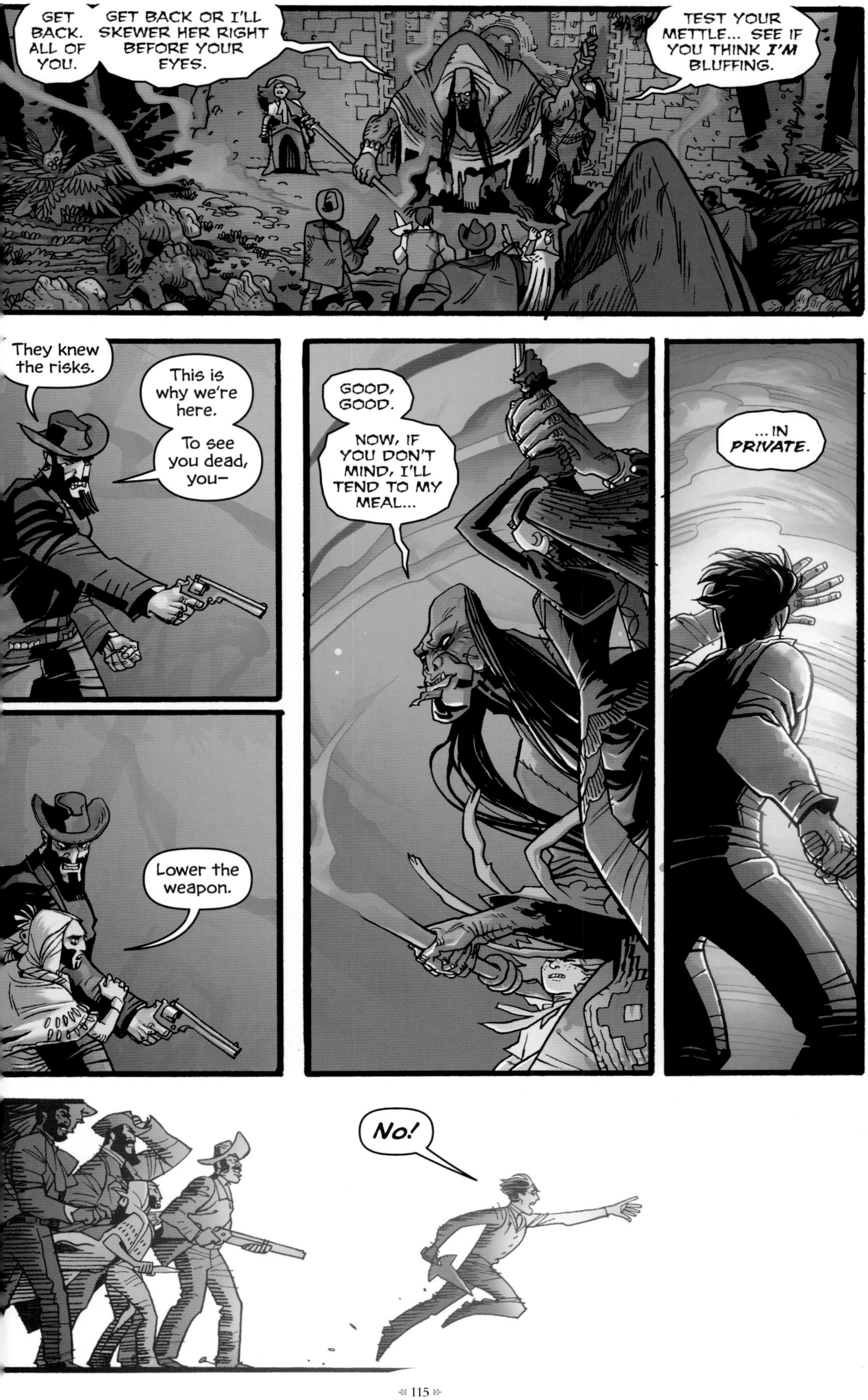
GET BACK. ALL OF YOU.
GET BACK OR I'LL SKEWER HER RIGHT BEFORE YOUR EYES.
TEST YOUR METTLE... SEE IF YOU THINK *I'M* BLUFFING.
They knew the risks.
This is why we're here.
To see you dead, you–
Lower the weapon.
GOOD, GOOD.
NOW, IF YOU DON'T MIND, I'LL TEND TO MY MEAL...
...IN *PRIVATE*.
No!

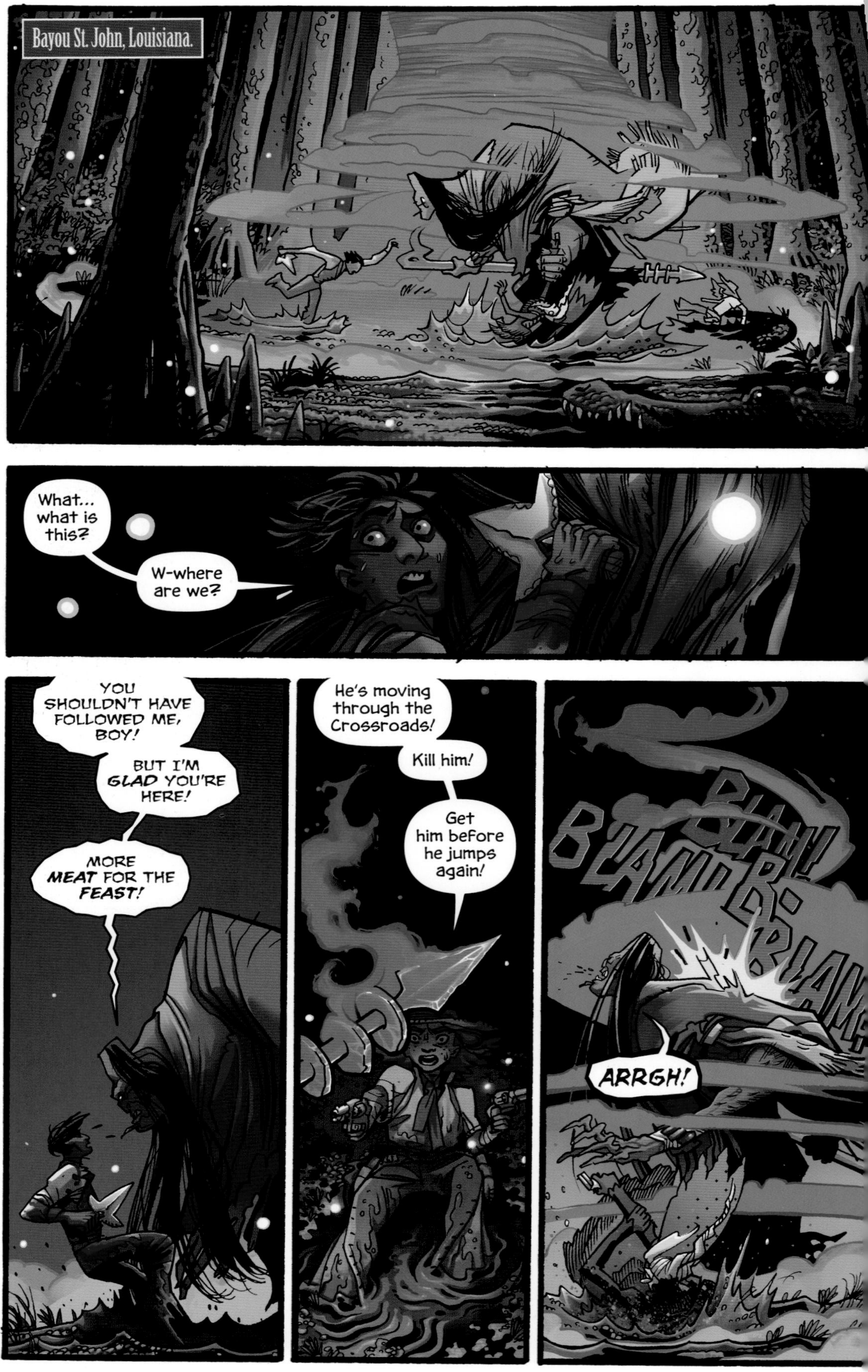

Bayou St. John, Louisiana.
What... what is this?
W-where are we?
YOU SHOULDN'T HAVE FOLLOWED ME, BOY!
BUT I'M *GLAD* YOU'RE HERE!
MORE *MEAT* FOR THE *FEAST!*
He's moving through the Crossroads!
Kill him!
Get him before he jumps again!
BLAM!
ARRGH!

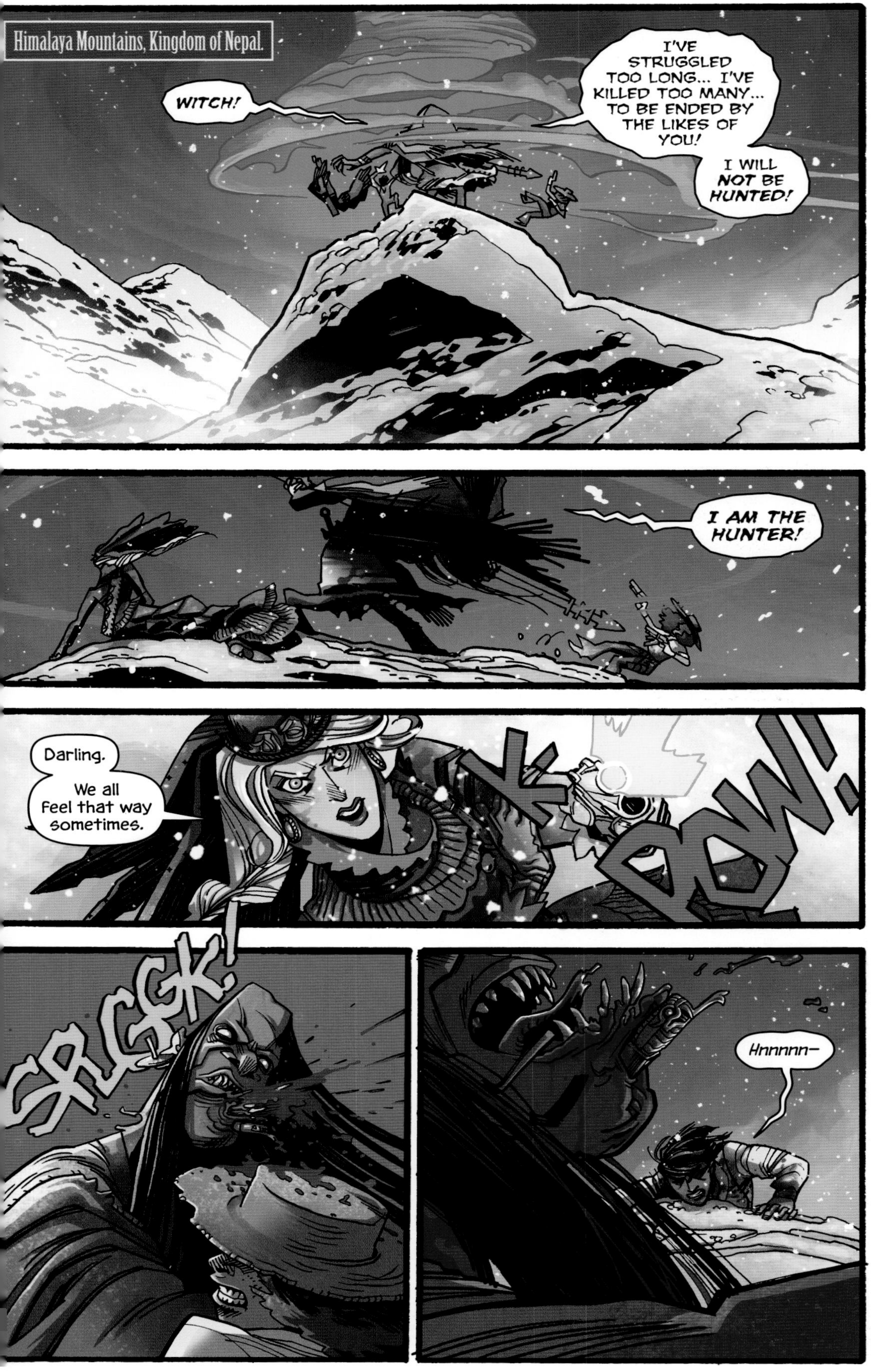
Himalaya Mountains, Kingdom of Nepal.
WITCH!
I'VE STRUGGLED TOO LONG... I'VE KILLED TOO MANY... TO BE ENDED BY THE LIKES OF YOU!
I WILL NOT BE HUNTED!
I AM THE HUNTER!
Darling.
We all feel that way sometimes.
K-BOW!
SRCGK!
Hnnnnn–

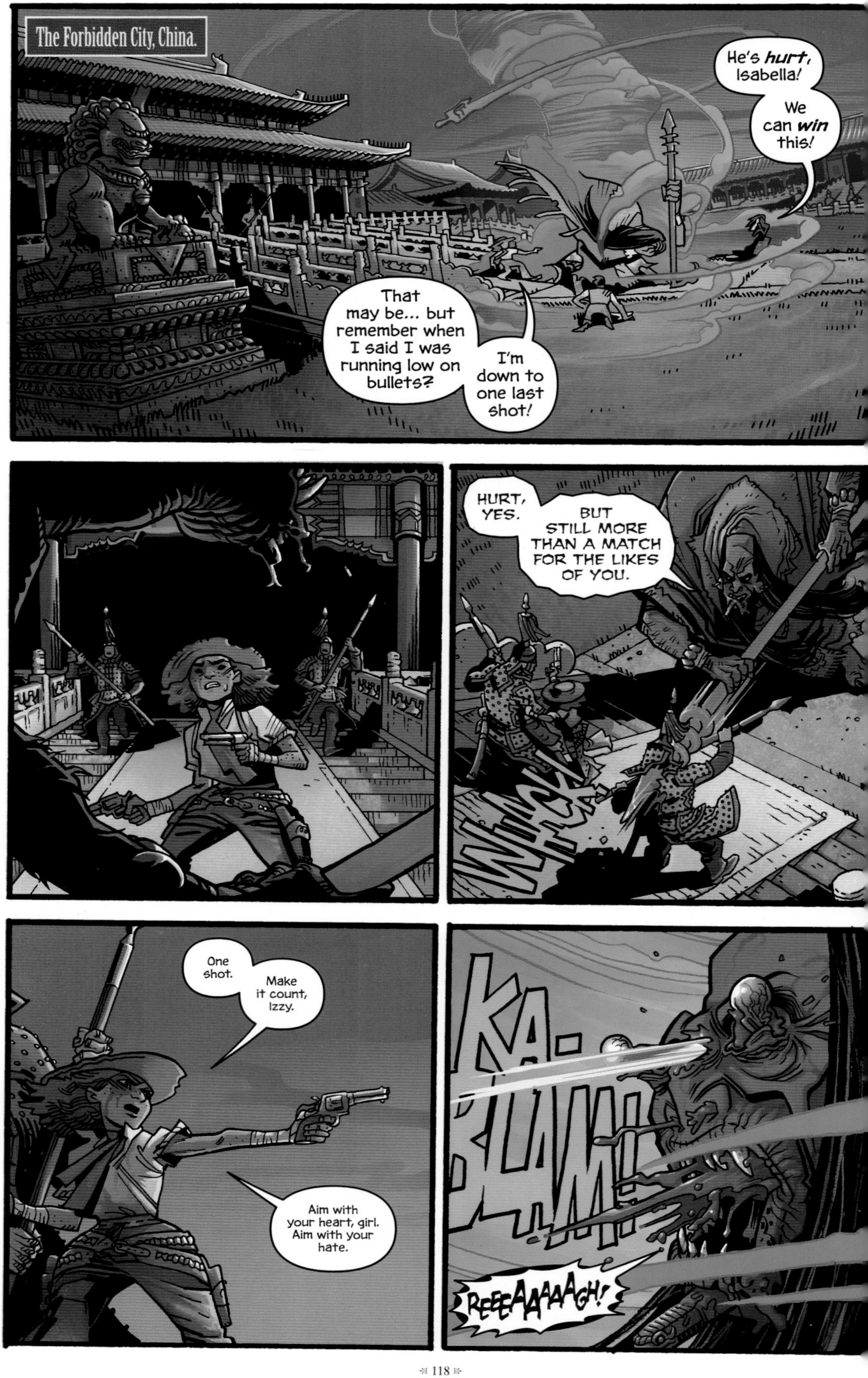
The Forbidden City, China.
He's *hurt*, Isabella!
We can *win* this!
That may be... but remember when I said I was running low on bullets?
I'm down to one last shot!
HURT, YES.
BUT STILL MORE THAN A MATCH FOR THE LIKES OF YOU.
One shot.
Make it count, Izzy.
Aim with your heart, girl. Aim with your hate.
KA-BLAM!
REEEAAAAAGH!

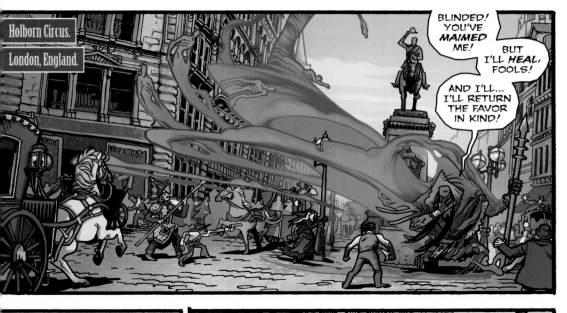

Holborn Circus.
London, England.

BLINDED! YOU'VE **MAIMED** ME!

BUT I'LL **HEAL**, FOOLS!

AND I'LL... I'LL RETURN THE FAVOR IN KIND!

London.

I'm... I'm home.

Henry! Don't just **stand** there!

The knife!

Kill him!

Right.

Oooof!

THWACK!

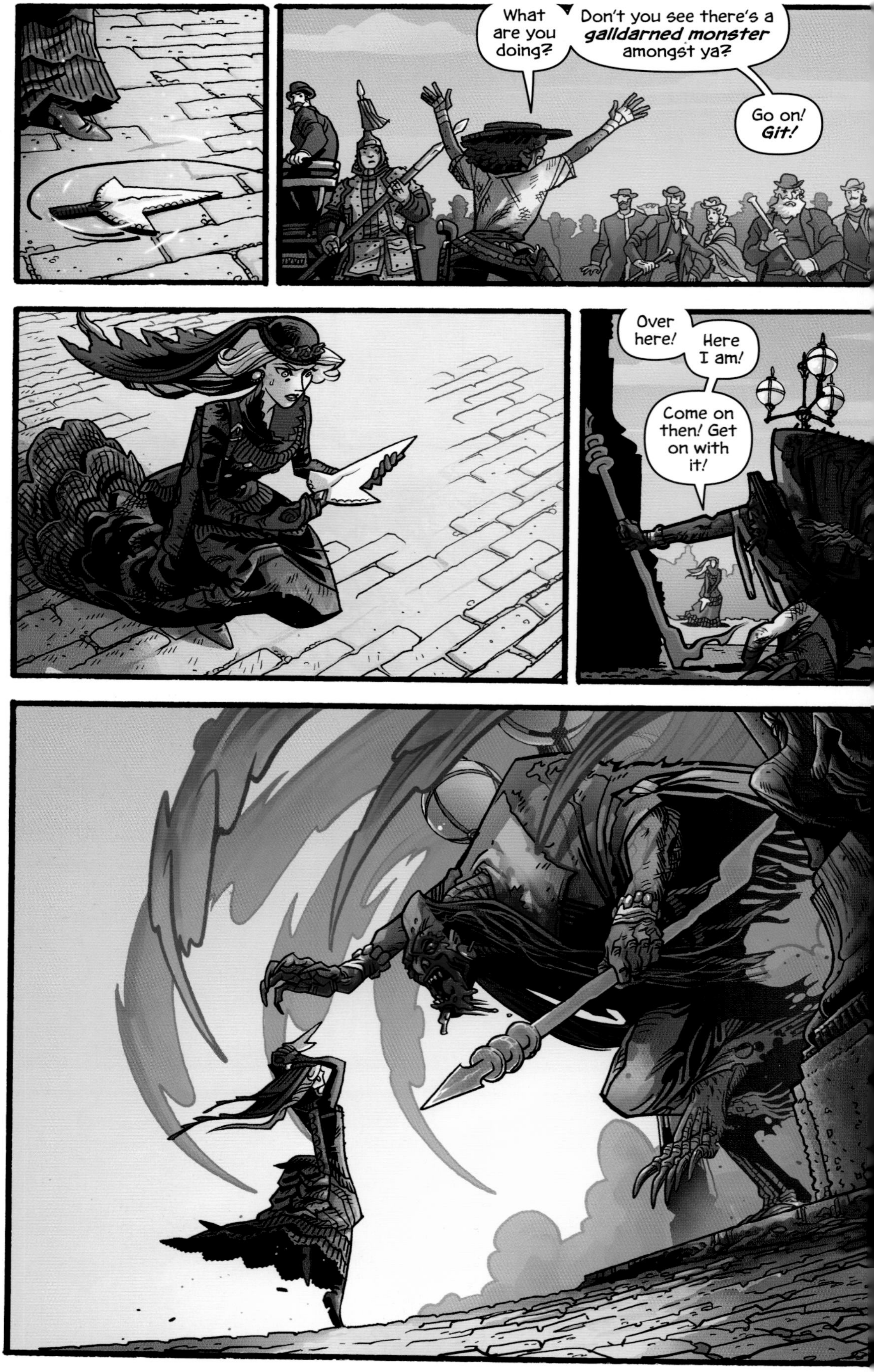
What are you doing?
Don't you see there's a *galldarned monster* amongst ya?
Go on! *Git!*
Over here!
Here I am!
Come on then! Get on with it!

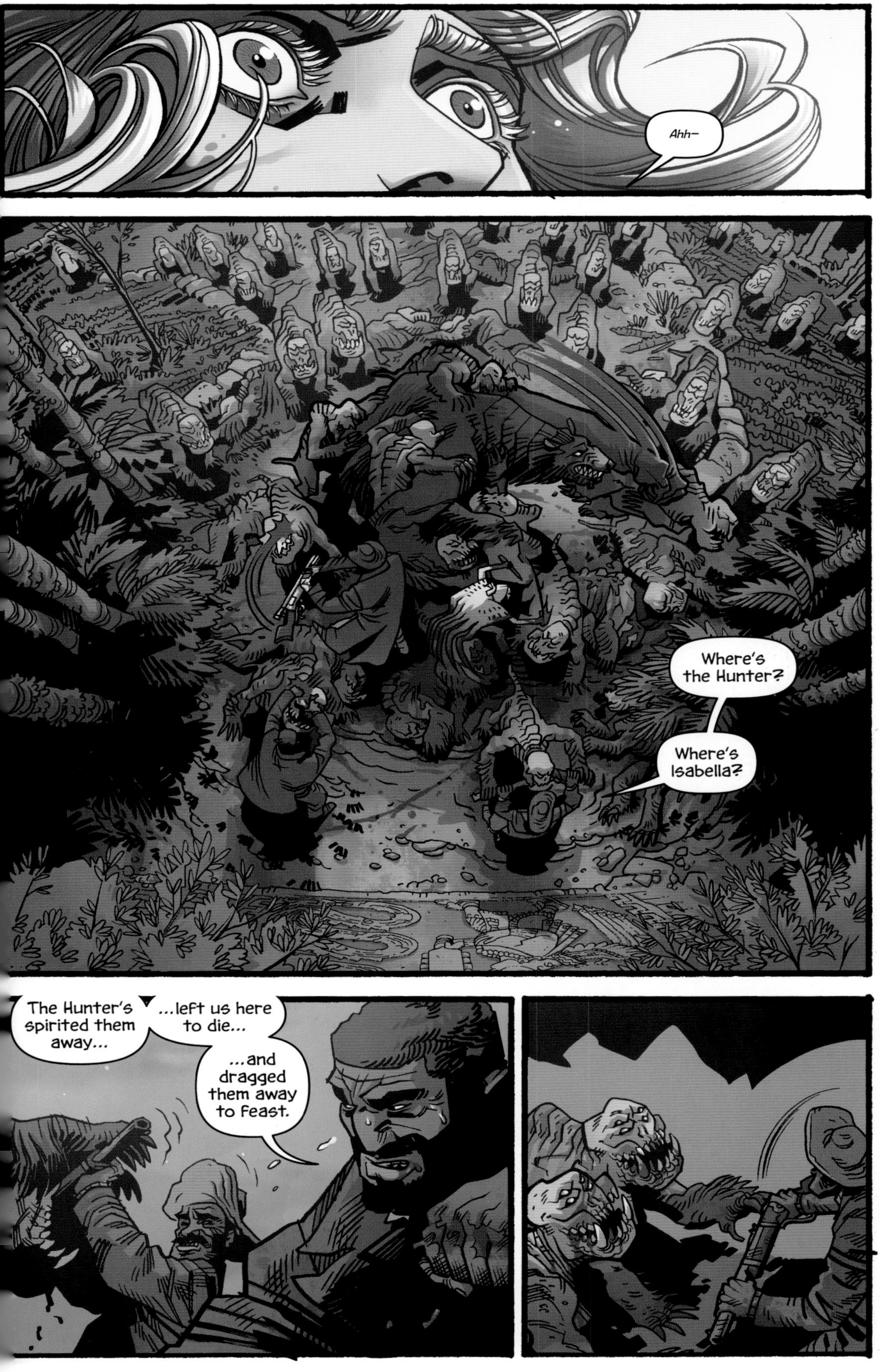
Ahh–
Where's the Hunter?
Where's Isabella?
The Hunter's spirited them away...
...left us here to die...
...and dragged them away to feast.

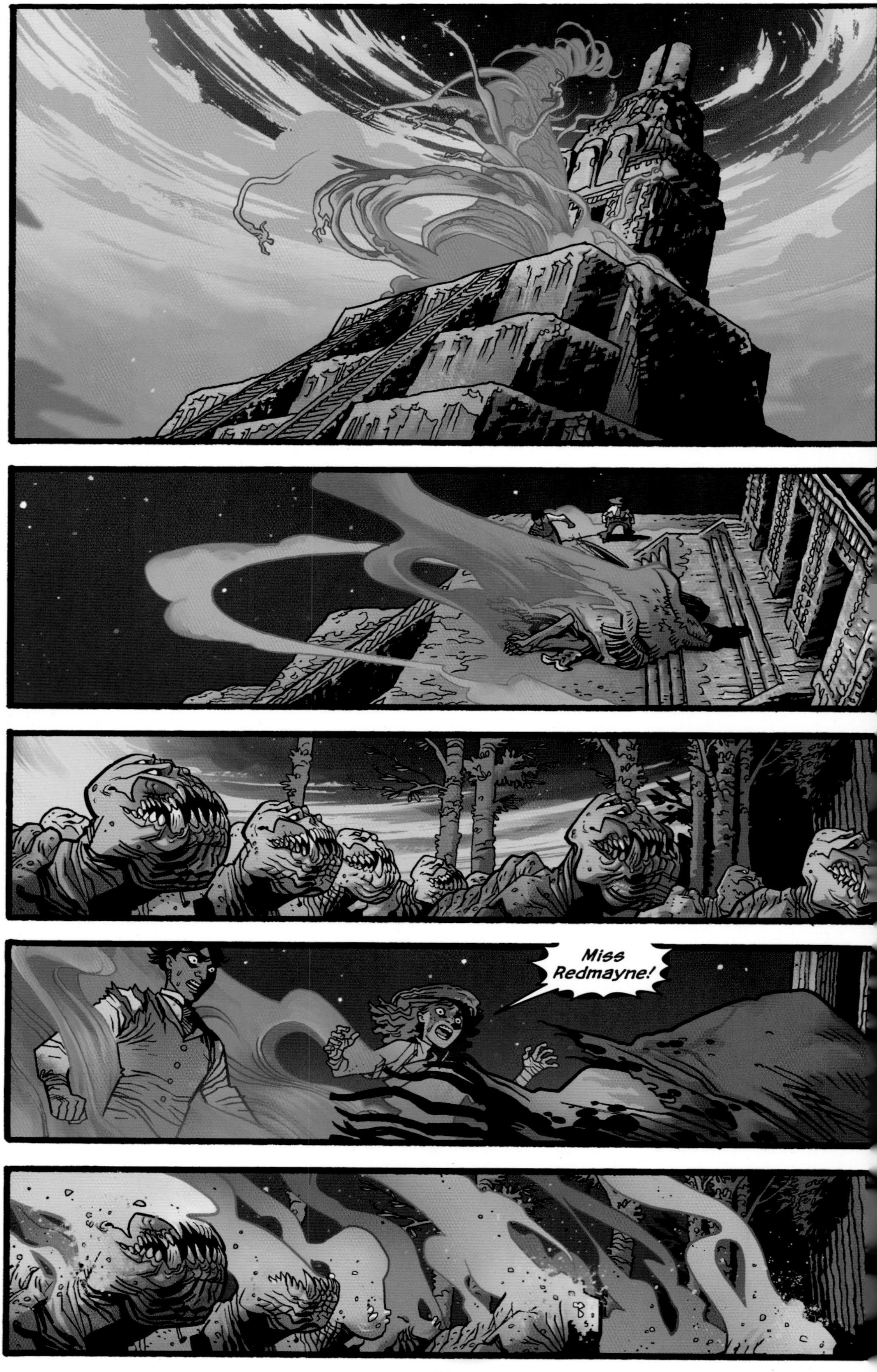
Miss Redmayne!

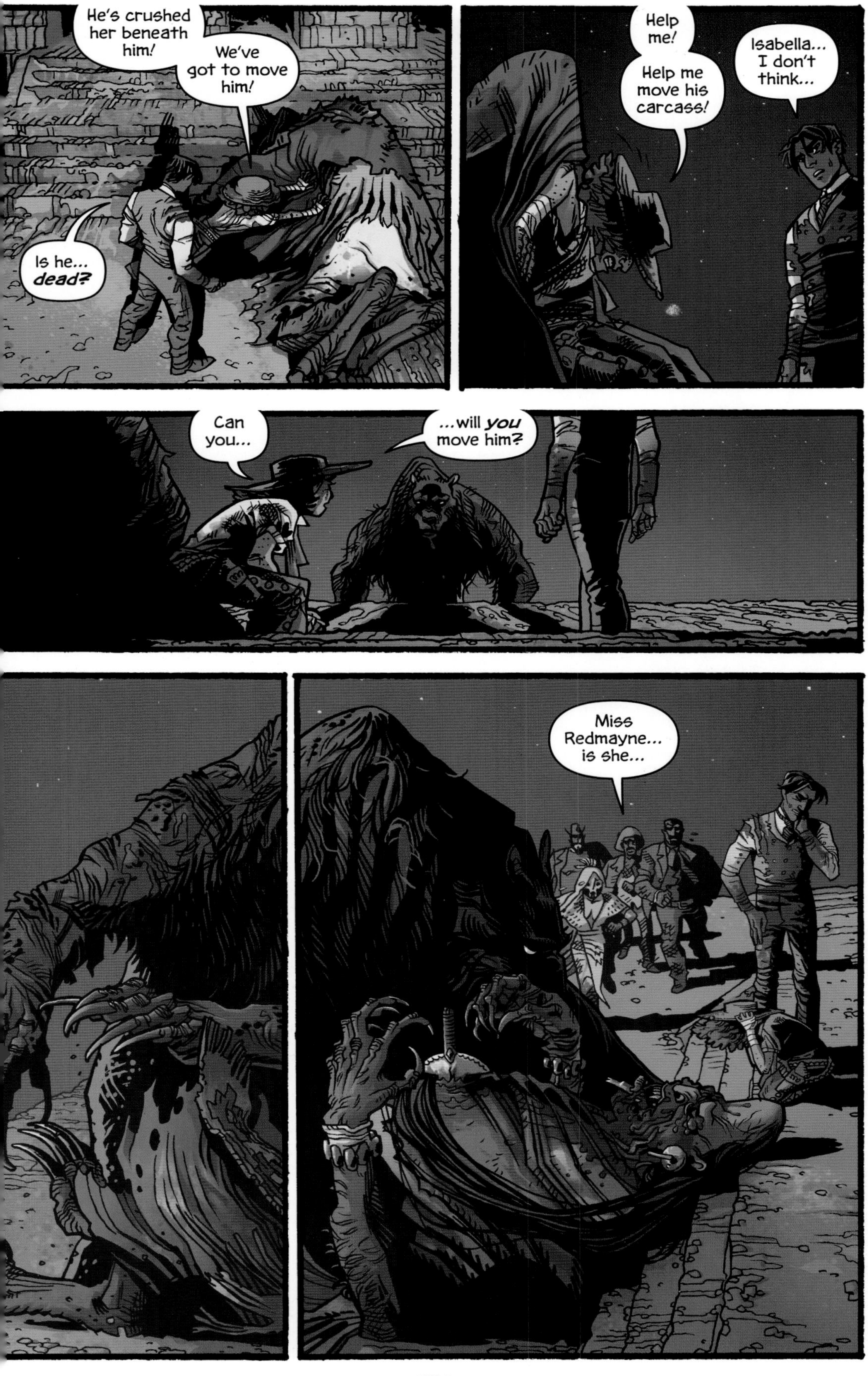
He's crushed her beneath him!
We've got to move him!
Is he... dead?
Help me!
Help me move his carcass!
Isabella... I don't think...
Can you...
...will you move him?
Miss Redmayne... is she...

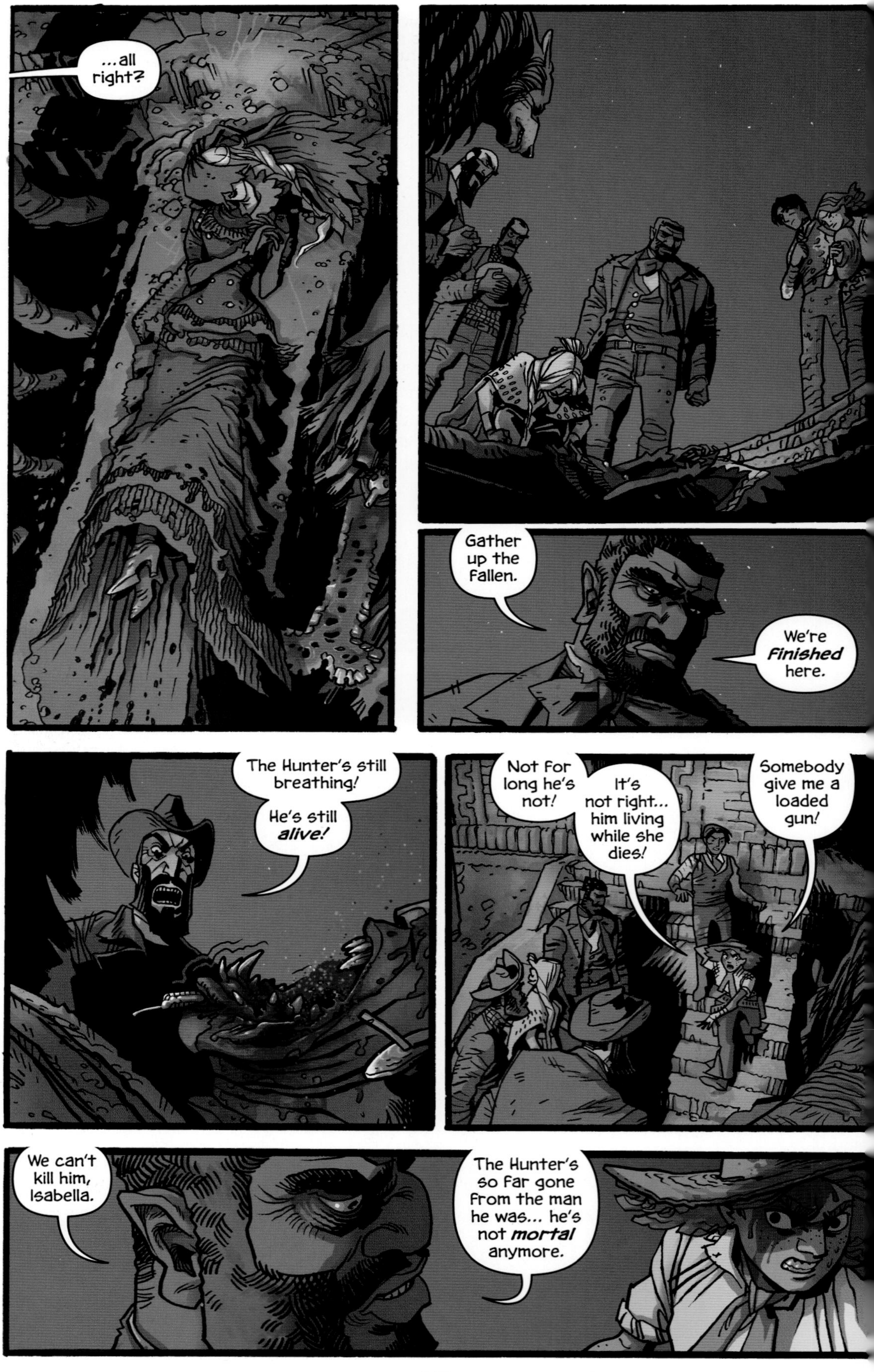
...all right?
Gather up the fallen.
We're *Finished* here.
The Hunter's still breathing!
He's still *alive!*
Not for long he's not!
It's not right... him living while she dies!
Somebody give me a loaded gun!
We can't kill him, Isabella.
The Hunter's so far gone from the man he was... he's not *mortal* anymore.

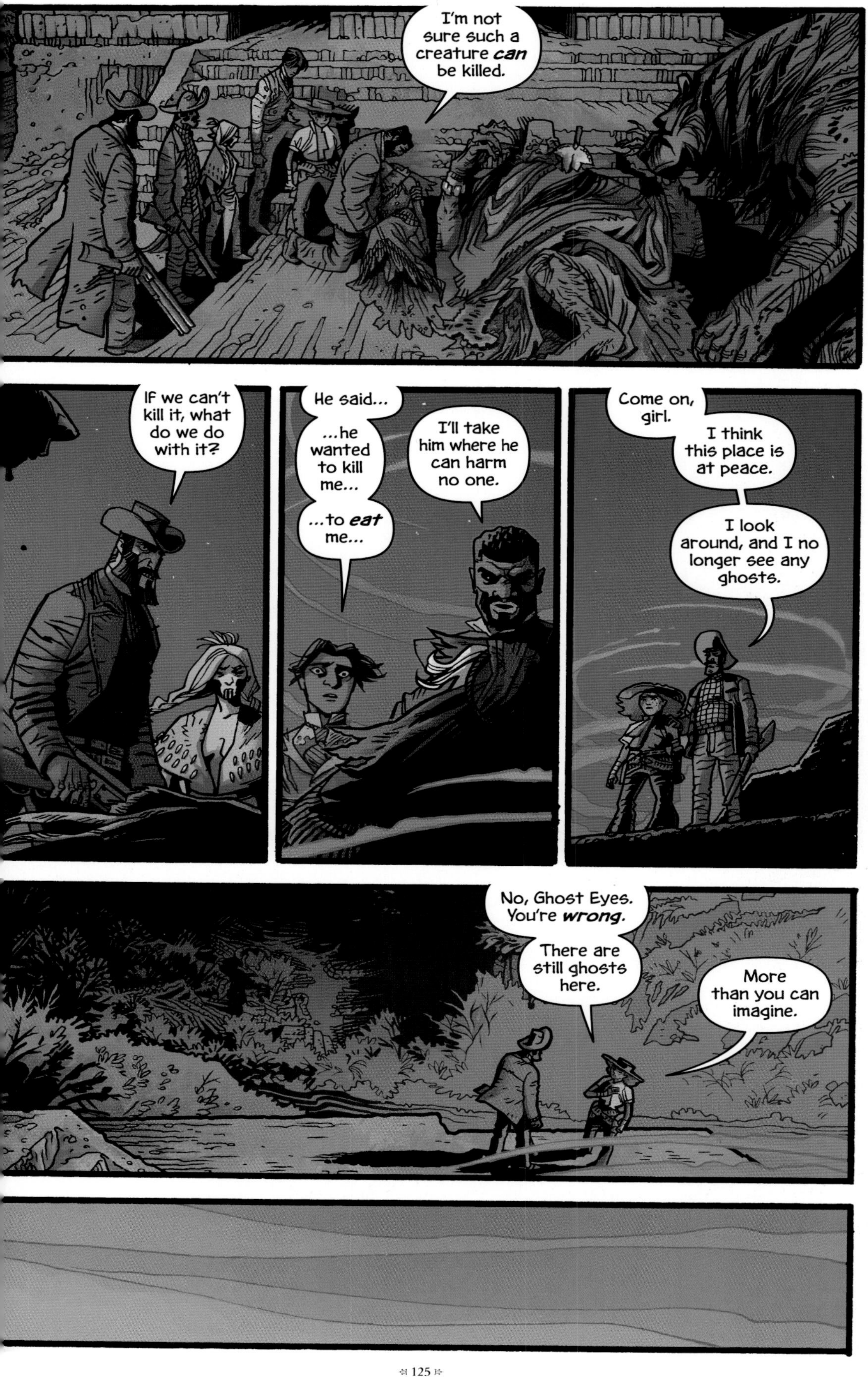
I'm not sure such a creature *can* be killed.
If we can't kill it, what do we do with it?
He said...
...he wanted to kill me...
...to *eat* me...
I'll take him where he can harm no one.
Come on, girl.
I think this place is at peace.
I look around, and I no longer see any ghosts.
No, Ghost Eyes. You're *wrong*.
There are still ghosts here.
More than you can imagine.

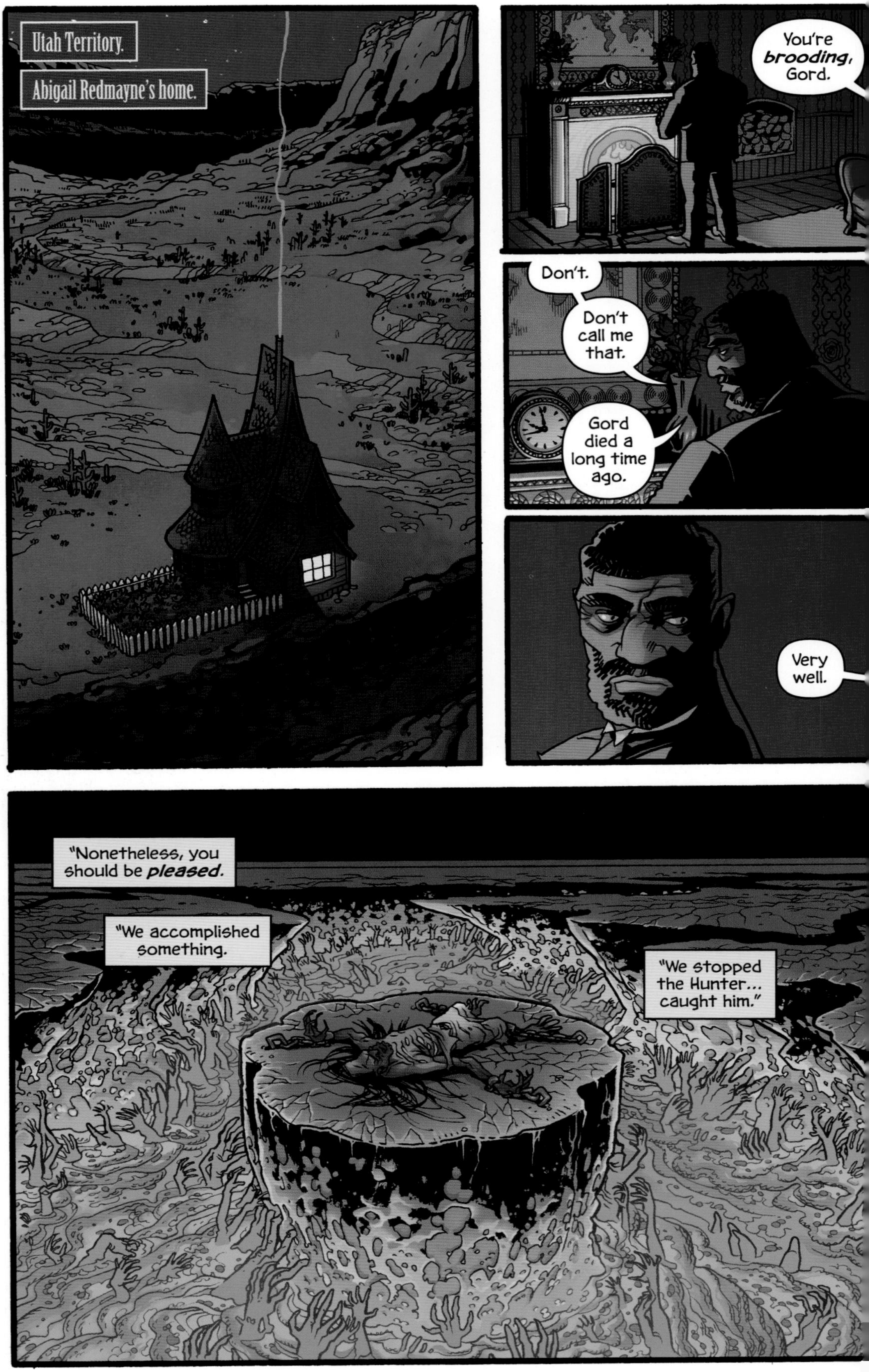

Utah Territory.
Abigail Redmayne's home.
You're *brooding,* Gord.
Don't.
Don't call me that.
Gord died a long time ago.
Very well.
"Nonetheless, you should be *pleased.*
"We accomplished something.
"We stopped the Hunter... caught him."

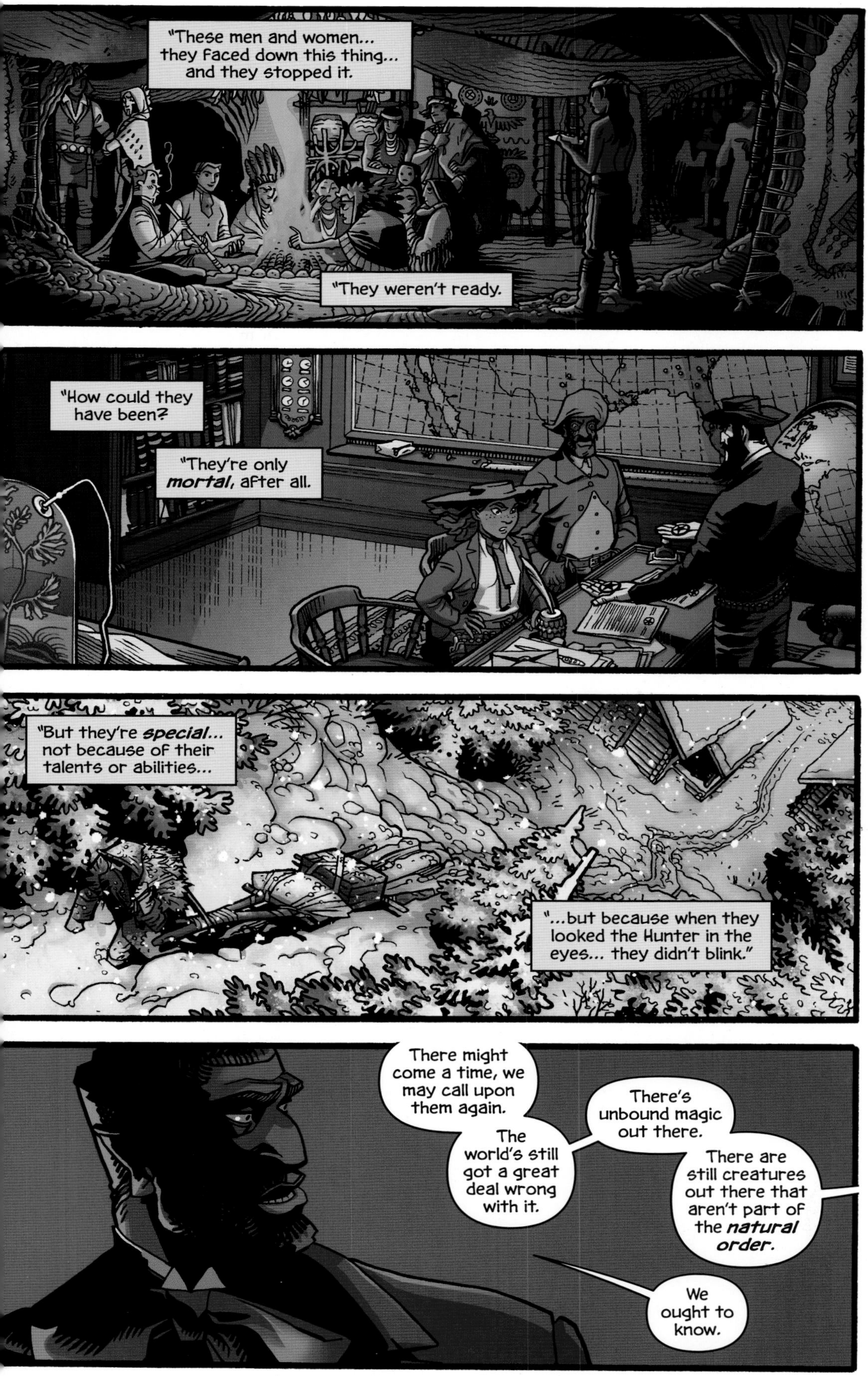
"These men and women... they faced down this thing... and they stopped it.
"They weren't ready.
"How could they have been?
"They're only *mortal*, after all.
"But they're *special*... not because of their talents or abilities...
"...but because when they looked the Hunter in the eyes... they didn't blink."
There might come a time, we may call upon them again.
The world's still got a great deal wrong with it.
There's unbound magic out there.
There are still creatures out there that aren't part of the *natural order*.
We ought to know.

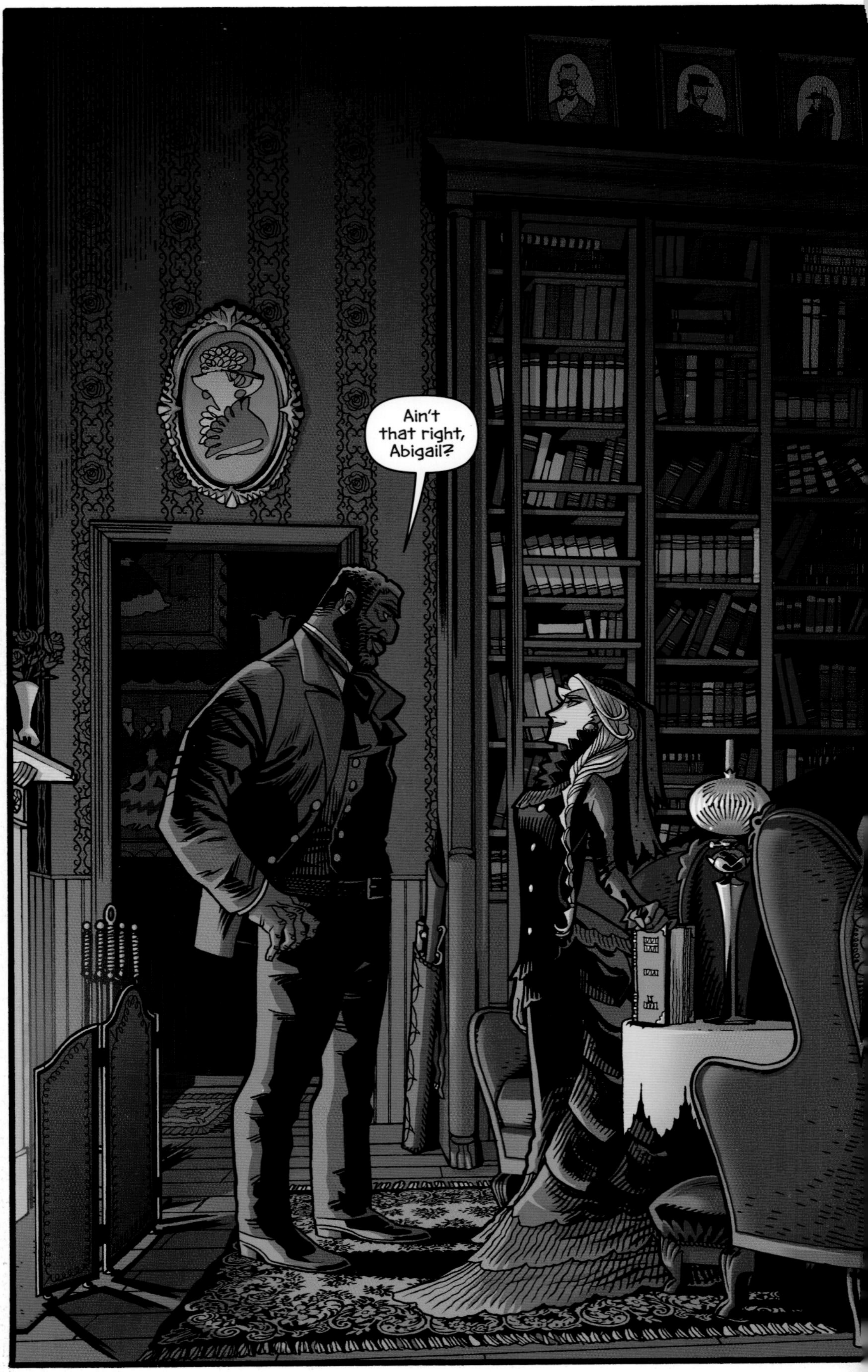
Ain't that right, Abigail?

SKETCH GALLERY

ILLUSTRATED BY
A.C. ZAMUDIO
AND
CARLOS N. ZAMUDIO

Since Carlos is a master of creature design, I often find it advantageous to let him have at the creatures in my stead. So for *Shadow Roads*, he took on the designs for the hounds and the Hunter's final design while I took on the rest.

I didn't give him all of the beasties—I claimed the bear man for myself. I had a certain look in mind. The amount of work I do to design a character varies depending on how naturally they come to me. For example, I knew I wanted Henry to look simple and handsome, so I just drew him once. Barry, in fact, didn't get a design at all; I didn't receive a character description for him prior to receiving the script, so the first time I drew him was on the page. Others, like Ghost Eyes, took a lot of feeling out to match what Cullen and Brian envisioned. His personality and life experience, I think, demand the most unique appearance among the cast. I'm glad we took our time with him, because he turned into one of my favorite characters to draw in the story.

—A.C. Zamudio

I think a big part of what I was trying to do with the designs for the hounds was to connect them to the Hunter in some way. We ended up going with one of the more canine looks, but with a face resembling an Aztec death whistle (a war horn, of sorts, that's said to sound like human screams). You can actually occasionally see a ceremonial weapon hanging from the Hunter's belt that has a death whistle attached to it. Some of my favorite unused versions of the hounds were actually more insectoid, because I wanted to tie them to a weird factoid Cullen told me about the Hunter. Turns out the red dust the Hunter left behind is supposed to be reminiscent of flea dirt, and plays off his parasitic nature. Man, I would've loved to have seen the flea-like versions skittering and jumping around the whole place during that first encounter in the train!

—Carlos N. Zamudio

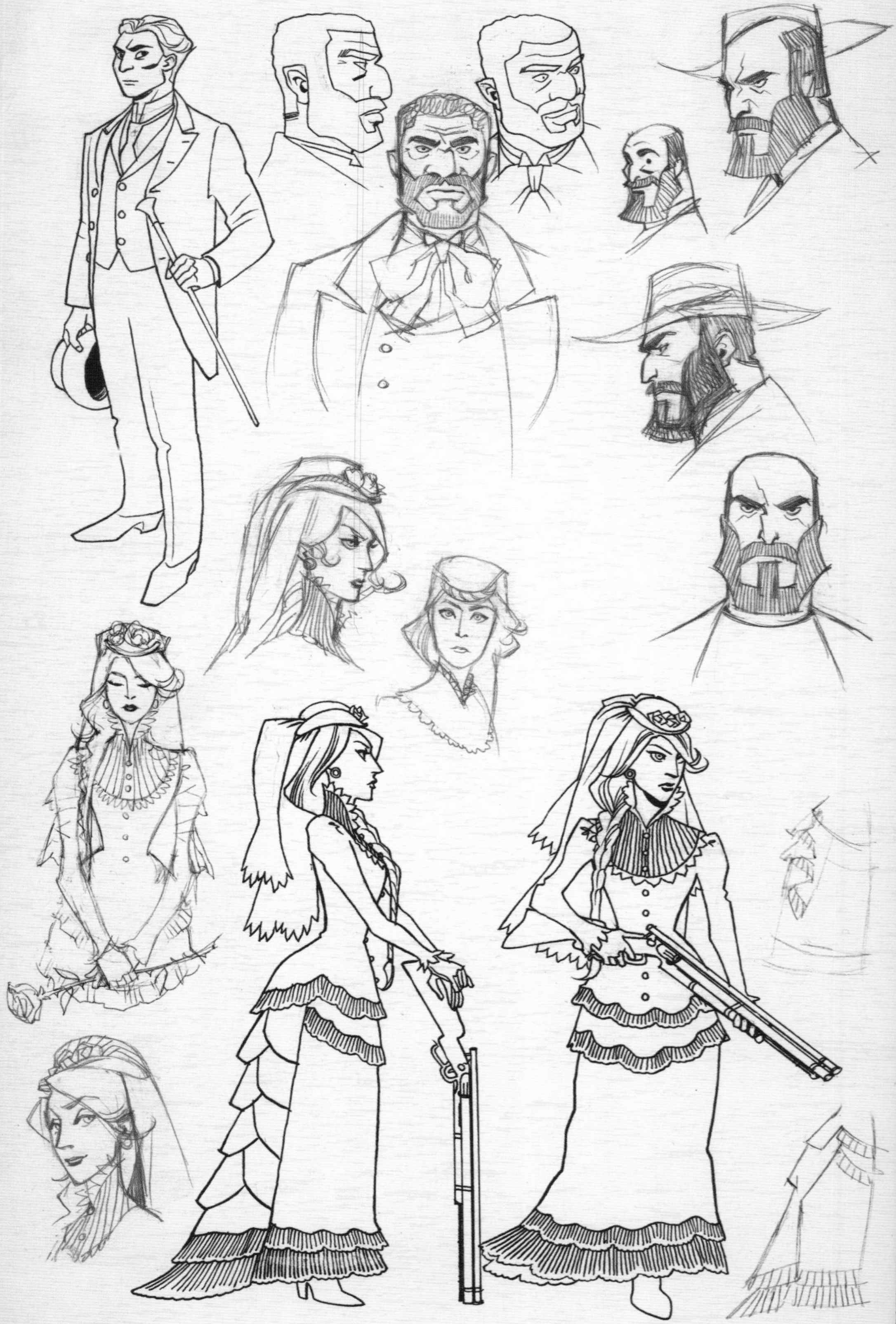

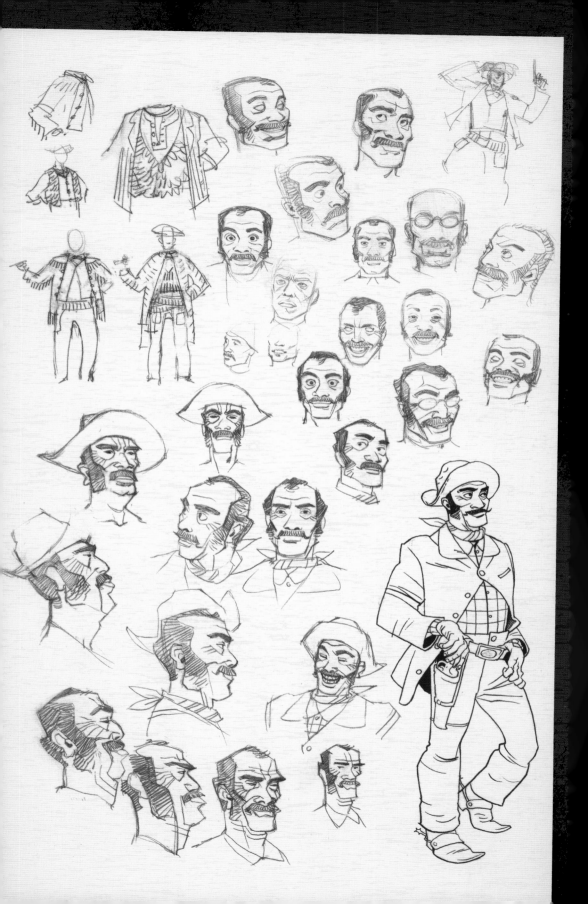

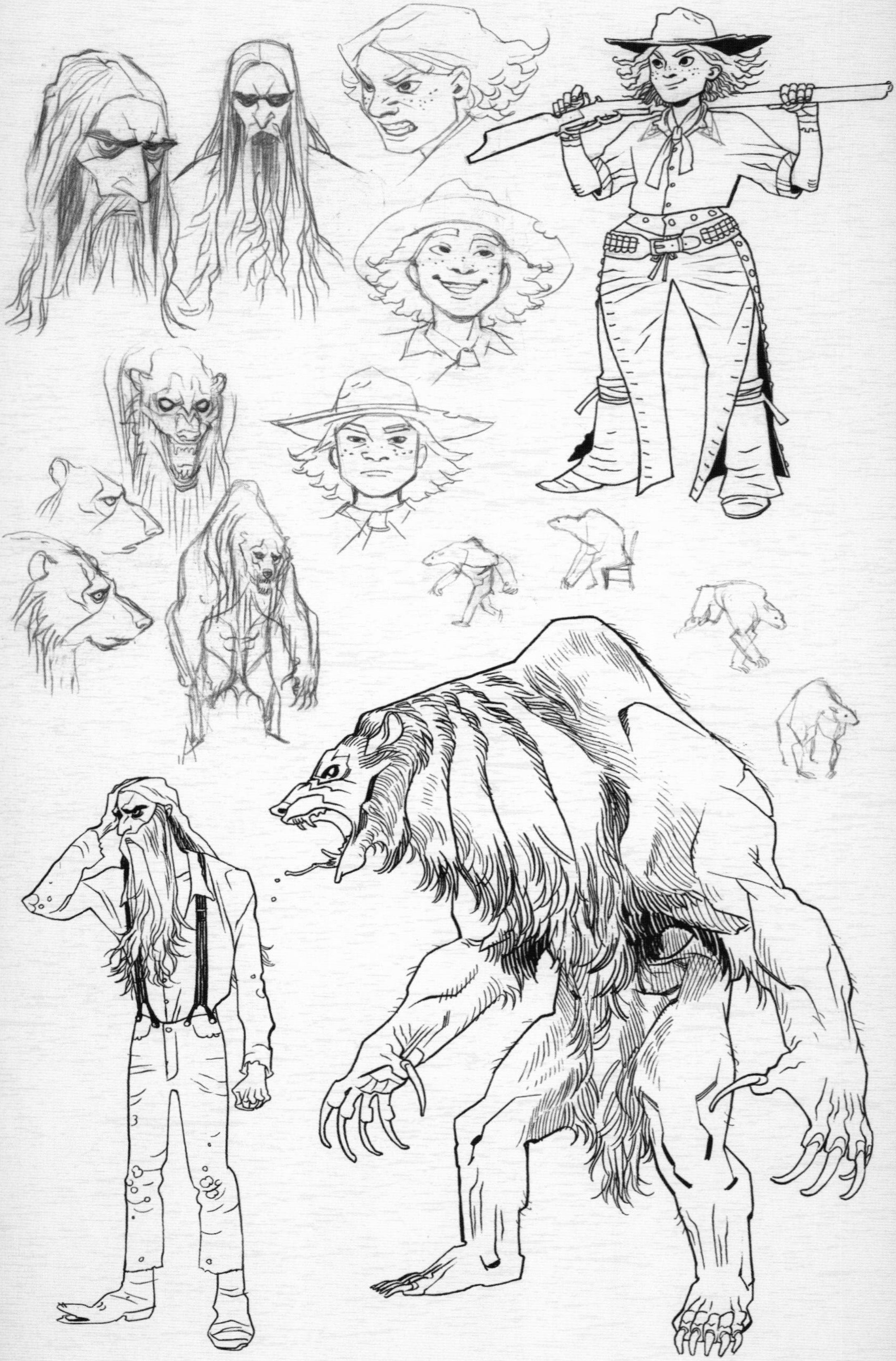

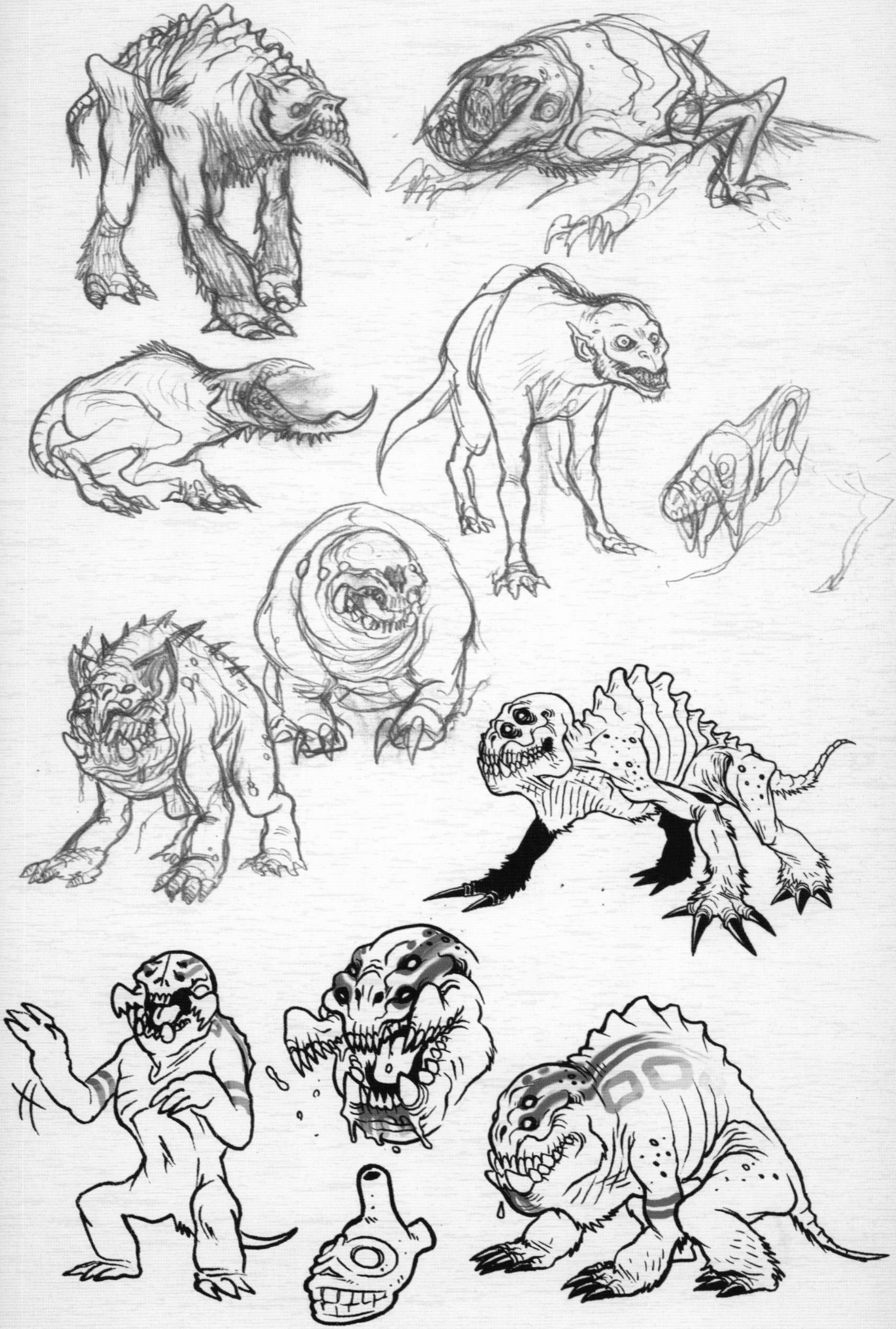

SHADOW ROADS CREATORS

CULLEN BUNN

Cullen Bunn is the writer of comic books such *The Sixth Gun*, *The Damned*, *Helheim*, and *The Tooth* for Oni Press. He has also written titles including *Harrow County* (Dark Horse), *Uncanny X-Men*, and *Deadpool And The Mercs For Money* (Marvel).

Cullen claims to have worked as an Alien Autopsy Specialist, Rodeo Clown, Pro Wrestling Manager, and Sasquatch Wrangler. He has fought for his life against mountain lions and performed on stage as the World's Youngest Hypnotist. Buy him a drink sometime, and he'll tell you all about it.

cullenbunn.com · Twitter: @cullenbunn

BRIAN HURTT

Brian Hurtt is an artist/writer who has spent most of his career working on collaborative creator-owned projects. His first such collaboration was in 2006 when Brian teamed with writer Cullen Bunn to create the Prohibition-era, monster-noir, cult classic, *The Damned*. A few years later the two teamed up again to create *The Sixth Gun*—a weird-west, epic supernatural fantasy. Brian also contributes to the popular webcomic *Table Titans*, in which he is the writer and artist of the stories "Whispers of Dragons" and "Road to Embers."

Brian lives and works in St. Louis, Missouri.

brihurtt.com · Twitter: @brihurtt · Instagram: @brihurtt · Tabletitans.com

A.C. ZAMUDIO

A.C. Zamudio is an art school dropout who didn't need no degree to chase her dreams of making comics. All she really needed was Cullen Bunn and Brian Hurtt to rope her into their end of the business. She's best known for *Death Follows* and *The Sixth Gun: Valley of Death* and couldn't be happier drawing corpses and dirty cowboys.

She grew up in Eugene, OR, and met up with her future husband and favorite collaborator Carlos N. Zamudio at college in Atlanta, GA. Since then, he's whisked her away to Bogotá, Colombia where she still hasn't caught up on her Spanish practice.

aczamudio.blogspot.com · Twitter: @aczamudio

CARLOS N. ZAMUDIO

Carlos Nicolas Zamudio has always loved drawing monsters, demons, and dragons above all else to the point that he used to refuse drawing anything else as a kid. Even now that he's accepted that sometimes people like characters in their stories, he's still easily swayed to work on comics with gore and monsters. He's best known for working as cover artist and colorist on Dark Horse's *Death Follows*, colorist on Boom! Studios' *Welcome Back*, and most recently as colorist and creature designer on Oni Press' *Shadow Roads*. If you spot him at a convention, know that the guy's not much of a talker, usually preferring to instead listen to the conversation on a table as he pulls out a pen and a sketchbook to draw. That is, unless someone decides to bring up comics, monsters, or board games!

ink-imp.blogspot.com · Twitter: @inkimpnick

CHRIS CRANK

Hi! I go by crank! You might know my work from several recent Oni books like *The Sixth Gun*, *Letter 44*, *Redline*, and *Rick and Morty™*. Maybe you've seen my letters in *Revival*, *HACK/slash*, *Spread*, or *God Hates Astronauts* (Image). Perhaps you've read *Lady Killer*, *Ghost Fleet*, or *Sundowners* (Dark Horse). Heck, you might even be reading the award-winning *Battlepug* (battlepug.com) right now! If you're weird you could have heard me online at crankcast.net where I talk with Mike Norton, Tim Seeley, Sean Dove and Jenny Frison weekly about things that are sometimes comics related. If you're super-obscure you've heard me play music with the Vladimirs or Sono Morti (sonomorti.bandcamp.com).

Twitter: @ccrank

Experience the epic adventures of Drake Sinclair, Becky Montcrief, Gord Cantrell, Billjohn O'Henry, and The Six in the collected editions of the Eisner-nominated series, *The Sixth Gun*!

THE SIXTH GUN
CULLEN BUNN
BRIAN HURTT

THE SIXTH GUN: BOOK 1:
COLD DEAD FINGERS
By Cullen Bunn, Brian Hurtt,
& Bill Crabtree
6 pages, softcover, color interiors
99 US • ISBN 978-1-934964-60-6

THE SIXTH GUN
CULLEN BUNN
BRIAN HURTT
BILL CRABTREE

THE SIXTH GUN: BOOK 2:
CROSSROADS
By Cullen Bunn, Brian Hurtt,
& Bill Crabtree
136 pages, softcover, color interiors
$19.99 US • ISBN 978-1-934964-67-5

THE SIXTH GUN
CULLEN BUNN
BRIAN HURTT
TYLER CROOK
BILL CRABTREE

THE SIXTH GUN: BOOK 3:
BOUND
By Cullen Bunn, Brian Hurtt,
Tyler Crook, & Bill Crabtree
160 pages, softcover, color interiors
$19.99 US • ISBN 978-1-934964-78-1

THE SIXTH GUN
CULLEN BUNN
BRIAN HURTT
TYLER CROOK
BILL CRABTREE

THE SIXTH GUN: BOOK 4:
A TOWN CALLED PENANCE
By Cullen Bunn, Brian Hurtt,
Tyler Crook, & Bill Crabtree
168 pages, softcover, color interiors
$19.99 US • ISBN 978-1-934964-95-

THE SIXTH GUN
CULLEN BUNN
BRIAN HURTT
BILL CRABTREE

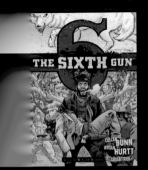

THE SIXTH GUN: BOOK 5:
WINTER WOLVES
By Cullen Bunn, Brian Hurtt,
& Bill Crabtree
0 pages, softcover, color interiors
99 US • ISBN 978-1-62010-077-6

THE SIXTH GUN
CULLEN BUNN
BRIAN HURTT
BILL CRABTREE

THE SIXTH GUN: BOOK 6:
GHOST DANCE
By Cullen Bunn, Brian Hurtt,
& Bill Crabtree
168 pages, softcover, color interiors
$19.99 US • ISBN 978-1-62010-016-5

THE SIXTH GUN
CULLEN BUNN
BRIAN HURTT
TYLER CROOK
BILL CRABTREE

THE SIXTH GUN: BOOK 7:
NOT THE BULLET, BUT THE FALL
By Cullen Bunn, Brian Hurtt,
Tyler Crook, & Bill Crabtree
160 pages, softcover, color interiors
$19.99 US • ISBN 978-1-62010-141-4

THE SIXTH GUN
CULLEN BUNN
BRIAN HURTT
BILL CRABTREE

THE SIXTH GUN: BOOK 8:
HELL AND HIGH WATER
By Cullen Bunn, Brian Hurtt,
& Bill Crabtree
160 pages, softcover, color interiors
$19.99 US • ISBN 978-1-62010-246

THE SIXTH GUN
CULLEN BUNN
BRIAN HURTT
BILL CRABTREE

THE SIXTH GUN: BOOK 9:
BOOT HILL
By Cullen Bunn, Brian Hurtt,
& Bill Crabtree
8 pages, softcover, color interiors
99 US • ISBN 978-1-62010-299-2

THE SIXTH GUN
SONS OF THE GUN
CULLEN BUNN BRIAN HURTT
BRIAN CHURILLA BILL CRABTREE

THE SIXTH GUN:
SONS OF THE GUN
By Cullen Bunn, Brian Hurtt,
Brian Churilla, & Bill Crabtree
136 pages, softcover, color interiors
$19.99 US • ISBN 978-1-62010-099-8

THE SIXTH GUN
DAYS OF THE DEAD
CULLEN BUNN BRIAN HURTT
MIKE NORTON BILL CRABTREE

THE SIXTH GUN:
DAYS OF THE DEAD
By Cullen Bunn, Brian Hurtt,
Mike Norton, & Bill Crabtree
136 pages, softcover, color interiors
$19.99 US • ISBN 978-1-62010-238-1

THE SIXTH GUN
DUST TO DEATH
BRIAN HURTT A.C. ZAMUDIO RYAN HILL
CULLEN BUNN TYLER CROOK BILL CRABTREE

THE SIXTH GUN:
DUST TO DEATH
By Cullen Bunn, Brian Hurtt, Tyler Cr
A.C. Zamudio, Bill Crabtree, & Ryan I
184 pages, softcover, color interiors
$19.99 US • ISBN 978-1-62010-268